A BEAUTY THAT HURTS

We set out for San Mateo Ixtatán, a ride of about nine leagues. . . .
We climbed the side of a long, high ridge, followed it and then . . .
came into a shaggy, rugged country of fine, tall pines and uncanny
live-oak groves, fog, cold, wheat, sheep, and very Indian-looking
Indians. . . . The clouds wove in and out of huge firs. . . . We had a
glimpse of Tibet-like houses, then the clouds shut down and the rain
began. . . . A tall, black cross came out of nowhere, and we began to
descend. On our right, close at hand, the other side of a new valley rose
like a wall of emerald-green pastureland seen through a shifting film
of cloud. . . . We climbed a hill, just enough to get back into the mist,
and entered San Mateo, getting glimpses of roses and shingle-roofed
houses. . . . The place was mournful with rain and the constant
rush of water. . . . But we felt our health and spirits revive . . .
and all that country was so beautiful it hurt.

OLIVER LA FARGE AND DOUGLAS BYERS,
THE YEAR BEARER'S PEOPLE (1931)

"The Angel," used as a poster for the John Sayles film Men With Guns.
Photograph by Luis González Palma.

The Linda Schele Series in Maya and Pre-Columbian Studies

This series was made possible through the generosity of William C. Nowlin, Jr., and Bettye H. Nowlin, the National Endowment for the Humanities, and various individual donors.

A BEAUTY THAT HURTS

Life and Death in Guatemala

W. GEORGE LOVELL

UNIVERSITY OF TEXAS PRESS
Austin

Second revised edition, 2010

Requests for permission to reproduce material from this work should be sent to:
Permissions
University of Texas Press
P.O. Box 7819
Austin, TX 78713-7819
utpress.utexas.edu/index.php/rp-form

Every reasonable effort has been made to identify copyright holders. The University of
Texas Press would be pleased to have any errors or omissions brought to its attention.

Permission to quote from the following works is acknowledged: Rigoberta Menchú,
I, Rigoberta Menchú: An Indian Woman in Guatemala (London: Verso, 1984); Victor
Montejo, *Testimony: Death of a Guatemalan Village* (Willimantic, CT: Curbstone Press,
1987); and Jean-Marie Simon, *Guatemala: Eternal Spring, Eternal Tyranny*
(New York: W. W. Norton and Co., 1987).

Royalties from the sale of this book help support educational opportunities in
Guatemala. For further information contact the Maya Educational Foundation, P.O.
Box 38, Route 106, South Woodstock, Vermont 05071–0038, www.mayaedufound.org.

Cover photograph: Daniel Hernández-Salazar
Map of Guatemala, p. 2: Jennifer Grek Martin

∞ The paper used in this book meets the minimum requirements of
ANSI/NISO Z39.48-1992 (R1997) (Permanence of Paper).

Library of Congress Cataloging-in-Publication Data
Lovell, W. George (William George), 1951–
A beauty that hurts : life and death in Guatemala /
W. George Lovell. — 2nd rev. ed.
p.   cm.
Includes bibliographical references and index.
ISBN 978-0-292-72183-8
1. Guatemala—History—1945–1985.   2. Guatemala—History—1985–   3. Mayas—
Guatemala—Government relations.   4. Indians of Central America—Guatemala—
Government relations.   5. Human rights—Guatemala.   I. Title.
F1466.5.L68   2010
972.8105′2—dc22
2009033444

*For my mother and my father, who are always with me,
and in fond memory of María Vilanova de Arbenz (1915–2009)*

CONTENTS

PREFACE

The privileges of university life are many. One that I hold in special regard is the luxury of sabbatical leave. Released from routine and duty on one such leave, I was able to devote myself entirely to writing, sitting at my desk without any need to prepare lectures, attend meetings, counsel students, grade papers, examine and supervise theses, evaluate grant proposals, compose letters of recommendation, or simply be at hand to deal with all sorts of matters—and crises, real or imagined. I found peace and quiet in the woods of Vermont, where I dared to think of myself not as teacher or colleague, academic adviser or member of committee, but simply as a writer. The distinction may mean nothing to anyone else, but a Rubicon it was, and remains, for me.

My father saw things differently. When I went home for Christmas the no-nonsense ways of Glasgow were soon asserted. "Yer mother tells me yer on a year's holiday." Normally a reliable filter, on this occasion my mother had let me down badly. The words had been uttered half as a statement, half as inquiry, lost on all the occupants of the Old Stag Inn but myself. I wondered, not for the first time, how to respond to my father's perception of what it is I do, what it is I am.

I began to explain, as my Dean would expect and as best I could, the gulf between "holiday" and "sabbatical," reeling off a litany of tasks I wished to accomplish before my year's leave was over. My father listened patiently. When I stopped talking it was time for another round. He wiped from his moustache the creamy froth of a fresh half-pint of Guinness. "Sounds like a holiday tae me, son!" he declared. The woman working behind the bar smiled at the sound of our laughter. Against what did my father measure his son's lucky lot? The years he spent at sea? After the merchant navy, the years spent running our family shop? After the shop closed, the years of swallowed pride sweeping the streets of Govan? As we made our way home, I felt more privileged than ever.

The flip side of privilege, however, is responsibility: responsibility to one-self, to one's family and friends, to the people and places we cherish and love, to the ideals we hope to live by. While more at ease in a university setting than in any other I have encountered, I have never felt comfortable with certain academic conventions. Among those that trouble me most is the bent that views scholarly work as a kind of cabal, as the ability to engage with a select group of fellow intellectuals in conversation, in print, or in an online forum. Even if I had the inclination to express myself in such a fashion, I doubt if I would derive any pleasure from knowing that whatever I had to say could be understood, and cared about, only by a handful of like-minded specialists. The academy, at times more than I consider tolerable, revels in exclusion.

So it was that, early on in my career as professor, I began to lead a double life, publishing research findings that cater to more erudite tastes while at the same time producing the odd essay, review, or opinion piece for media with more public terms of reference. I enjoy both parts of my double life and have never considered them mutually exclusive. This book is an attempt to link and integrate the two. It is a measure of the freedom that university life allows that, during my sabbatical leave, I could channel energy into a book like this, one that draws on academic training and hopes to have something to offer a specialist clientele, but not at the expense of an interested general readership. It is also, for me, a peculiar measure of what Canada represents that much of the time I spend there is taken up coming to terms with Guate-mala, a country I stumbled on almost by accident over three decades ago.

Did I choose Guatemala or did Guatemala choose me? I had been in Canada less than a year, having left Scotland to pursue graduate studies in Latin American geography at the University of Alberta. Classes in anthro-pology and history, to say nothing of the bite of that first Canadian winter, only fuelled my desire to flee Edmonton and head south. Responding to my supervisor's instructions — "Finish your fieldwork in Mexico and get down to Central America" — I arrived in Guatemala on June 25, 1974, not really knowing what might happen. I was twenty-three, hitching rides or travelling on second-class buses, wide-eyed and ripe for new experience. Within days Guatemala had cast its spell and seduced me, offering not just a fleeting summer's reward but fulfilling work for a lifetime. I had found something I longed for, something I knew would endure. I could feel it in my heart, be part of it as I walked through the hills and the corn, observe it everywhere in the bonds of land and life.

Thereafter, rites of academic passage called for a dissertation, then a mono-graph, with articles, conference presentations, a teaching job, and graduate supervisions along the way. Soon after being awarded my doctorate, however,

I felt that something was missing, that the contract I had struck with Guatemala called for me to develop the knowledge I had picked up as a scholar, to cultivate a rapport with a non-specialist audience. This occurred in 1981, when the political situation in Guatemala (seldom good) began to deteriorate, when friends whose safety was threatened made plans to leave, when people I knew and respected were killed. Things started to unravel, spun tragically out of control. That year, as civil war flared up, I made my first foray into journalism and began to accept invitations to speak at public meetings in which issues of human rights were addressed.

Guatemala is a complex country. In trying to make sense of it, I make no claims of providing definitive, unassailable interpretations. Evidence can be presented; knowing the full extent of the truth is another matter. "Así es, púes. . . . That's just how it is," is a popular Guatemalan way of putting it. For me, it's an *un*just way of how things should be. The fallout of the war years will be manifest for decades to come. I heard it put even more obliquely once, after I made what I thought was the most straightforward of inquiries. "Claro no sí hay." I checked, via eye contact, with the graduate student whom I was visiting in Guatemala City to make sure I had heard correctly. She nodded, mouth open. "Yes, it's clear that it isn't" is the best I can approximate.

This book has three parts. In Part One I let Guatemala come into focus through the lives of disparate individuals, several of them indigenous Mayas, whose circumstances differ but whose stories tell of hardship and adversity. These individuals share a common need to bear witness, a belief that abuse and injustice can at least be confronted if not overcome. Some have been given pseudonyms to protect their identities, others not. I have no rule of thumb in this regard besides allowing people to decide for themselves, and feel comfortable about that, before I opt for maximum caution. The main protagonists of Chapters 1 and 4, for instance, expressed a preference to be known by their real names after I had taken the pseudonym route. In the case of Doña Magdalena, her grandson Paulino told me: "My grandmother says that we did nothing wrong and so have nothing to hide. Let people know who we are, tell them what happened to us." It is the strength and courage of its inhabitants that I find most inspiring about Guatemala.

Part Two offers a series of temporal vignettes that deal with politics and human rights in Guatemala between 1981 and 1995. For this look at the country I lean heavily for information on Guatemalan newspaper sources, because I believe that what appears each day on the printed page, however incongruous, however incomplete, is important and revealing. The period between 1995 and the present is dealt with similarly in the Epilogue.

In Part Three, I step back from journalistic forays to assess the histori-

cal forces that shape, and the cultural context that frames, current predica-
ments, especially those of Maya communities. I draw here on my familiarity
with archival documents and scholarly literature to inject the narrative with
contemporary viewpoints and observations. I also indulge in a little playful
fieldwork, which I hope lightens the load of more onerous discussion about
the vicissitudes of Maya survival. Wherever possible I bring elements of the
Guatemalan story back to Canada, where I have lived and worked for more
than thirty years. Canadians, as much as Americans, need to know more
about life and death in a country that is closer to Toronto than Vancouver
is. NAFTA, which is responsible for all sorts of geographical transformations,
made Guatemala our next-door neighbor.

As with most projects, this book reflects the help, influence, and encouragement of many people. First mention belongs to my parents, who always
stressed the importance of getting an education and who worked hard to
afford me opportunities that they themselves never had. In Scotland, at least
in the part of Glasgow where I grew up, it was possible then to move through
primary and secondary schooling and on to university without being too
much of a burden on family resources. This is the greatest gift I was given,
and the one I value most. Both my mother and my father lived long enough
to see me leave home and make my way in the wider world beyond. Now
they are gone, I no longer worry about them worrying about me, but I miss
them more than I ever could have imagined.

In Canada, a special vote of thanks belongs to Roger Bainbridge. As editor
of Kingston's *Whig-Standard Magazine,* he welcomed my very first submis-
sion on Guatemala in 1981. It was Roger who suggested that I write under
a pen name, for he grasped right away the nature of my involvement—that
I would always want to go back to Guatemala. We settled on Donald Mc-
Alpine, a combination of the maiden names of my mother and my grandmother. My *alter ego* was published in the Kingston newspaper several times.
He even managed, on a couple of occasions, to migrate from the Saturday
magazine to the editorial page, where his views were enshrined, if not en-
dorsed, by the then lively, independent-minded *Whig.* In 1982, after I testified on the armed conflict in Guatemala before a parliamentary committee
in Ottawa, at which representatives of the Guatemalan government were also
in attendance, Donald McAlpine was made redundant. It also made sense not
to return to Guatemala for a while. Roger, however, believed it was his job to
keep readers informed as well as entertained, as did the *Whig*'s literary editor,
Larry Scanlan. From the time of McAlpine on, several times a year, I have

written or spoken about human rights in Guatemala in the hope of making it a concrete issue, not a distant abstraction, for the Kingston community and others across Canada, the United States, and Europe.

In addition to Roger and Larry, other *Whig* associates nudged me along at key junctures, among them Barbara Carey, Amy Friedman, David Prosser, David Pulver, Jennie Punter, and Harvey Schachter. Maureen McCallum Garvie, who first caught my eye when she worked at the *Whig*, is the best editor anyone could hope for, and is now my treasured partner. I thank her for putting up with me, and with my constant comings and goings.

Don Akenson of McGill-Queen's University Press was the first person to tell me that writing a book and getting it published was not beyond me, an early vote of confidence I will always appreciate. A colleague at Queen's University, Brian S. Osborne, listens with an open, supportive mind each time I return angry, sad, or confused from Guatemala. A former Queen's colleague, John Walker, insisted some time ago that I acknowledge and deal with these emotions. Numerous other university associates, at Queen's and elsewhere, I leave unnamed but not unappreciated.

My job allows me the opportunity to talk about Guatemala in the classes I teach. Students pay me the greatest compliment when their curiosity actually takes them there, or elsewhere in Latin America. I have learned a great deal over the years from the graduate students I have supervised or somehow been involved with, in particular Jeff Bellinger, Wayne Burke, David Carr, Peter Cleary, Susan E. Davis, Mireya Folch-Serra, Roberto Garcia Ferreira, Patricia Foxen, Victoria L. Henderson, Sarah Hill, Krista L. House, Leah A. Huff, Wendy Kramer, Aracely Martínez, Karin Monasterios, Erin Morin, Catherine Nolin Hanlon, Kari M. Pries, Jim Reinhart, Finola Shankar, Michelle Switzer, Giselle Valarezo, Paul Van Zant, and Rohini Wilkie. Time spent in their company, on the road and in the field, has been especially rewarding. "The lesson," writes Keith Reid of Procol Harum, "lies in learning, and by teaching I'll be taught." He got that one right, as he has so many other observations about the essence of life.

Over the years my work on Guatemala has been supported by the Office of Research Services at Queen's University, the Killam Program of the Canada Council, the Social Sciences and Humanities Research Council of Canada, the John Carter Brown Library, and the Andrew W. Mellon Foundation. Mary Ellen Davis always responds in her own inimitable way. So do an esteemed assortment of others, among them Armando J. Alfonzo, Wayne Bernhardson, Kathrin and Brian Cooper, Ray Craib, Krystyna Deuss, Mark Fried, Eduardo Galeano, Wayne Grady, Linda Green, Jim Handy, Daniel Hernández-Salazar, John M. Kirk, Christopher H. Lutz, Oscar Maldonado,

María Laura Massolo, Ken Mills, Marilyn Moors, Dougie Munroe, Diane M. Nelson, Michael Polushin, Tom Pow, Alasdair Robertson, Merilyn Simonds, Carolyn Smart, Michael Steinberg, Matthew Taylor, and Ronald Wright. As strategic sources of information, I can always count on Victoria Henderson and Celeste MacKenzie. Conversations in Guatemala with Patrick Ball, Paul Kobrak, Trudy H. Peterson, and Jane E. Swezey got me thinking and made me investigate further. The sisters belonging to Hermanas de la Providencia have been generous not only with their hospitality but also with their quirky sense of humor, a trait necessary for survival in most places, few more so than Guatemala. Earlier drafts of the book profited from the scrutiny of Douglas Fetherling, Michael Shawcross, and Jamie Swift. The copyediting talents of Christopher D. Chung and Robert Clarke worked wonders with structure and organization. Helen Phelan, Sharon Mohammed, and Leah "Mesha" Huff created textual order out of handwritten and digital chaos. Lesley and Bill Taylor encouraged an association with the *Toronto Star,* Carl Neustaedter and Scott Anderson likewise with, respectively, *The Globe and Mail* and the *Ottawa Citizen.* Alastair Reid continues to be model and mentor, and I never pick up an issue of *The New Yorker* without thinking of him. Friends in Seville, among them Antonio Acosta, Alexandra Parma and Noble David Cook, Cristina García Bernal, Juan Gil, Carmen Gómez, José Hernández Palomo, Juan Marchena Fernández, José Manuel Peña Girón, Antonio Reyes del Pulgar, Julián Ruiz Rivera, Pilar Sanchiz, Consuelo Varela, and Elías Zamora, make my sojourns in that marvelous city ever more memorable. Marie Delattre graciously allows her home in Antigua to serve as my base while I am in Guatemala, where I have long enjoyed a rewarding affiliation with the Centro de Investigaciones Regionales de Mesoamérica.

A book, I have come to appreciate, often assumes a precarious existence upon publication. I am delighted that Between the Lines, who first published *A Beauty That Hurts* in 1995, kept faith with it and moved ahead with plans for a subsequent edition, co-published with the University of Texas Press in 2000. This edition is the undertaking of the University of Texas Press alone, where Bill Bishel and Theresa May have been pivotal in keeping titles about Guatemala at the forefront of scholarly attention. I am also pleased that, given reviews of the first two editions, my desire for the book to appeal to both an academic and general readership has apparently been realized.

In devising the present edition I have expanded the Epilogue well into the twenty-first century, with the signing of the peace accord on December 29, 1996, serving as my point of departure. All the chapters that precede it have been augmented to incorporate new information or to elaborate on what I previously had to say. I have added more than sixty titles to my "Sources and Commentary," where I evaluate a growing and evolving English-language literature on Guatemala. The photographic appendix, "A Guatemalan Gallery," has also been expanded. Jennifer Grek Martin redrafted a map of places mentioned in the text and Luis González Palma kindly gave me permission to use his image of *The Angel* (1992) as a frontispiece. The cover photograph of church and parishioners at San Mateo Ixtatán comes courtesy of Daniel Hernández-Salazar.

What follows is a small token for all that Guatemala, and Guatemalans, have given me. It is, however, the payment I am perhaps best suited to make. Words alone will never change Guatemala, but they do afford contemplation of a gnarled, captivating land, as stunning to look at as it is painful to know.

PART ONE

STRUGGLE AND SURVIVAL

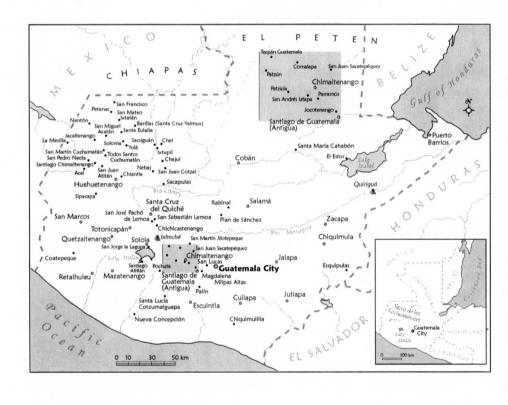

MEXICO

CHIAPAS

EL PETEN

BELIZE

Gulf of Honduras

Tecpán Guatemala
Comalapa   San Juan Sacatepéquez
Patzún
Chimaltenango
Patzicía
San Andrés Iztapa   Parramos
Jocotenango
Santiago de Guatemala
(Antigua)

San Francisco
Petanac   San Mateo
Ixtatán
Nentón
San Miguel   Barillas (Santa Cruz Yalmux)
Acatán
Jacaltenango
La Mesilla   Soloma   Sacsiguán   Chel
Yulá
San Martín Cuchumatán   Ixtupil
San Pedro Necta   Todos Santos   Chajul
Cuchumatán
Santiago Chimaltenango   San Juan   Nebaj   San Juan Cotzal
Acal   Atitán   Chiantla
Sacapulas
Huehuetenango

Cobán
Santa María Cahabón
El Estor
Lake
Izabal

Puerto
Barrios

Quiriguá

HONDURAS

Río Chixoy

Sipacapa

San Marcos

Santa Cruz
del Quiché   Rabinal   Salamá

San José Pachó
de Lemoa   San Sebastián Lemoa   Plan de Sánchez
Chichicastenango   Zacapa

Totonicapán   Chiquimula
Quetzaltenango   Solola   Ixlmché
San Martín Jilotepeque
San Jorge la Laguna   San Juan Sacatepéquez
Coatepeque   Lake Atitlán   Chimaltenango   Jalapa
Santiago   Pochuta   San Lucas
Atitlán   **Guatemala City**   Esquipulas
Retalhuleu   Mazatenango   Santiago de   Magdalena
Guatemala   Milpas Altas
(Antigua)   Palín
Santa Lucía   Cuilapa
Cotzumalguapa   Escuintla   Jutiapa

Nueva Concepción   Chiquimulilla

Río Motagua

Pacific
Ocean

EL SALVADOR

0 10   30   50 km

MEXICO
GUATEMALA
Caribbean Sea
Sierra de los
Cuchumatones
Lake
Atitlá   Guatemala
City
HONDURAS
EL SALVADOR

0   100 km

ONE

Q'ANJOB'AL CANADIAN

Genaro Castañeda was only four years old when, in 1974, I first saw the Cuchumatanes Mountains that are home to him and another quarter-million Q'anjob'al Mayas. The life that awaited him in Canada was a long way off, and Spanish still as foreign a tongue as the English he now speaks fluently. His father, murdered at thirty-six, had only two more years to live.

We first became acquainted in 1987. Genaro was working as a busboy at a Kingston restaurant, looking after tables in the summer patio. Someone at the restaurant had mentioned my name and told him about my interest in Guatemala. Genaro knew, for instance, that I had written a book about the experience of his people and neighboring Mayas under Spanish colonial rule. A puzzled expression crossed his face when I said I had spent ten years researching and writing that book. He paused, then asked, "How is it possible to write a book about my people without knowing our language, without speaking Q'anjob'al?"

The question caught me off guard. I mumbled something about how "ethnohistory" and "engaged fieldwork" could elicit "the native's point of view," but I mostly felt the relevance of these notions shrivel in his stare. Whether or not Genaro was enlightened by my response, he didn't say. We became friends. Genaro moved in and shared my house with me. During our time together he told me about his long journey north, about how a Maya from Guatemala came to be in Canada.

Genaro was born and raised in Yulá, a small Cuchumatán village of about two hundred people. Its name in Q'anjob'al translates as "in the water" or "in the place where there is water." Pre-Columbian in origin, Yulá today forms part of a municipal and parish division called Soloma, which is also the name of a nearby town undergoing radical transformation as remittances sent home by former residents now living and working in the United States reshape traditional patterns of economic and social life. Soloma is itself administered as a *municipio,* or township, of the Department of Huehuetenango. The city called Huehuetenango, which locals refer to simply as "Huehue," lies about sixty kilometers of treacherous mountain road away. An important administrative hub designed to serve the political objectives of the government of Guatemala over the entire northwestern highlands, Huehue's influence stretches to the border with adjacent Mexico. Its population is made up predominantly of Spanish-speaking mixed bloods known in Guatemala as Ladinos. The city has modern facilities such as banks, hotels, e-mail cafés, and video arcades, yet still feels like another world compared to the rural areas surrounding it.

Genaro's people, the Q'anjob'al, are one of twenty different Maya groups who make up roughly half of Guatemala's national population. Their conspicuous presence underscores a dynamic of survival that few Native American peoples have been able to sustain. Maya survival hinges on how, from 1524 on, natives in Guatemala resisted Spanish intrusion by warfare, flight, disobedience, and deception. Elsewhere in the Americas, especially in Mexico and in Peru, the lure of gold and silver guaranteed intense Spanish exploitation. Guatemala, by contrast, became something of a backwater, a land where Spanish conquistadors could expect only modest, marginal rewards for their adventures. In 1570, for example, a Crown official described the countryside around Yulá as "poor and unfruitful land," a place where the only commodities in abundance were "corn and chickens," hardly the stuff of which an El Dorado could be forged. Paltry resources in remote terrain often resulted in symbolic Spanish colonization, not obliterating conquest. The Q'anjob'al and other Maya peoples were thus able to create for themselves a culture of refuge that was a blend of pre-Columbian and Spanish ways, to take shelter in a culture of resistance with long-term benefits for group survival.

Far more destructive to Maya life in Guatemala than Spanish brutality or greed were outbreaks of disease. Sicknesses brought in from outside, passed from European and African carriers to vulnerable native hosts, served as lethal accomplices of conquest. Maya numbers dropped 90 percent or more during the first century of Spanish rule. Population recovery was slow and sporadic for centuries thereafter.

Some years ago in an uncared-for archive in Guatemala City, I unearthed a letter about the ravages of disease among the Maya of Soloma. Dated May 5, 1806, and written by a Ladino constable named Marcos Castañeda, the letter fills me with immense sadness, for such suffering as it describes fell again on Soloma more recently, albeit for ideological rather than epidemiological reasons. The disease in question was typhus, a historic scourge of the poor. Castañeda's Bosch-like imagery and Dickensian tone of concern, the latter a rather risky attitude for a petty official to assume, evoke a grim picture of what Genaro's ancestors were up against:

> For four years now in the parish of Soloma there has been great distress on account of the mortality caused by the typhus epidemic, which kills the Indians without relief or remedy, leaving them only in dire hardship. Through fear of death, my brother and I fled with our families to the solitude of the mountains, suffering there from extremities of climate, leaving our houses and possessions abandoned in Soloma. But God having seen fit to end this terrible affliction, we have returned once again to our homes. We find that most Indian inhabitants have perished and lie un-buried all over the place, their decaying corpses eaten by animals that stalk the countryside.
>
> What grieves us most, however, as it would any pious heart, is to see orphaned children crying for the laps of their parents, asking for bread without having anyone to receive it from; to behold widows and widowers mourning the loss of their consorts; and to watch old people lament the death of their offspring. After so much hard work, these unfortunate Indi-ans have been reduced to a life of misery. Having returned from afar, those who survived are without homes to live in, for these were burned to rid them of the contagion. They are also without resources to pay their taxes and without corn to feed themselves.
>
> If no measures are taken to assist these wretched people, they will most certainly starve to death, because they did not plant corn in the places where they sought refuge and so have nothing to live on, both this year and next, for it is now too late to plant their fields. It is a common thing in this parish to encounter Indians, old and young alike, walking from town to town, from house to house, begging or searching for corn and charity. Others seek loans, leaving as security one of their children, for they have nothing else to offer.
>
> For the sake of God and a sign of his mercy, assistance should be ex-tended to the Indians of this parish. At the very least the people could be exempted from paying taxes for the years during which they suffered such great misfortune.

Castañeda's appeal, penned to the district governor, met with wilful disre-gard, a customary response. Not much changed in Soloma after Guatemala attained independence from Spain in 1821. Only in the late nineteenth century did the culture of refuge shaped by the Maya during colonial times begin to break down.

Under land and labor reforms initiated in 1871 by President Justo Rufino Barrios, Guatemala became not so much a "banana republic" as a "coffee republic." Native lands, especially along the Pacific piedmont and in the Verapaz highlands, were taken over by enterprising coffee planters, who also demanded that native hands be made available to perform agricultural labor. Barrios imposed on Guatemala the liberal vision of modernity, a blueprint that would ensure plenty for a few and little for many. His double plunder, very importantly, did not affect all Maya communities to an equal extent. The territorial and social integrity of some disappeared or was dissipated by the joint operation of land and labor encroachments in locales suitable for the cultivation of coffee. In other communities, including Genaro's, land expropriation was tempered by their being situated at elevations that were not conducive to intensive coffee growing.

The land base of Genaro's community may not have been usurped, but after the Barrios reforms his people began to spend part of each year working as wage laborers who migrate to Pacific plantations to help harvest coffee. Maya culture today, however, tends to be particularly resilient in communities that, like Genaro's, guarded their land as best they could against seizure and encroachment, even if labor was (and still is) procured for plantation deployment.

Unlike many Maya families, Genaro's still has some land around which to improvise an existence. The holder of forty *cuerdas,* about eight acres, Genaro's father was a wealthy man by the standards of his community. Genaro's family also had access to another ten *cuerdas* his mother shared with her two brothers.

Land is something Mayas in Guatemala relate to in ways that transcend most Western notions of astute property management. For them land is like air and sunlight, a God-given resource over which no one exercises exclusive proprietary rights. Custom dictates that it be worked, protected, and passed on to offspring as a sacred gift handed down from the ancestors with that end in mind. Mayas consider themselves not so much owners as caretakers of land.

Not surprisingly, it is in relation to land that Genaro's earliest memories are lodged: "I grew up on land by the side of the river. On it we raised corn, beans, chilli peppers, tomatoes, carrots, beetroot, and potatoes. Some wheat too, higher up. For fruit we had apples, cherries, plums, and even some peaches. On our land my father kept many animals. With my sister I looked after sheep, watching out for coyotes when my father was away."

Genaro's father, it seems, was away quite often. The reasons for his absence were not always made clear. What Genaro remembers about his father comes not so much from lived experience—he was six years old when his father was murdered—as from what family and friends told him afterward, when he was growing up.

To earn a living, Genaro's father worked the family land, as Maya men habitually have done; but he also spent time in the Ixcán, a coffee-growing region to the north of Yulá. There, unlike most other natives, he did not pick coffee but bought it for resale elsewhere in Guatemala, primarily to merchants who shipped it overseas. Genaro's father was able to carve out a comfortable niche as a small-time middleman because of the capital he acquired from bootlegging, an activity that provided funds for an initial investment in the coffee business and a steady supply of cash thereafter. Bootlegging not only attracted men from all over to Genaro's home—men seeking refreshment or escape—but also gave his father another excuse for being on the road a lot, selling *kusha,* homemade liquor, in neighboring villages.

In one of these villages Genaro's father met and formed a relationship with another woman, who gave birth in the course of the union to two daughters. Keeping a *segunda casa,* a second home, is not an uncommon practice in Guatemala. Genaro's father is said to have been as dependable a material provider for his "second family" as for his first.

Such situations, however, inevitably create problems. In the case of Genaro's father, relatives of the woman with whom he kept a *segunda casa*— her estranged husband and four drink-loving brothers—reckoned after a while that the liaison was an insult to family honor. Family honor in Guatemala is restored in several ways. One of them is murder. Whether the husband and brothers actually killed Genaro's father by their own hands, or arranged for others to do so, has never been established: life, most people believe, is the most precious gift of all, but it can be bought very inexpensively in Guatemala. Genaro does not rule out the possibility that his father's involvement in the *kusha* racket or his role as a coffee middleman may have been responsible for the murder. The treasury police employed by the government to track down bootleggers are notoriously vicious. Likewise, guerrillas who had infiltrated the Ixcán in the 1970s would not have considered Genaro's father's moneymaking ventures to be politically sound.

Death leaves so much unasked, so much unanswered. Genaro has an enduring image of his father riding off on horseback, departing on one of his many trips. He recalls traveling once with his father to Barillas, shortly before the murder, on a coffee-buying expedition. His memories of those days are sketchy, but for Genaro it is important to remember his father as someone who could support his family without having to sell his labor cheaply, without having to be bossed about by others.

Genaro's sheltered life within Yulá changed when he started school. School in Yulá was then a two-room hut, attended by about thirty-five children who were taught exclusively in Spanish by two Ladino teachers. One of the teachers also ran the local store.

Acquiring Spanish is not something all Maya children achieve with equal proficiency. Boys tend to be pushed along more forcibly during the learning process than girls, usually because they are the ones who, as grown men, will have more to account for to the Ladino, Spanish-speaking state. Genaro's hushed, sing-song Spanish is considerably more articulate than that of most indigenous Guatemalans, many of whom command only a skeletal vocabulary of oft-repeated words, phrases, and curses. His efforts to learn and be at ease in the language of the conqueror have served him well.

Attending school brought exposure to the world beyond home and community, the world beyond the horizon. Before the trip with his father to Barillas there were shorter school outings to play soccer against the teams of surrounding villages, villages only a few hours' walk away through the fields and the forests, in valleys beyond the mountains.

Few events, however, get people moving more happily from one place to another in Guatemala than a fiesta, especially one held in association with the worship of a patron saint. Genaro has a warm recollection of walking from Soloma to Santa Eulalia as part of a procession that carried a statue of San Pedro from one town to the next. Equally memorable was his first trip to Huehuetenango. As a small boy he went there with his uncle to sell apples at market. Huehuetenango remains one of his favorite places.

Maya children are expected to start working early. For girls this usually involves innumerable household chores: helping with babies and younger children, fetching water, washing clothes, and preparing corn to be made into *tortillas*. It may also involve learning to weave commercial items for the tourist trade. Often it means entering into domestic service in distant Ladino households, where they are rarely treated well and can be sexually harassed or even initiated while barely adolescent.

For boys, priority training is coming to grips with how best to work the family plot, especially the rudiments of corn cultivation. Genaro was no exception. It is also common for a boy nine or ten years of age to go with his father to a plantation to be guided on how to pick coffee or cotton, shown what kind of working conditions and living arrangements to expect, and generally exposed under paternal supervision to wage employment in the Ladino world.

But when Genaro was exposed, soon after his tenth birthday, to the travails of plantation labor, his father was already several years dead. His first experience of it occurred in the company of five others from his village on a cotton plantation to the south of Retalhuleu. He lived there, along with sixty fellow workers, in a large wooden shack beside the cotton fields. Like many Indians accustomed to the cool climate of the highlands, he did not do well in the suffocating heat of the Pacific coast. He fell sick with fever and within weeks was shipped back home, where it took him months to recover.

He fared much better the next year on a coffee plantation near Santa Lucía Cotzumalguapa. There, at an altitude salubriously above the coastal plain, he worked a full forty days, earning about two dollars each day. Food and water at this plantation were less of a problem than on the cotton farm; the lodgings were cleaner and more spacious, with fewer occupants.

Genaro's most enjoyable and most lucrative spell as a wage laborer was on a coffee plantation, Finca La Florida, near Pochuta. He speaks almost fondly of his time there: hard work, for sure, but good pay, tasty meals, comfortable beds, and a river nearby to bathe and even to frolic in. At Finca La Florida, in the company of his best friend, who met and later married a young woman who also worked on the plantation, Genaro fulfilled an eighty-day contract before returning to school in Yulá.

By age twelve he had gained enough confidence and experience to test even deeper Ladino waters. Huehuetenango, which he had visited or passed through on several occasions, would have been challenge enough. Even more so was Guatemala City.

La capital. Perhaps the most striking feature about Guatemala City is how it appears to bear very little relation to the land and people over which and whom it presides. If Nero fiddled as Rome burned, then the government of Guatemala is a symphony orchestra playing in the midst of even greater conflagration. What do the bright lights and commercial paraphernalia of downtown Guatemala City, the multinational consumerism and chic glitter of Sixth Avenue, the elegant mansions and flashy nightclubs of Zone 9, have to do with the events and circumstances of a life like Genaro's?

I struggle with the contradictions of its capital city each time I visit Guatemala. When I mention this to Genaro, he shrugs. Why did he go there, what did he do there, how long did he stay there? *"Para ver.* To see what it was like. I worked as a *lustrador,* a shoeshine boy. I cleaned boots (fifty cents), and shoes (twenty-five cents) for about six weeks. During the week I looked for customers at the main bus terminal, where I'd make two to three dollars a day. On Sundays I'd go to the zoo, where I'd usually make four dollars, sometimes even five. I had a bed in a room with two other boys in a house in Zone 4. It wasn't bad."

He talks into the tape recorder so casually. It is a warm summer day in southern Ontario. The sky is blue and cloudless. Birds sing. Squirrels scramble across the lawn. The flowers gleam, the grass soaks up water, the trees provide shade. In the garden, as I listen and scribble, it crosses my mind that I first left Scotland at the same age Genaro left Yulá for Guatemala City. I travelled with my youth club from Glasgow to Stranraer and then across the Irish Sea to Belfast. There, playing soccer, we beat a team of boys representing a youth club on the Ormeau Road. We celebrated and slept in their church hall. We toured the premises where Cantrell and Cochrane made pop and visited Gallagher's cigarette factory. I drank free samples at the pop place, but did not have the nerve to smoke the cigarettes some of my teammates plundered at Gallagher's. I certainly would not have had the courage to head off for an unknown city and chance my hand at shining shoes.

When Genaro returned home from Guatemala City, the countryside around Yulá had become a dangerous place to be. By 1982 insurgents who had earlier set up a base of operation in the Ixcán, the Guerrilla Army of the Poor, were at the peak of their strength. Their actions, along with those of another insurgent group, the Organization of People in Arms, were so widespread that the Guatemalan army found itself losing control over entire areas of the western highlands. A desperate situation called for drastic action. It came in the form of intimidation and slaughter in rural areas where, at the local level, the guerrillas had experienced some success in building popular support for their cause.

Maya communities paid dearly for their proximity to revolution. Genaro's village cannot be said to have suffered the worst of counterinsurgency. Some communities no longer exist, their houses burned, their fields untended, the pens of their animals empty. The people who used to live in them are dead, scattered, or haunted still by their being herded into "model villages" set up by the army as a means of social control. Dreadful things happened, and much also that will never be known.

What Genaro knows is that guerrillas passed through Yulá late one night and painted slogans on the walls of the bridge, the church, the school, and some houses. They melted back into the darkness before dawn. The following morning the villagers awoke and looked in horror at the graffiti defacing their community.

Terrified that an army patrol might arrive and think their village a guerrilla stronghold, people set to work, daubing over propaganda with mud, paint, and whitewash. Fear lurked for days, for by then they well knew what could happen to a community suspected by the army of cooperating with the insurgents. It mattered little to the army how cooperation was gained, that it arose in many instances from the same fear of guerrillas that people had of government soldiers. Whether voluntary or coerced, sympathy for the insurgent cause, however the army chose to define it, was punishable in the most barbarous ways imaginable.

Some villagers feared that the guerrillas might return first and, seeing their slogans erased, accuse people of casting their lot with the army, of being on the side of counterinsurgency. But this was deemed the lesser risk, for although the guerrillas were known to assassinate collaborators or undesirables—a woman who ran a bar in the village had been killed after she ignored warnings to stop selling cheap liquor—their cause could never be served by indiscriminate slaughter or full-scale massacre.

The army itself did not arrive in Yulá, but an order from the regional commander did. It called for all able-bodied men between sixteen and sixty years of age to form a civil defense patrol that would act, under army supervision, as a buffer between soldiers fighting for the government and guerrillas fighting to overthrow it.

Although civil defense patrols originated with the counterinsurgency measures of President Romeo Lucas García, it was under the rule of his successor, General Efraín Ríos Montt, that they were most actively and successfully promoted. Now disbanded, though some of them have become the nucleus of local development committees, they existed in many areas, allegedly functioning as a means of community self-protection.

Most Maya men resented civil defense duty. Besides forcing them to align with, and possibly even fight alongside, the national armed forces, patrol service disrupted normal working routines. It took people away from their fields. It made it difficult to plan projects or lengthened their time of completion. It stifled mobility. It especially created problems when a patrol member had to be absent from his community, in which case permission had to be solicited, a travel permit obtained, and a suitable replacement found, persuaded, and paid to act as a substitute.

Even before Genaro reached the age of eligibility, he was pressed into service in the local civil defense patrol. He served as an emergency recruit, standing guard at the outskirts of Yulá while more senior patrol members were engaged in a distant reconnaissance. Not to have served, to have run away as some youths did, was to be considered subversive.

It was a scary experience. Given antiquated guns but no instructions about how to use them, one underage patrol member accidentally shot himself in the leg. Most frightening of all for Genaro was when he had to leave the checkpoint at the entrance to Yulá and comb surrounding hills in search of guerrillas. He had heard about exchanges of fire between insurgents and civil defense patrols in which the patrols, poorly trained and ill-equipped, had been wiped out. Although no such skirmish occurred, Genaro began to worry that, inevitably, one day he would qualify for regular duty in the civil defense patrol. After that loomed conscription, forced membership in an army that, as he put it, "would teach me to hate, teach me to kill."

His fear and confusion turned to panic when, in a town called Chiquimulilla, he was apprehended by the army, thrown in jail, and interrogated. What was he doing so far from his village? Why wasn't he there serving in the civil defense patrol? Was he travelling alone or with someone else? Who did he know here in town? Where were his papers? Just awful, *muy horrible*, is how Genaro describes the experience of being locked up overnight, waiting for daybreak with about two hundred others in a compound that had no bunks or toilets, only enough room to stand upright.

Genaro had gone to Chiquimulilla with one of his relations, Cruz Sebastián, to sell ice cream at the annual fair. With earnings and some help from his mother, he and Cruz had purchased a small ice-cream maker, transported it by bus from Soloma to Chiquimulilla, found a local supply of ingredients, and set up shop. Before the army picked him up Genaro and Cruz had sold out their ice cream day after day. Business was terrific. He smiles as he remembers, then turns quiet and forlorn.

Luckily for Genaro, he was carrying a pass signed by the commissioner in charge of the civil defense patrol, which authorized him to be absent from his home for up to forty days. Cruz had taken pains to attend to this matter before he and Genaro had left Yulá. The pass convinced the officers who questioned Genaro that he was not evading service in the civil defense patrol or engaged in subversive activities in Chiquimulilla. He was later released, unharmed but shaken.

The experience was a pivotal one. He decided to act. What he decided, at an age perhaps shy of parental consent but certainly not personal courage, meant leaving things behind: his home, his mother and sister, his friends, a land, a people, a way of life. Genaro resolved to flee Guatemala altogether, to escape forever from the clutches of the army, first to Mexico and then to the United States.

He moved quickly. From Chiquimulilla he and Cruz travelled back to Huehuetenango. There was no time, in the rush of action, to return to Yulá and say goodbye. His mother and sister, furthermore, would try to persuade him to stay, even though they realized the inevitability of some kind of military service and Genaro's fears of such involvement. He asked Cruz, who was going back, to explain the situation as best he could. In Huehuetenango, Genaro applied for papers that would enable him to enter Mexico, legally, for a short while. These he obtained without difficulty, although he lied about his age and why he wanted to leave Guatemala: he said he wanted to visit a friend in Chiapas. He sold some of his clothes, a suitcase, and the ice-cream-making equipment, not making much money. Cruz went with him to the bus station, and after purchasing a ticket Genaro was left with fifty *quetzales,* then about twenty dollars, to his name. From Huehuetenango he travelled by bus west to the border town of La Mesilla.

The first rains had already fallen. Green with corn, the Sierra de los Cuchumatanes rose like a fortress from the banks of the Río Selegua. Genaro crossed into Mexico, turning his back on the past.

Borders are not just lines on a map. They are mental as much as geographical constructs, states of mind, not mere arrangements in space. A border is something we carry inside ourselves, so the realms that lie on either side are in part our own creation.

Genaro was headed toward one of the most palpable borders in existence, the border between Mexico and the United States. Mexican writer Carlos Fuentes considers the line marked by the Río Grande less a border than a scar, a scar that divides the rich from the poor, the strong from the weak, those whom history has blessed from those whom history has damned. The scar separates not only Mexico from the United States but also the United States from all of Latin America. It is a scar that still bleeds, and the blood runs north.

Like many people from Latin America, Genaro first formed an image of the United States from hearsay: "I was told it was a free place, a place where there was no war, a place where you could work and study in peace. I was told that life there was easier." His perceptions were reinforced by a group of fellow Mayas he met in the Mexican city of Villahermosa. One of them, Tomás, had actually been to the United States. Like Genaro, Tomás and his friends had fled Guatemala—they lived in San Miguel Acatán, a town not far from Soloma—to escape the violence. Genaro benefited considerably from their support in Mexico. He found work as a gardener and for two months planted flowers in parks, plazas, and other public places. One of his jobs was to design the display for a floral clock. Staying in Villahermosa, however, was risky. If he was stopped by the Mexican authorities, Genaro was told, he would most likely be relieved of his savings and shipped off to one of the refugee camps that had sprung up in Chiapas close to the Guatemalan border. Farther north he would be safer, so with Tomás and his friends he journeyed all the way to the border city of Reynosa. There they made plans to cross the Río Grande into the United States. The savvy Tomás said there was no need to hire a *coyote* to guide them; besides, there was no way they could afford one.

Their plans worked out. Genaro is short in stature, but the river was low enough that one night he was able to wade across it, balancing his possessions in a bag he carried on his head. No border patrol lurked on the other side. With two other Guatemalans he walked from early morning until about three in the afternoon, when they arrived at a country store. There they pooled money and called a taxi, which drove them to McAllen, Texas. Not yet fourteen, Genaro had made it to *El Norte*.

His good luck continued, mostly because he stuck close to Tomás, who put his wits to good use: first, a place to stay; next, a job to pay the rent. Genaro found work on a farm between McAllen and Edinburg. He fed chickens some of the time, fed fighting cocks the rest. Weeks passed uneventfully, and then his luck ran out.

Outside a store in Edinburg, where he had gone to buy groceries, officers from the U.S. Border Patrol questioned him politely, but insistently. Unable to produce papers, Genaro simply informed them he was Mexican. The officers escorted him by car to the border and watched as he walked across the bridge back into Mexico.

Deportation was only a momentary setback, for it was clear to Genaro that what he had done once he could easily do again. Early next morning, near Hidalgo, he waded once more across the Río Grande. His second stint in Texas, where he watered orange groves near Edinburg, lasted about a month before *la migra*, U.S. Immigration Services, caught up with him. Genaro once more declared he was Mexican, and so was again delivered back to Reynosa. This time he stayed longer, thinking things over. The trick, it seemed, was not just to cross the border but to get far enough inland to a bigger place than either McAllen or Edinburg, to a place where the work of *la migra* might be less efficient. He looked at a map and opted for Houston.

He waded one last time across the Río Grande. After drying off in Texas he made his way to the Greyhound station in Edinburg, where he caught a bus that sped up Highway 281. He had gone about seventy miles inland to Falfurrias when a border patrol flagged down the bus. An officer boarded, approached Genaro, and asked him his nationality. This time he told the truth: *"Guatemalteco."* Guatemalan, not Mexican. The officer did not believe him. Genaro was ordered off the bus and put in a waiting patrol car. He was taken to headquarters in Falfurrias where, when questioned, he repeated he was Guatemalan. His truthfulness was finally taken seriously. Instead of being accompanied back to the border, he was driven to a detention camp for Central American aliens located halfway between Brownsville and Harlingen, near a place called Los Fresnos.

For an entire month Genaro fretted in detention. During this time he was noticed by a visitor to the Los Fresnos camp, his youthful Maya features standing out among the older, predominantly *mestizo* (mixed Spanish-indigenous) traits of other Latin detainees. The visitor contacted a local church group that had decided to challenge U.S. immigration law by offering sanctuary to individuals and families, especially from Central America, who had fled their homes through fear only to be denied refugee status in the United States. Through the mediation of the sanctuary movement, Genaro was released from detention; a bond was posted with U.S. Immigration Services to guarantee future knowledge of his whereabouts. He was taken to Baton Rouge, Louisiana, where he was placed in the care of Quakers, who welcomed him as one of their own.

Genaro lived with the Quakers for three years. In Baton Rouge he began adjusting to life in El Norte. Different sights, different sounds. Different wants, different needs. A different sense of time, a different sense of place. Different premises to wake up to in the morning, different expectations to go to bed with at night. It was all, he says, just so vastly different, especially the language. Learning English was not easy, but immersion in school and at home—he spent hours and hours in front of the television—soon produced encouraging results. Today, Genaro's spoken English is impressive, softly voiced and less noticeably accented than that of most Latin American immigrants.

He had two options concerning how to secure the legal right to remain in the United States. The first was to apply for status as a resident alien, a costly, protracted procedure, one that might not produce the desired outcome. The second was to be adopted officially as a member of the family he was living with in Baton Rouge. Of the two options the second carried the best chance of success, but it necessitated formal severance of ties with his natural mother—and acknowledgment of this step on her part as well as his.

The paperwork for option two was pursued, but Genaro could not bring himself to follow it through. It represented an emotional barrier far more difficult to traverse than trekking through Mexico and crossing the Río Grande.

Moreover, he worried that his legal adoption in the United States would get his mother into trouble, for word had reached him that she had been questioned about his absence from Yulá.

As the dilemma grew, another option materialized. A church organization in Georgia found out about Genaro's case and suggested that permission to enter and reside in Canada might be more readily attained than applying for resident alien status in the United States. Contact was made with a refugee support group in Kingston, Ontario, whose members were informed of the particulars of his situation. Despite changes to Canadian immigration law, an application to allow him to enter Canada as a landed immigrant was processed favorably in six months. Judging from the scores of cases I've been consulted about since, I reckon that getting his immigration papers in prompt, satisfactory order was a stroke of considerable luck.

Genaro took leave of the Quaker family in Baton Rouge. He did not want to go, but neither did he wish to squander an opportunity to enter another country on a firm legal footing. He boarded a plane and arrived in Toronto several hours later. At age seventeen, four years after he fled Guatemala, Genaro's life as a Q'anjob'al Canadian had begun.

TWO

NOBEL K'ICHE'

I heard Rigoberta Menchú speak for the first time in Toronto on February 6, 1988. That very day *The Globe and Mail* ran a travel feature with the headline "Guatemala in Style for a Mere $5 a Day." Whether she or the organizers of the human rights conference she came to address noticed the coincidence, I don't know. I suspect, however, that the image of Guatemala it projected would not have been to their liking.

It is unclear from the piece whether the writer, Margaret Piton, had actually visited Guatemala: she provides the prospective tourist with a long list of enticements, but these are mostly culled from Paul Glassman's *Guatemala Guide*. Piton packages Guatemala as cheap, romantic, and not to be missed by anyone interested in an exotic travel experience. She writes:

> The ideal travel destination would probably be a country with beautiful scenery, a spring-like climate, nice beaches, historic buildings and ruins, fine handicrafts, and low prices. Such a country does exist—and it isn't on the other side of the world. Guatemala has all the above attributes and can be easily reached in a day's travel.

Piton goes on at length about the glories of Guatemala. Then, toward the end of her piece, she offers the following reflection:

> There is no such thing as a perfect travel destination and Guatemala, like every country, has problems. Poverty is widespread and petty theft is common in some areas—especially markets. Political violence flares up from time to time, although the situation seems to have improved with the present civilian government.

The Guatemala that Rigoberta Menchú speaks of is far removed from the "low prices," "beautiful beaches," and "tasty, filling meals" that Margaret

Piton writes about. Menchú's message to the people gathered in Toronto's Church of the Holy Trinity—that we live in a careless world, one that acts wantonly and forgets too easily—could not have been more opportune.

Menchú first recounted the details of her life in Guatemala in an oral history given shape, structure, and the authority of print by Elisabeth Burgos-Debray, a Venezuelan scholar who pieced together, in autobiographical form, interviews she conducted with Menchú in Paris in 1982. After the publication of her testimony in Spanish in 1983—an English translation, *I, Rigoberta Menchú: An Indian Woman in Guatemala,* appeared a year later—Menchú began to travel across Europe and North America speaking about her beloved but tormented Guatemala. Her work as a human rights activist was instrumental in her being awarded the 1992 Nobel Peace Prize.

An indigenous Guatemalan of K'iche' Maya lineage, Menchú was twenty-three years old when she and Burgos-Debray recorded her testimony. Burgos-Debray recalls:

> Rigoberta spent a week in Paris. In order to make things easier and to make the best possible use of her time, she came to stay with me. Every day for a week, we began to record her story at nine in the morning, broke for lunch about one, and then continued until six in the evening. We often worked after dinner too, either making more recordings or preparing questions for the next day. At the end of the week I had twenty-four hours of conversation on tape.

The transition from spoken to written word, Burgos-Debray informs us, involved two key stages:

> I began by transcribing all the tapes. By that I mean that nothing was left out, not a word, even if it was used incorrectly or was later changed. I altered neither the style nor the sentence structure. The Spanish original covers almost five hundred pages of typescript.

Burgos-Debray then set about the tricky job of editing Menchú's words in order to lend them narrative coherence:

> I soon reached the decision to give the manuscript the form of a monologue: that was how it came back to me as I re-read it. I therefore decided to delete all my questions. By doing so I became what I really was: Rigoberta's listener. I allowed her to speak and then became her instrument, her

double. . . . This decision made my task more difficult, as I had to insert linking passages if the manuscript was to read like a monologue, like one continuous narrative. I then divided it into chapters organized around the themes I had already identified. I followed my original chronological outline, even though our conversations had not done so, so as to make the text more accessible to the reader.

The text created by Burgos-Debray, like that of most oral histories, is not without its flaws. Menchú is at times repetitious, obscure, vague, and inconsistent. She collapses separate episodes into a single event, mixing time and place in ways that incense academic purists, especially those who believe in the myth of objective social science. Collective memory is of necessity selective memory, subjective memory. Such ways of remembering are simply how the K'iche' and other oral cultures operate. They are also, in large measure, the reason why Menchú's testimony has such universal appeal: the voice that working with Burgos-Debray has given her speaks as much for an entire people as for one person. Her experiences in Guatemala also form the centerpiece of a documentary film, *When the Mountains Tremble* (1983). Soon after her week in Paris with Burgos-Debray, long before the heady days of the Nobel laureate, Menchú became an important cultural icon.

This unusual status for a Maya woman is linked directly to the power of her testimony. Menchú begins by telling about her father, mother, brothers, and sisters, and about growing up not just in the remote highland village where she was born but also on plantations on the Pacific coast where her family, like most Maya families, spent part of each year picking coffee or cotton. The trip from the *altiplano*, or highlands, down to the plantations, known in Guatemala as *fincas*, is not one for a delicate stomach:

> I remember the journey by lorry very well. . . . The lorry holds about forty people. But in with the people go the animals (dogs, cats, chickens), which the people from the *altiplano* take with them while they are in the *finca*. . . . It sometimes took two nights and a day from my village to the coast. During the trip the animals and the small children used to dirty the lorry and you'd get people vomiting and wetting themselves. . . . The lorry is covered with a tarpaulin so you can't see the countryside you're passing through. . . . The stuffiness inside the lorry with the cover on, and the smell of urine and vomit, make you want to be sick yourself just from being in there. By the time we got to the *finca*, we were totally stupefied; we were like chickens coming out of a pot.

Time spent working on *fincas,* Menchú tells us, was followed by a spell serving as a maid in a well-to-do household. Menchú's recollection of domestic service abounds in details of abuse and degradation:

> The food they gave me was a few beans with some very hard *tortillas.* There was a dog in the house, a pretty, white, fat dog. When I saw the maid bring out the dog's food—bits of meat, rice, things that the family ate—and they gave me a few beans and hard *tortillas,* that hurt me very much. The dog had a good meal and I didn't deserve as good a meal as the dog.

Washing dishes and mopping floors, however, was not without reward, for it was in such exploited keep that Menchú groped toward a better knowledge of Spanish.

Becoming fluent in Spanish changed her life. Following the example of her father, a community activist, in 1977 Menchú joined a peasant organization responsible for raising the political consciousness of rural workers. Being bilingual meant that as well as canvassing in her own and other K'iche'-speaking communities, she could travel throughout Guatemala and communicate with Spanish-speaking Ladinos who, in her words, "also live in terrible conditions, the same as we [Mayas] do." By the late 1970s, as civil war between guerrillas and the national armed forces began to take a heavy toll, Menchú aligned herself firmly on the side of the insurgents, committed to revolution as the only means of achieving peasant demands for human rights and social justice.

Counterinsurgency war has scarred Menchú's life, like that of many Guatemalans, in horrific ways. Of a list of family members numbering fifteen, seven met their death violently, including her parents, Vicente and Juana. Her father was burned alive on January 31, 1980, in a blaze that gutted the Spanish embassy in Guatemala City when it was fired at by government security forces ordered to end a peaceful occupation by leaders protesting against repression in the countryside. Several weeks later her mother was kidnapped, beaten, and raped, left to die after being dumped by the army on a deserted hillside far from the Menchú family home:

> When my mother died, the soldiers stood over her and urinated in her mouth; even after she was dead! Then they left a permanent sentry there to guard her body so that no-one could take it away, not even what was left of it. The soldiers were there right by her body, and they could smell my mother when she started to smell very strongly. They were there right by

her; they ate near her, and, if the animals will excuse me, I believe not even animals act like that, like those savages in the army. After that, my mother was eaten by animals; by dogs, by all the *zopilotes* [vultures].

Menchú states that the soldiers stayed at the site for four months, "until they saw that not a bit of my mother was left, not even her bones, and then they went away."

In *Crossing Borders,* a sequel to *I, Rigoberta Menchú* published in 1998, Menchú informs us that her mother's death occurred soon after she fled Guatemala for the safety of exile in Mexico. Of that last farewell, she writes:

I will never get over the trauma of having left my mother so shortly before her death. It was my last chance to feel a mother's warmth. If I had known, I would at least have paused to look at her, to gaze at her face for the last time. I would have tried, to the very last, to learn more about her. All I could think of in my misery was that I had to go away.

Since the publication of her life story, Menchú has been criticized on the grounds of authority and accuracy by several commentators, most notably (and at greatest length) by anthropologist David Stoll in his book *Rigoberta Menchú and the Story of All Poor Guatemalans* (1999). Menchú reveals in *Crossing Borders* that Guatemalan historian Arturo Taracena "was the one who persuaded me to write my book." Menchú took Taracena's advice "because he had followed the whole story and thought it would be an injustice to a time and a people if we didn't relate it." She confesses, "After the text was compiled, I spent about two months trying to understand it," and also divulges that "seeing it on paper is very different from talking into a tape recorder." Menchú elaborates:

I realize now how shy I was. I still am, but not as much as I used to be. In those days I was innocent and naive. When I wrote that book, I simply did not know the commercial rules. I was just happy to be alive to tell my story. I had no idea about an author's copyright. I had to ask the *compañeros* in Mexico to help me understand the text, and it was painful to have to relive the content of the book. I censured several parts that might have been dangerous for people. I took out bits that referred to my village, details about my brothers and sisters, and names of people. That is why the book lacks a more specific identity and I feel it will be my duty to provide this before I die.

Her dream, she says, is to reach an agreement with Burgos-Debray and the French publisher Editions Gallimard "to recover the rights to *I, Rigoberta Menchú* and to expand it," because she wants "to give it back to Guatemala and the coming generations as part of their history."

Stoll's problem with Menchú's testimony, as rendered by Burgos-Debray, revolves around his assertion that "her story is not the eyewitness account that it purports to be." He links a good deal of his argument, and attributes much of his being disquieted in the first place, to Menchú's depiction of the killing of her sixteen-year-old brother, Petrocinio. In *I, Rigoberta Menchú* she tells us:

> The lorry with the tortured came in. They started to take them out one by one. . . . Each of the tortured had different wounds . . . but my mother recognized her son, my little brother, among them. . . . My brother was very badly tortured, he could hardly stand up. . . . He was cut in various places. His head was shaved and slashed. He had no nails. He had no soles to his feet. The earlier wounds were suppurating from infection. . . . I found it impossible to concentrate, seeing that this could be. You could only think that these were human beings and what pain those bodies had felt to arrive at that unrecognizable state. . . . My mother wept. She almost risked her own life by going to embrace my brother. My other brothers and my father held her back so she wouldn't endanger herself. . . . The captain said, "This isn't the last of their punishments, there's another one yet. . . ." They lined up the tortured and poured petrol on them; and then the soldiers set fire to each one of them.

In the course of his fieldwork Stoll interviewed a number of people about the episode, and records a variation in how this particular event is remembered: "When I brought up Rigoberta's story of prisoners being burned alive in the plaza of Chajul, all I harvested were quizzical looks." Stoll favors another version of events, one gathered while he was investigating the affair and which he corroborates with information contained in an "Open Letter," dated January 31, 1980, distributed by the Democratic Front Against Repression. One man recalled the following scene, which took place after the Guatemalan army had killed a number of guerrilla suspects:

> From a military truck they threw down the cadavers, one by one. I think there were seven. They rang the church bell and summoned the people, to say that [the dead] were guerrillas. The army also said that they were from San Miguel Uspantán. This was done to make the people afraid, to make an

example [of the victims]. . . . Yes, they burned a body. But he was already dead; he wasn't alive.

Stoll himself acknowledges that "as best anyone can determine," the people killed at Chajul "included her [Menchú's] brother." He also concedes, "In and of itself, the contrast between Rigoberta's account and everyone else's is not very significant." None of this, however, deters him from subjecting Menchú's version of certain events and circumstances to sustained scrutiny, for motives he never makes entirely clear.

Does it matter whether the Guatemalan army shot Menchú's brother or tortured him before burning him alive? Does it matter that Menchú says one thing about how Petrocinio was executed and Stoll's informant says something slightly different? Is not the most pertinent information the incontestable fact that murder was committed in an atmosphere of terror that both sources not only agree upon but can also describe with as much convergence as divergence of opinion? "There can rarely be a definitive version of the past and rarely a particular truth," Merilyn Simonds has written, "only the larger truths of existence." Menchú's account, like others of the testimonial genre to which it belongs, conforms to this existential criterion. What should concern us most is the authority with which her testimony bears collective, representative witness, not its inability to meet standards of verifiable proof invoked by the magnifying glass of western social science, quite simply a spurious canon by which to judge a composite viewpoint.

Stoll's dissection of *I, Rigoberta Menchú* is all the more difficult to fathom given that Menchú emphasizes, in the book's opening paragraph, that her testimony rests as much on communal experiences as eyewitness credentials. She spells out:

> This is my testimony. I didn't learn it from a book and I didn't learn it alone. I'd like to stress that it's not only *my* life, it's also the testimony of my people. It's hard for me to remember everything in my life that's happened to me since there have been many very bad times but, yes, moments of joy as well. The important thing is that what happened to me has happened to many other people too. . . . My experience is the reality of a whole people.

The communal emphasis of Menchú's words, made apparent at the very outset of her testimony, makes redundant or at least renders less valid Stoll's lugubrious exercise in fact-checking, which he conducts as if Menchu's account was exclusively cast as that of single, infallible narrator.

As a text, one that has been read in translation in over a dozen languages, Menchú's testimony has reached a global audience and has had an immense impact in drawing international attention to the atrocities committed against Maya peoples in Guatemala. How she comes across in print, however, does not compare with the experience of hearing her in person. When she spoke that evening in Toronto, clad in a colorful wraparound skirt and a sleeveless *huipil* that defied the February cold, she was sitting around a table among fellow Guatemalan exiles, joking as well as consoling, laughing one minute, somber the next. As I listened to the passion with which she kept her family alive by the telling of the horror of their deaths, I was struck more than ever by the enormity of Maya survival, by the spirit of her people in the face of calamity. That vital human trait, one that declares "We are still here," is what she articulates in remarkable personal fashion and communicates to her listeners.

Two years after hearing her speak in Toronto, I was asked to translate for Menchú while she was doing a speaking engagement in Kingston. Moves to nominate her for the Nobel Peace Prize had just begun. It was a gala community event, complete with a potluck supper, attendance by the mayor, and a book signing turned into a marathon by her earnest desire to inscribe each copy of her book with the best wishes of the author. My inscription reads: "*Con mucho cariño para Jorge* . . . For George, with great affection, this keepsake from my people to you. It is the cause of our struggle and a small part of our memory. With all my heart, Rigoberta Menchú." It was nearly eight o'clock when the audience settled down to hear her speak.

The church hall had few empty seats. We sat side by side on the stage. "*Me llamo Rigoberta Menchú y este es mi testimonio*. . . . My name is Rigoberta Menchú and this is my testimony." Her voice was calm but plaintive, her words measured, sure, precise. She spoke for almost three hours, which exhausted me more than it did her. Then she fielded questions. It was well after eleven when the evening ended.

After the audience had dispersed, Menchú thanked me for my services and apologized for the number of instances she had spoken beyond the length of time suitable for ideal translation. She then said something that will stay with me always.

"You understand, Jorge," she whispered, "that I can't tell them everything I know, everything that happened. If I do that, they might not believe me. I can only tell so much. It's better that way."

Much to her credit, Menchú used the prize money that accompanied her Nobel award to establish a foundation whose mission is summed up in an eloquent code of ethics: "There can be no peace without justice, no justice without equality, no equality without development, no development without democracy, and no democracy without respect for the dignity and identity of all cultures and peoples." Driven by this code of ethics, Menchú has lobbied at considerable risk for the prosecution of government leaders under whose rule the crimes to which she bore witness were carried out. Well aware that such an indictment was unlikely to come from the Guatemalan judiciary, she pursued the matter overseas, her efforts resulting in a decision by the Spanish Constitutional Court to proceed with the trial of former government officials for "crimes of genocide, torture, murder, and illegal imprisonment committed in Guatemala between 1978 and 1986." The Constitutional Court, the highest legal entity in Spain, decreed in 2005 that "the principle of universal jurisdiction takes precedence over the existence or not of national interests." One year later it called for the extradition of two notorious heads of state in the 1980s, General Efraín Ríos Montt and his successor, General Oscar Humberto Mejía Víctores. While it is unlikely that either of them will be judged in a Spanish court of law, Menchu's persistence at least resulted in the moral victory of Ríos Montt being placed under house arrest, no small feat given the impunity he and military leaders like him enjoy in Guatemala.

Menchú has political ambitions of her own. She ran in the presidential election of 2007 for the party Encuentro por Guatemala (Together for Guatemala), placing a distant seventh in the first round of voting held on September 7. Though her share of ballots cast was a mere 3 percent, 101,316 votes in total, her idealism remains undiminished. Menchú's hope is that the movement of indigenous leaders she helped to found, Winaq, will be better placed to compete in the election scheduled for 2011. That a Maya woman may one day serve as the president of Guatemala is surely now no harder to imagine than a Maya woman already having won the Nobel Peace Prize.

THREE

JAKALTEK AMERICAN

Jacaltenango is a remote, unkempt-looking town at the western edge of the Cuchumatanes Mountains close to the Guatemalan border with Mexico. It is known to the scholarly world as a stop on the route taken in 1925 by Frans Blom and Oliver La Farge, who afterward produced a two-volume record, *Tribes and Temples* (1926, 1927), about their reconnaissance. La Farge returned to Jacaltenango two years later with fellow researcher Douglas Byers, with whom he penned *The Year Bearer's People* (1931), another classic contribution in the field of Mesoamerican anthropology.

Both works, especially the latter, document an intriguing array of Maya survivals. One of the most remarkable was the persistence in Jacaltenango of a method of observing the passage of time according to a pre-Columbian calendar, complete with rites and ceremonies that date back centuries, if not millennia. In his introductory remarks to *The Year Bearer's People*, Blom aptly likened the intent of La Farge and Byers "to that of a man trying to become familiar with the ritual of a Masonic Lodge without becoming a Mason himself." All three men spent long and distinguished careers studying indigenous cultures in Guatemala and other parts of the Americas.

As part of the decolonization of academic life in Guatemala, Jacaltenango is now being written about not by visiting anthropologists but by one of its native sons. Before he himself trained and became accredited in the discipline while studying in the United States, Victor Montejo engaged local lore and storytelling in two books, *El Kanil: Man of Lightning* (1984) and *The Bird Who Cleans the World* (1991). The first book presents an elaborate legend that La Farge and Byers recorded only fragments of; the second is a collection of fables that resonate with the moral authority of Aesop, Jakaltek folk tales that Montejo heard as a boy from his mother and community elders. In *Testimony* (1987), however, social not magical realism prevails as he grapples with Jacaltenango's grim lot during counterinsurgency operations in 1982.

On the morning of September 9 that year, a Friday, Montejo woke in a small village some distance from Jacaltenango. His job then was to teach village children as resident schoolmaster. Friday, he writes, "has always been a happy day for me, full of anticipation," for after class he would set off to return home to Jacaltenango to spend the weekend with his wife and children. An elementary school teacher, Montejo had worked for ten years as a government employee in the Department of Education, preferring to take a humble post within reasonable reach of his home rather than seek employment in a more illustrious setting farther away. Montejo was satisfied with his decision to go back to his roots after graduating from teacher's college.

That Friday class unfolded as usual until one of the villagers burst into the schoolhouse and screamed, "The guerrillas are approaching. . . . Everyone get ready!" The peal of the church bell confirmed the danger. Montejo recalls:

> I consulted my watch and saw it was eleven in the morning. At almost the same instant I heard the first shot fired. Behind it came a volley of machine gun fire. The peaceful community broke into confusion. The women wept and prayed to God to protect their husbands and older sons who had been forced to join the civil [defense] patrol.
>
> I ordered the students to stretch out on the floor and barred the door and windows with old broomsticks. The invaders had encircled the village and the hills echoed the furious explosions of grenades and the sputter of bullets that whistled past the corrugated tin roof of the schoolhouse.
>
> "Don't make a sound," I ordered my children. Some began to weep and others trembled with fear. Their fathers were in the midst of that gunfire, armed with sticks, stones, and slingshots and the children were fully aware of the danger they were in.

It turned out to be a tragic case of mistaken identity. The local civil defense patrol had seen an armed group of men moving through village territory and assumed that they were guerrillas. The patrol opened fire, wounding one of the intruders, but then noticed that the guns the intruders replied with emitted the distinctive "coughing noise of Galil rifles," the standard Israeli-made issue of the Guatemalan army. Realizing their error, the members of the civil patrol fled to escape retaliation.

Chaos erupted as the army attacked the village. After a while the shooting died down, and Montejo deemed it safe enough to dismiss his students, who "fled like deer out the door" and raced off to find their parents. He then joined other villagers ordered by the army to assemble in the school patio. There and in the space adjoining the village church the army was getting ready for a public execution, rounding up local militiamen who had been captured and accused of being guerrillas. They tied five men to a row of pillars. Montejo attempted to intervene and explain to the enraged officer in charge just what had happened:

> "Good afternoon, my lieutenant," I said respectfully. . . .
>
> "What do you want, you—" he snapped.
>
> "I am the schoolmaster in this village and have come to let you know that the people you're holding captive are members of the civil patrol. By accident they mistook you for guerrillas."
>
> "Don't come to me with those stories. These sons of bitches are guerrillas. That's why they attacked us, and I am going to execute every damn one of them."
>
> I went on, unperturbed. "Up there by the chapel the rest of the men are waiting to clear up the situation for you."
>
> "With me you have nothing to clear up. Everything is already clear. They've wounded one of my soldiers, and all of you will have to pay for it. What more do you want to know?"
>
> "I beseech my lieutenant to forgive these people. All the men are members of the patrol and guard the village day and night, as you have verified for yourself. What a pity they mistook you, because of your olive green uniforms."
>
> The commander made no reply, but went on inspecting [some] boxes and chests. . . . "This radio interests me. Take it along," he called out.

Montejo's intervention proved futile. The lean majesty of his prose, translated beautifully from Spanish into English by Victor Perera, only heightens the horror of what took place next, when the firing squad set about its work:

> The five condemned men turned to one another, uncomprehending. They set their eyes above the heads of the *kaibiles* [soldiers] who were lining up to discharge their weapons into their hearts. No one spoke. The hapless captives gazed toward the horizon, as though to bid farewell to the hills that had nurtured them. . . .
>
> As the commander prepared to give the fatal order, the condemned turned instinctively for a last look at their loved ones. Their hands were tied behind their back so they could give vent to their feelings only with strained smiles and bitter tears.
>
> "FIRE . . . !" The cavernous voice of the commander rang out, and the Galils exploded with thunderous fury.

The women raised a deafening howl. Dazed with grief, they tried to fling themselves on the bullet-ridden bodies of their beloved ones, but once again the *kaibiles* forced them to draw back by threatening them point blank.

The victims slumped and hung from the pillars as the warm, copious blood drenched their shirts.

After the execution Montejo's personal situation quickly deteriorated. Under torture a villager demented by pain gave Montejo's name as a guerrilla sympathizer, and so the schoolmaster was sought out, bound, beaten, and led "like a thief or a murderer" back to army headquarters in Jacaltenango, where he was interrogated and beaten again. Death, he believed, seemed inevitable:

> I was bothered by the knotted rope around my neck and stuck my fingers repeatedly under the noose to prevent it from choking me. My dignity as a schoolmaster, I said to myself. These bastards are making a display of me, as if I were an assassin, a thief or a common criminal. I spat my darkest unspoken thoughts on the ground. . . . In all my thirty years I had not known darker days than the present ones.

Fortune, however, favored him. Insisting always on his innocence, Montejo was eventually released from captivity, but only on the condition that he visit army headquarters and report on "every person" he thought might be "involved with the guerrillas." Repugnant though this condition was to him, he accepted it to protect himself and his family. Once home, living by his wits for weeks on end, he resisted being forced to inform on others until he was finally able to flee into exile and arrange for his wife and children to follow. The family lived for many years in California, eventually becoming American citizens. After Montejo departed Guatemala, suspicion fell on his parents, forcing them also to flee Jacaltenango. They lived for a while in Canada.

In recording his ordeal, Montejo is careful not to lapse into indiscriminate hatred. During his captivity, one soldier offered Montejo food and a blanket, causing him to reflect: "I thanked God that not every soldier was malevolent and devoid of human feelings. His gesture made me understand that in their own way—although they dare not say so—they too are victims of a violence that has become institutionalized." Judging by the way they spoke, Montejo was able to identify the soldiers involved in the operation as natives of Sololá or Totonicapán, Mayas like himself.

Heavy of heart, Montejo observes how terror sows division and distrust among Maya communities, how it corrodes group solidarity. The scorn with which the soldiers rebuked his pleas of reason — "you don't fool any of us with your high-sounding jabber" — illustrates how risky it is to value education in a country where knowledge or the gift of self-expression can be construed as an act of subversion.

Education was the bedrock upon which Montejo reinvented himself in the United States. With customary Maya resourcefulness, he learned English and enrolled in university, earning a bachelor's and master's degree from the State University of New York at Albany and, in 1993, a doctorate in anthropology from the University of Connecticut. Afterward, he took a faculty position at the University of California, where for eight years he served as Chair of Native American Studies. He reworked his Ph.D. dissertation into a substantive monograph, *Voices from Exile: Violence and Survival in Modern Maya History* (1999). To his already impressive literary output has been added a collection of poems, *Sculpted Stones* (1995), and an illustrated retelling, for children, of the *Popol Vuh* (1999), a sacred Maya text.

When I met up with Montejo and other Mayas in Chicago in 1991 — we were attending the annual meeting of the American Anthropological Association — I was able to arrange a visit to the Newberry Library, where we inspected a copy of the *Popol Vuh* made in the late seventeenth century by the Dominican friar Francisco Ximénez. The original is either lost or in safe keeping beyond our ken. It was a very emotional day. During a ceremony of symbolic repatriation, the Q'eqchi' spiritual leader and native rights activist Antonio Pop Caal was reduced to tears as he held the Maya bible and chanted a prayer. Don Antonio, who studied philosophy and theology at the University of Salamanca in Spain before returning to work in his Verapaz homeland, is now in the arms of his Maya makers: on December 17, 2002, having been abducted two months before, his decapitated body was found in a well.

For his part, Montejo has become a critic not only of American anthropology and Guatemalan politics but also of the indigenous movement to which he belongs, subjecting it to scrutiny in a trenchant book of essays, *Maya Intellectual Renaissance* (2005). As an assimilated American academic with a Fulbright scholarship among his many awards and distinctions, Montejo has faced the challenge of returning to Guatemala and getting involved in political life there. In elections held on December 28, 2003, he won a congressional seat and was later named by presidential winner Oscar Berger to serve in 2004 and 2005 as the newly created Minister of Peace. The corruption so endemic to holding any political post in Guatemala was one Montejo and his team managed to keep at bay, a trait recognized by the National Award for

Transparency in Office. In 2006 he was elected president of the Congressional Commission for Indigenous Issues.

"We have to emerge from this chaos," he once told Mary Jo McConahay in an interview with Pacific News Service. "We need people in this country who can create [a] strong relationship with the United States. The indigenous, for instance, will not simply tell Washington what it wants to hear."

A Jakaltek American has spoken.

FOUR

DOÑA MAGDALENA

We arrived in Santa Cruz del Quiché shortly before noon, drove slowly around the main square, then waited as instructed in front of the church. I spotted Tina before Lorenzo did. She made her way unhurriedly across the plaza, looking relaxed and composed. I found it remarkable to think that she had given birth to a baby girl only days before. Everything with Tina was the opposite of drama. She specialized in being matter of fact, which made her a reliable stringer.

I heard her call out our names as she approached the jeep. We nodded. "You're early," Tina said. "Doña Magdalena's eating lunch. The women from CONAVIGUA have still to arrive. You can order something to eat also before we head out to San José." Lorenzo's contacts had come through. We might yet get the film footage he most wanted.

Magdalena González, eighty-five years of age, polished off her soup but picked her way through the main course. She complained about the *tortillas,* which looked and tasted like burnt cardboard. She drank her Pepsi *al tiempo,* unchilled, straight out of the bottle. Flies buzzed around the table. Doña Magdalena declined coffee but accepted the offer of tea. She had the most weathered face I have ever seen, rutted with deep lines that absorbed shiny beads of perspiration. Her grey hair was braided in pigtails tied with strands of bright pink ribbon. We sat in the restaurant waiting for Josefa and Tomasa. The bus from Guatemala City, to no one's surprise, was late.

When the women from the widows' support group, CONAVIGUA, finally arrived, they too had to eat. While their meals were being prepared, they brought Doña Magdalena into the conversation, which our lack of K'iche' and her limited Spanish had hitherto prevented. All three Maya women chatted in their native tongue, with Josefa and Tomasa translating into Spanish for our benefit, as well as relaying questions into K'iche' for Doña Magdalena to answer. Doña Magdalena was clearly at ease with the two much younger women, who had helped her with her earlier petitions. The time we spent together in the restaurant set things up nicely for the on-camera sequences Lorenzo was to shoot in San José.

There was room in the jeep for one passenger only. Tomasa volunteered. Josefa rode with Doña Magdalena in Tina's car, along with Tina's baby girl and her nanny. We followed them for about half an hour along the dusty, dry-season road. Boys and men were hard at work readying the fields before the onset of rain. Tomasa explained to us her and Josefa's involvement in CONAVIGUA, which Doña Magdalena had contacted in her efforts to recover the bodies of her husband and her son.

San José Pachó de Lemoa is a hamlet of some twenty to thirty houses near the larger settlement of San Sebastián Lemoa. Doña Magdalena was born in San Sebastián and lived there until she married at age twenty. Her husband, Pablo, one year her junior, persuaded her to move to San José because his family compound offered more space and better access to land. Doña Magdalena's mother had died years before, and her father also soon after her marriage, so she convinced her husband that his orphaned in-laws, three girls and two boys, should also move to San José. The eldest of seven—one brother died early on, after becoming sick while working on a coffee plantation— Doña Magdalena kept an eye out for her siblings while looking after Pablo and raising Diego, their only child. The young couple were a hard-working team. Pablo tilled their land and sought contracts as a hired hand. What he loved most was to play the marimba. He was also an accomplished drummer, and thus an important member of the village band. Doña Magdalena is good with her hands too. Since age seven she has woven *trenzas*, narrow palm bands used to line the inside of hats. She rarely sits at home without the trappings of her craft scattered around her.

The family compound in San José is home to over fifteen people, from toddlers to the elderly. Paulino, one of Doña Magdalena's grandsons, was only eleven when his father was murdered. He takes us to a room and shows us his parents' wedding photo, which reveals bride and groom looking stiff and uncomfortable in clothes that don't seem to fit. Paulino says he looks at the photograph every day, pinned to a wall alongside a religious calendar and a poster of the Brazilian World Cup soccer squad.

Lorenzo flutters from one side of the compound to another, worse than the resident chickens. "I'm worried about the light," he says for the umpteenth time. "Two things. Ask the old lady if she can turn around a bit so her face is in the sun. And could she stop weaving hat bands? The rustling noise her hands make interferes with the sound of her voice. It'll muddy up the tape."

It is Tomasa's turn to be go-between. Doña Magdalena lays down her *trenza* at the same time Lorenzo lays down his camera. She reaches for the soft drink Tina has brought her, sipping through a straw from a plastic bag while Lorenzo loads a new battery.

"Right. Ask her when she's speaking *not* to look at the camera," he says to Tomasa. "Tell her to look over my shoulder." Doña Magdalena starts to talk again, in accordance with Lorenzo's wishes.

She speaks mostly about her son, Diego. A member of the local cooperative and church group called Catholic Action, he labored for the betterment not just of his family but for the whole community. It was Diego who lobbied to have San José connected by a dirt road to the main highway. He was the one who hounded the authorities in Santa Cruz del Quiché to install running water and build a school. Diego knew how to read and write and wanted others to learn also. After the earthquake in 1976, when the church was levelled and had to be rebuilt, he organized people to do the work. All these initiatives made him well known, distinguished him from the crowd. Diego was liked by most but not by all, for there were some in the community who thought him arrogant, smart, and pushy, too big for his boots.

"People who get things done make people who do nothing jealous. Jealousy breeds hatred. That's just how it is." Doña Magdalena's words ring true for more than just the small-town ways of San José.

Whenever she warned Diego about people talking about him, he shrugged it off. "I do what I think needs to be done," he would say. Even Diego, however, admitted that it was best to maintain a low profile when the situation deteriorated in the early 1980s, for he was precisely the kind of individual whose social awareness was considered a threat, whose "Catholic Action" was interpreted as "communist subversion." When the worst of the killings were under way, Diego cooled his heels and even left San José for a while. His absence, unfortunately, only fuelled the local rumor mill and served to increase suspicion on the part of his enemies that he was up to something.

The date is etched forever in Doña Magdalena's mind. She mouths it with the reference of prayer: *"Era la tarde del día domingo veintiseis de diciembre milnovicientos ochenta y dos. . . .* It was the afternoon of Sunday, December 26, 1982." She and Pablo were at home when members of the civil defense patrol arrived, entered the family compound, and demanded to know the whereabouts of their son. Pablo answered that Diego had gone off to work in Guatemala City. The patrol members accused Pablo of lying. They threatened him in an attempt to get him to disclose the truth. Pablo insisted that he was telling them the truth, but still they would not believe him. When he resisted attempts to be bound and taken captive, he was punched and kicked. Then an old man in his seventies, he was soon overpowered. Led away with his hands tied behind his back, shoved and cursed, Pablo has not been seen since.

After the abduction, Doña Magdalena chose the same manner of dealing with the tragedy as countless thousands of Guatemalans: silence. Through fear of reprisal from denouncing the crime, she sought instead to cover it up. What she feared most was that Diego would hear of his father's disappearance and return to San José.

How word reached him she doesn't know, but Diego's response to the news, as expected, was to go home to see his mother. Doña Magdalena again has no difficulty remembering the date: February 12, 1983. The *orejas*—Spanish for "ears," meaning spies or informants—did their job with numbing efficiency. Soon after Diego entered the family compound, the civil defense patrol also arrived. He was surrounded, tied, beaten, then led under armed guard to the schoolhouse. Doña Magdalena followed all the way, weeping and pleading. Members of the patrol threatened to kill her unless she left immediately. *"Eschuché un disparo. . . .* I heard a gun go off and knew it was him, that my son was dead."

She pauses to wipe her eyes. Tomasa translates in a voice that becomes so quiet it is barely audible. Josefa takes over as Doña Magdalena resumes.

For almost ten years it was deemed unsafe and unwise to bring the matter to anyone's attention. Then a fear stronger than reprisal began to eat away at Doña Magdalena: that she herself would die without giving Diego a proper burial. Maya Catholicism can be an unorthodox, hybrid faith, but it is practiced at all times by people who believe that the dead must be buried with dignity and respect. Doña Magdalena got in touch with CONAVIGUA through her church. CONAVIGUA, in turn, engaged the interest of the forensic scientist Clyde Snow, whose research team took the case on as part of an attempt to come to terms with Guatemala's unwholesome past.

People in San José knew where to look. At the bottom of a ravine not far from Doña Magdalena's home only a thin layer of soil covered Diego and five other victims. She watched with members of her family as the bones were unearthed. A dozen or so locals also looked on. Exhumation allowed positive identification and the opportunity to allay grief with decent burial. Diego now rests in peace. Pablo's remains have yet to be found.

"Es raro," Paulino says. "It's strange. We know who killed my father. They are our neighbors. One lives right over there and two others just up here." He gestures with his arms this way and that, aware that his grandmother is listening.

"When we meet them out walking, we still say hello," he says. "We talk with them, but not about my father. He's never mentioned. We talk about other things: animals, the price of food, the rain, how the corn is doing. They know that we know. But they never have been brought to trial. I don't know why."

Doña Magdalena sighs, picks up her *trenza,* and starts to weave.

The first time I told this story, I considered it prudent not to use the real names of Doña Magdalena and her family. After the brokering of a peace agreement in 1996, however, human rights initiatives encouraged people to speak out, even if no guarantees could be made for their safety. During a subsequent visit to San José, I asked Paulino what he thought about the idea of my recounting events without resorting to pseudonyms, even including photographs of family members in the narration. Paulino, who by then had assumed the role of chief breadwinner, discussed my idea and later gave me collective family consent. I asked more questions and took lots of photographs: of Paulino and his wife, María, of their home surroundings, and of their many children. I noticed that Doña Magdalena was especially fond of one little girl in particular, her great-granddaughter Lucía. Their cooperation allowed me to feature the family in an earlier edition of this book. Even though it was published in a language no one in the family could understand, I looked forward to returning to San José and presenting it to them.

This I was eventually able to do a week before Christmas. Arriving unannounced, I walked along the trail that led from the school toward the family compound. A dog barked as I drew near. Two children peered from behind a line of washing to see who was approaching. I recognized little Lucía. She ran to fetch her father. Paulino wiped some dirt from his hand before he extended it in welcome.

"*Buenos días, Jorge.* You've come to visit us. We wondered when you would."

He invited me to sit down and offered me a cup of *atol,* a hot drink made of cornmeal and spiced with peppers. I sipped it while saying hello to family members of all ages who joined us in the patio. Out of a room adjacent to the compound entrance stepped Doña Magdalena, not looking any older than when last I saw her but limping more noticeably. Paulino helped her to a chair. I smiled at her as she made herself comfortable. Doña Magdalena smiled back at me.

"I have a present for you."

Paulino translated as I handed her a gift.

"And these are for you to share among the children," I said to Paulino.

The bag he took from me I had filled with crayons, notepads, candy, and chewing gum. A couple of youngsters rushed to Paulino's side. Doña Magdalena, meanwhile, held the small package as if she didn't quite know what to do, looking at it until Paulino's wife helped her undo the wrapping.

"It's a book. A book with photographs for you to look at," I said.

Since neither woman could read, I took the book and opened it at the section containing photographs. I pointed to the image on the upper right of the first page.

"*Es la abuela!*" Paulino's wife exclaimed. "*Es la abuela con Lucía!*"

The youngsters dipping their hands into the bag I'd given Paulino scurried to their mother's side to see for themselves. Their shouts brought more children gathering around. Doña Magdalena joined in with her own cries. Then she fell quiet, examined the photograph below the one of herself and Lucía, and let out the loudest cry of all.

"What's she saying?" I asked Paulino.

Beneath the image of Doña Magdalena and her great-granddaughter was a photograph of Rigoberta Menchú. Before any human rights initiatives were feasible, it bears repeating, it was Rigoberta's testimony that alerted the outside world to the horrors of civil war in Guatemala. Doña Magdalena brandished the book over her head, and spoke, her voice tinged with sadness.

"She says she won't be as famous as Rigoberta Menchú," Paulino explained to me, "but people will see them in the book and know they shared the same experiences."

When I next visited San José, the village storekeeper watched me park the jeep and came over to tell me before I took the path to the family compound that Doña Magdalena had died. I thanked her and cursed myself for not having made the trip sooner.

I walked to the family compound, which was eerily empty. Not even a dog barked in warning. I called aloud several times, but nobody replied. A radio had been left on. The drone of marimba music was a fitting lament.

Knowing that the children were still in school—I had heard a class chant a multiplication table as I walked past—I returned to wait in the playground. During recess I asked a teacher if he could help me identify one of Paulino's boys or girls. "I've been out to the house," I explained, "but no one's home. I'd like to pay my respects. Someone I knew in the family is dead."

The teacher helped me locate the eldest of Paulino's daughters. "My father is working in Santa Cruz and won't be back until dark," she told me. "My mother is over at my aunt's. I'll go and get her for you."

The girl crossed the playground to a house that lay behind the village store. I followed. Paulino's wife, María, appeared and greeted me.

"I'm sorry to hear about Doña Magdalena," I said. "I understand that Paulino won't be back until later this evening. Would it be possible for you to take me to see her grave?"

María agreed. She led me to a plot of ground about a mile away. The family had buried Doña Magdalena not in the local cemetery, where the killers of her husband and her son one day might be, but in a clearing we walked to through fields of towering corn.

A wooden cross, painted red, distinguishes Doña Magdalena's grave from a handful of others. María approached and stood over it. A baby peered out from the shawl tied to her back. A barefoot toddler held on to her mother's skirt. Laid to rest in a clearing by a cornfield, Doña Magdalena had to struggle no longer.

We returned in silence to San José. The school that Diego helped to build was emptying out. Children ran and yelled and larked about, several of Paulino and María's among them. The sight of so much life cheered me up.

When it was time for me to leave, María asked if she could have a copy of my book. Fortunately, I'd thought to bring one with me.

"Here you are, María. But remember, I left a book with Doña Magdalena when I passed through on my last visit. We all admired the photograph of her, the one with her sitting next to little Lucía."

María looked at me and said, "*El libro está en la caja, Jorge. Está en la caja con la abuela.*"

The family had buried Doña Magdalena with the book.

FIVE

THROUGH A LENS, DARKLY

Imagine the naked body of a young woman. Her head is turned to one side, eyes closed, lips apart, mouth half-open. She is dead. A soiled cloth has been laid across her genitals. Her arms, in repose, are arranged across her chest, but they have no hands. These have been cut off, one placed beneath her right arm, another on top of her stomach. The left side of her face shows she was pretty, but the right side has been mutilated. Three deep gashes on her right arm stand out amidst myriad other lacerations. She must have departed life, had it taken from her, in a frenzy of agony. An ooze of yellow matter, uncontained by stitches sewn from skin to skin by the mortician, runs along what was once the top of her breasts. The polish with which she painted her toenails somehow withstood the torture inflicted on her, for the nail of her big toe, left foot, has a fleck of red unmistakably lighter in color than her dry, crusted blood.

Her name is Eugenia Beatriz Barrios Marroquín. Like Guatemala itself, this image of one of its citizens, one of its victims, screams in silence, a tragedy we glimpse through the steely eyes of Jean-Marie Simon. She photographed the corpse in the morgue at Escuintla. It is important that Canadians in particular know something about the facts of this case, for Beatriz Barrios had solicited, and received, formal permission to enter Canada as a political refugee. She had been issued a visa and was abducted only a day or so before she was due to leave Guatemala for Canada. In *Guatemala: Eternal Spring, Eternal Tyranny* (1987), Simon writes:

On December 10, 1985, two days after [Vinicio] Cerezo's presidential victory, 26-year-old Eugenia Beatriz Barrios Marroquín, a school teacher and mother to two small children, called for a taxi to go to a friend's home.

Minutes after she left in the taxi, she and the driver were stopped by a car carrying three armed men, who forced her out of the taxi and into their vehicle. Barrios had either been under heavy surveillance or the call that she made to the taxi dispatcher had been monitored by government intelligence. Although the taxi driver returned to tell her friend about the abduction, it was too late.

Her body was found the following day, near Palín, Escuintla, by the painted quetzal-bird rock: it had been hacked, her face carved out, her hands severed at the wrists. A piece of cardboard found near the body carried her name and the words "more to come." When security agents arrived to take fingerprints from her severed hands, Captain Armando Villegas, head of the Honor Guard G-2 intelligence office, was already there. When they asked him, "Muchá, what happened?" Villegas responded by taking out a card on which he had written Barrios's name, and told them that it was she. The writing on Villegas's card matched that on the cardboard message.

In her book Simon documents the sweep of events that, between 1982 and 1987, saw Guatemala pass through "two presidential elections, two military coups, two states of alert, two Constitutions, an eleven-month state of siege, at least four amnesty periods, and four heads of state—three of them army generals." A quarter century on, even though a civilian government is in place, the military continues to exercise tremendous clout. Nowhere in Guatemala during the war years was this more apparent than in the so-called "Ixil triangle" of the Sierra de los Cuchumatanes, a combat zone whose fields, folklore, people, and communities are highlighted throughout Simon's riveting photo essay.

It was in Ixil country, at the Pensión Tres Hermanas in Nebaj, that I last got to speak with Simon, a couple of years after her book had been published. I'd noticed her from afar earlier in the day, walking across the town square in quick, determined bursts, watchful and alert. I had some sad news to tell her, of the death of a dear friend of mine, someone she also knew, who in fact had introduced us years before at a bookstore in Antigua. I figured I'd bump into her later on, for Nebaj is like that. We ended up eating supper together in the kitchen of the *pensión*. Our conversation was somewhat hushed, for Tres Hermanas attracted soldiers from the army barracks only blocks away, who rented rooms for their trysts with visiting prostitutes.

Simon was careful not to tell me too much about what she was doing in Nebaj, but she was there to say goodbye. The country she first visited in 1980, only a year after she had started out in photography, had consumed her talents for the better part of a decade. A gutsy, driven individual, willing to confront face-to-face the unpredictable horror that death in Guatemala can assume, Simon had taken risks in getting her photographs that not many would be prepared to incur. It was time to move on—marriage and law school were on the horizon—before Guatemala caught up with her.

We said goodnight. I found myself thinking, what, as a photojournalist, does Jean-Marie Simon leave behind as a record of her years in Guatemala?

As a photographer she has an eclectic range. Her touch is varied, her vision confident and keen. She moves skilfully from dark to light, capturing in the mood of her pictures the chameleon landscape with which she wrestles—tender, cruel, cathartic, bleak, a pattern with no fixed design. She is careful to make us celebrate as well as mourn. Her photographs demand that we rejoice, not just lament, for "a nation of prisoners" is also "a nation of survivors."

As a journalist, a consultant to Americas Watch and Amnesty International, she focused on issues of human rights. Their flagrant, incessant, and bestial violation in Guatemala had in Simon a dogged, uncompromising reporter. The text of her book is informative, but her photographs are what set her apart. They are indeed striking, and they constitute a stunning collection. An Ixil mother, child in her arms, circled by government soldiers, stares toward us during interrogation. Stopped at a roadblock, a passenger on board a bus peers from the window. Dawn at Nebaj, where the walls of the church rise above the mist that shrouds rooftops and cornfields. A member of the armed forces dances with a young girl at a party, a machine gun slung across his back.

Think about what you see, her images beseech, when you look at the world. Let your gaze not be idle. Through the eyes of Jean-Marie Simon, Guatemala unsettles and disturbs, insinuates and kills.

SIX

DEVILS AND ANGELS

Just as the photographs of Jean-Marie Simon cut to the heart of Guatemala's dark reality, so too do three features by documentary filmmaker Mary Ellen Davis. Her Maya trilogy spans a decade of faltering transition from war to peace. In *The Devil's Dream* (1992), *Tierra Madre* (1996), and *Haunted Land* (2002), Davis contemplates a deeply troubled past and tries to imagine how Guatemala might one day be anything other than its tortured, unresolved self.

A staunch believer in narrative, Davis informs the viewer by the trust she places in having her protagonists tell stories. She seldom resorts to off-screen voiceovers, restricting them mostly to the questions we hear her ask quietly while on location. We are made to feel at all times part of an intimate conversation. One watches without the sense of intrusion that often pervades the documentary genre. Davis takes care not to rush her subjects. Instead, she lets them present us with information in a layered, cumulative fashion. She insists that the viewer, like herself and her crew in the field, be patient, observant, and discerning, above all else disposed to mull things over before reaching a conclusion. The viewer, in short, is forced to think, not remain passive and inert as words, sounds, and images are articulated and screened.

The Devil's Dream, operating on two very different but powerfully connected levels, is perhaps the most challenging of the three films to watch. At one level, Davis utilizes footage of "The Dance of the Twenty-Four Devils," a popular drama enacted on the streets of Ciudad Vieja, to create a vast, symbolic allegory: having declared war on humanity, the Devils form a pact with Death and seek to capture human souls with the avowed goal of bringing to an end the human species. As the Dance of Death unfolds—kitschy folkloric music accompanies campy theatrical performances—the iniquities of everyday life in Guatemala are interspersed in a series of grounded, self-contained vignettes: the assassination of José María Ixcayá, once an active member of a native rights association; the migration of entire Maya families from their homes in the mountains down to lowland plantations, where they work in the scorching heat for starvation wages; the concern of Maya mothers that the children they bring into the world, destined to be inadequately fed and thus prone to constant sickness, will not survive infancy; and the massacre perpetrated at Santiago Atitlán by government soldiers stationed there on December 2, 1990. Almost everywhere Davis looks, she observes a military presence: parading from the presidential balcony, grim-faced and sun-glassed, dressed in camouflage or cloaked in medals; overseeing with macho pride the Miss Guatemala beauty pageant; patrolling a fairground, guns at the ready, during a village fiesta; and blocking roads so that a demonstration planned by striking workers will at least be disrupted, if not abandoned altogether before violence erupts.

A fragment of conversation in *The Devil's Dream* furnishes Davis with the subject matter she pursues at length in *Tierra Madre:* native views of the relationship in Guatemala between land and life, especially how Maya values in this regard are at odds with non-Maya ones. At one juncture in *The Devil's Dream*, Rosalina Tuyuc, a leading figure in the widows' rights group CONAVIGUA, puts it thus: "Without land there is no life." This point of view, and the deeply rooted beliefs that anchor it, are developed in *Tierra Madre* by a number of individuals, among them a Maya Catholic priest, Darío Caal Xí, and a Ladino lawyer, Fredy Ochaeta. We listen to Caal speak as the lens of Guillermo Escalón, Davis's cameraman for all three films, pans the landscape and captures bits and pieces of Guatemala's haunting beauty:

> The earth is our mother. She gives life to humanity. The land belongs to God. It belongs to the people. We don't view the land as private property. We understand land as a divinity and as a mother. The earth divinity— *tierra madre, madre tierra*—is also bonded to human kind. The land nourishes humanity. The land allows us to live, to survive.

Caal, a Q'eqchi' Maya, stresses the spiritual, collective dimension of land/life relations. The perception of land as community, not commodity, ties together people living off the land, linking them back to their ancestors' past and forward to their offsprings' future. It is a relationship that, because it cherishes land as having a nonmaterial, inalienable essence, conflicts with the fundamental tenets of Western, liberal ideology upon which an export-oriented "coffee republic" was first established in Guatemala in the nineteenth century and upon which the country has been exploited and run ever since, at the expense of many for the benefit of a few. Ochaeta elaborates:

43

Our authorities have never asked themselves what it really means for native people to live and work in a community. Instead, they insist on imposing programs, studies, and so-called "agrarian laws" based on the individual, not on the community. The notion of private property does not figure in native people's thought, in their view of the world. They see, instead, a bond between the earth and mankind.

While it is the relationship between native land and native life that is emphasized in *Tierra Madre,* Davis is careful also to focus on the plight of poor Ladinos, who make up roughly the other half of Guatemala's national population. Many Ladino families in rural areas have to contend with the same deplorable conditions as their Maya counterparts, often with the added psychological burden of not having as strong a sense of community and identity to sustain them. As we listen to native voices, Davis reminds us not to forget about decent, humble, Ladino ones as well.

She does this by reconstructing the events and circumstances surrounding what happened in the settlement of Las Dos Erres, The Two Rs, on December 7, 1982. Located in the rainforests of the Petén, Las Dos Erres is inhabited by impoverished Ladinos who moved there decades ago from other parts of Guatemala in search of a better life, clearing land and building new homes in what was once remote, frontier terrain. In the early 1980s, however, Las Dos Erres found itself caught up in the civil war, having to send male members of its population to serve in a civil defense patrol organized by the army in a neighboring settlement some distance away. At first the people of Las Dos Erres complied, but later they refused to participate, arguing that if guerrilla forces were operating in the vicinity, then the male members of the settlement were best to remain near their families and their fields to protect them from possible attack. This line of reasoning did not please the army, which accused the people of Las Dos Erres of sympathizing with enemy forces, indeed, of actually *being* guerrillas. Hundreds of men, women, and children lost their lives in a bloody massacre. As we watch the remains of victims, years later, being recovered from the depths of a well, Davis asks a survivor who he thinks was responsible.

"It's clear," he says in a hushed voice. "The army."

Toward the end of *Tierra Madre* we hear one of its protagonists declare that "peace is not a magic word." If peace is to have any future in Guatemala, then the land issues that are at the core of the country's woes will have to be dealt with. This means not only listening to but also responding to native points of view, bearing in mind that poor Ladinos also have concerns that need to be heard and addressed. Anyone familiar with Guatemala knows how difficult a task this is.

For *Haunted Land,* Davis locates the film's narrative not only in Guatemala but also in Canada, where she introduces us to Mateo Pablo, a Chuj Maya whom she met in her native Montreal. Mateo had fled Guatemala at the height of the repression, one of only thirteen survivors of a massacre perpetrated on July 14, 1982, in Petanac, a village perched high in the clouds of the Sierra de los Cuchumatanes. Davis decides to document Mateo's return to Petanac after an absence of almost two decades. Few road movies take us on such a challenging journey, morally and existentially, as that traversed in *Haunted Land.*

Like all good artists, Davis is keen on improvisation, open to incorporating ideas compatible with her own. In Guatemala she meets up with Daniel Hernández-Salazar, a photographer committed to the documentation of human rights violations. Davis convinces Daniel to join her and Mateo on the journey to Petanac, where a team of forensic scientists is to exhume the bodies of those massacred. Among them are Mateo's wife, Catalina Pérez, and their two small children. In an inspired piece of juxtaposition, Daniel had earlier grafted a shoulder blade recovered from an exhumation onto a series of male figures, creating images of four angels used as book covers for the Catholic Church's accounting of the war years, *Guatemala: Nunca Más* (1998). The angels become a central motif in the film.

Mateo and Daniel connect and relate as soul mates, Maya and Ladino made Guatemalan in the way that matters most: on the grounds of lived experience. Davis, meanwhile, elicits moving testimony, which bolsters the findings of the forensic scientists, that as many as seventy-six people were slaughtered at Petanac, half of them children under twelve years of age. After the massacre, which Mateo witnessed from a hillside on his way home, Petanac was burned to the ground, its twenty-two families left to decay in the charred debris of their houses.

We see Mateo wander through a graveyard on the brow of a hill. Its small white sepulchers emerge for a moment from the mist. Children slice the air with long poles, netting a clutch of dragonflies. As Mateo clambers over the tombstones, Daniel's angels hover in the eyes of the living, in the bones of the dead, during the mass burial of disinterred and now identified remains. A man recognizes what is left of his father, thrown in a heap with three other murdered villagers, by the make of his shoes, by the color of his shirt and trousers.

"That's him," the man says. "I know that's him. That's my father."

Another man tells how, like Mateo, he lost his entire family—his wife, his children, his parents, his brothers and sisters. Everyone. "I was left alone, with nobody. I was an orphan, with no place to go. So I sought refuge in Mexico. I still feel this pain, which has never gone away."

A woman who shares a similar fate hangs her head and laments, "I live here in poverty, under the curse of the dead."

Candles are lit. A Chuj Maya prayer-maker asks the dead to forgive the living for disturbing them to remove them to a final place of rest. Dozens of wooden coffins are carried to a nearby cemetery, where they are sealed in narrow tombs.

At the close of *Haunted Land,* one of Daniel's angels cups his hands around his mouth. "So that all shall know," he declares. His message resounds, the driving force of truth, a dynamic epitomized by Mary Ellen Davis and her work in documentary film.

PART TWO

BLOOD AND INK

SEVEN

THE DELIVERY MAN

Joselino arrives with the newspapers every morning shortly after seven. He prefers to ring the doorbell rather than summon attention with the brass knocker cast in the shape of a hand. When I open the door, I usually find him flicking through the pages, stealing a glance at the headlines between call and answer. His bicycle is propped against the curb on the side where the foot pedal is missing, an entire day's delivery stacked in the wooden box fitted above his rear wheel. After work Joselino rides a flashy motorbike, as impressive to behold in the streets of Antigua as his handsome, kiss-them-and-leave-them looks. He peers up at me from beneath the peak of his baseball cap and grins. His dark eyes sparkle, but it's the gleam from the gold in his teeth that dazzles most. *"Buenos días, Jorge!"* he declares, even though the news he delivers makes for anything but a good morning.

Knowing that I live in Canada, Joselino informs me that there's nothing about it mentioned in today's papers. I recall once reading about a "Brain" Mulroney attending a summit meeting, and the sports section occasionally announces the scores and standings of the Blue Jays and the Expos. But not much news about Canada filters south to Guatemala.

One morning Joselino asked if Canadian papers carry news about Guatemala. Not very often, I told him. I also told him that, as part of my job, I write from time to time about Guatemala, but that the content and style of my efforts are usually quite different than the standard fare of the Guatemalan press. With a cry of *"Hasta mañana!"* he jumped back on his bicycle and resumed his round.

I thought afterward about Joselino's question and the kind of news that daily fills the delivery box on his bicycle. I also thought about the dozens of times I get asked, "How was Guatemala?" on my return to Canada. I clip bits and pieces from the newspapers that Joselino delivers each time I visit Guatemala, and later I file them with my field notes as a record of the trip. Those yellowed clippings and scribbled logs allow me to look back and remember.

EIGHT

INTO THE FIRE (1981)

The man sitting next to me in the sauna is a doctor from Guatemala City. He has come out to Jocotenango in the hope that he can cleanse himself of more than just the capital's filth. The story he tells me concerns one of his colleagues, Raúl Matamoros, also a doctor, an odontologist trained in Spain who afterward returned to practise his specialty in Guatemala. They had grown up together, gone through medical school together, worked at the same hospital together, and were the best of friends.

"I said good-bye to him on Thursday around noon. Next morning, when he didn't show up for his shift, people asked me if I knew where he was. I told them I had no idea; he left to go home when I did. Later on Friday his secretary called me; they found his car in Zone 10 and his body in Zone 14. He'd been shot, one bullet fired into each side of his head. And knife wounds too."

A woman on the other side of the metal partition shouts, "*Más leña, por favor.*" I hear a door creak open and a man curse as he stokes the fire. The doctor shakes his head.

"I'll never understand it," he says. "He lived properly and correctly. He cared for people. He loved sports and was good at his job."

The lumps of wood thrown in below us start to crackle. The metal partition ticks.

"We buried him yesterday," the doctor continues. "He was my age, thirty-two, with a wife and two little girls."

I ask the doctor if he knew of a reason. Another shake of the head.

"*Listo para su masaje!*" I hear a voice holler. Yes, I'm ready for a massage. I excuse myself with a quiet "*Con permiso.*" The blood of one doctor is the sweat and tears of another.

That night I catch up on a backlog of newspapers. An article in *El Gráfico* of May 31 suggests that the killing was "*una equivocación,*" a mistake, but reveals that Raúl Matamoros was a prominent figure in soliciting relief funds for the needy after the earthquake of February 4, 1976.

If Guatemala can ill afford the loss of a caring doctor, so too the life of a rural schoolteacher. The June 2 edition of *El Imparcial* reports:

TEACHER GUNNED DOWN
IN FRONT OF 40 SCHOOL CHILDREN

A primary school teacher was shot to death by unknown assassins in the village of Sanjón, in the Department of San Marcos, in full view of forty of his pupils, according to local authorities.

The victim was identified as Adolfo Recinos Ramos, thirty-seven years of age, who was shot a number of times, dying instantly at the scene of the attack.

Recinos, moments before, had left the small country schoolhouse of Sanjón and was walking to the bus that would have taken him to his home in nearby Malacatán.

With him walked some forty of his pupils, who were accompanying Ramos to the bus stop. Two unknown men suddenly blocked his way and opened fire.

The body of the murdered schoolteacher was taken to the morgue of San Marcos national hospital at 8:30 p.m., three hours after the shooting.

Teachers, it seems, are often prime targets for "unknown assassins." The headline in *El Gráfico* on June 4 announced: "Five Teachers Gunned Down: One in San Lucas, Three in Nueva Concepción, and One More in the Capital." Particularly hard-hit is Guatemala's national university, the Universidad de San Carlos, one of the oldest universities in the Americas, now a skeleton of learning: scores of its professors and students have been murdered or intimidated into silence, while others have sought refuge outside the country. Some have taken to the hills to join the guerrilla insurgency. On June 25, celebrated throughout Guatemala as Teachers Day, leaflet bombs that exploded in a number of cities declared the founding of the Frente Revolucionario de Maestros, the Revolutionary Teachers Front.

Not all teachers targeted for elimination are killed on the spot. Some mysteriously "disappear," only to show up dead a week, a month, a year later. In the June 4 edition of *El Gráfico* we learn:

KIDNAPPED TEACHER FOUND DEAD

The schoolteacher Bertha Alicia Morán González, twenty-three years of age, who was abducted on Saturday, May 23, was found dead in the early hours of the morning at 14th Avenue and 8th Street in Zone 6 of Guatemala City.

Beside the teacher's body there was also the corpse of a forty-year-old man, as yet unidentified. The family of the deceased teacher visited the morgue at San Vicente hospital, where they identified her body.

The teacher had been abducted on May 23 after leaving her home to attend a birthday party to be held in her honor at a neighbor's house.

Her body was found with the same clothes she had on at the time of her abduction.

In this case the report mentions no evidence of rape or torture, but sexual assault and disfigurement frequently await the victim between disappearance and death. Another account, from the *Prensa Libre* of May 25, records the murder of journalist Fulvio Alirio Mejía, who worked for the newspaper *La Nación*. Journalism, like teaching, can easily be interpreted as "subversive" and is therefore a profession that is practised under censure of death. Alirio Mejía's death is again but one example of many:

JOURNALIST WAS DISFIGURED
BODIES OF OTHER PERSONS ALSO FOUND BUTCHERED

The body of the journalist Fulvio Alirio Mejía, which mysteriously appeared in Cuilapa, Santa Rosa, along with the bodies of various other persons, showed signs of cruel torture. His disfigurement is attributed primarily to blows from a *machete*.

His face was a mass of deep wounds, apparently perpetrated so as to prevent recognition. He was also stripped of his clothes, but his wife, Esmeralda Chavarría de Mejía, was eventually able to identify him.

He and the people found with him had received the same treatment as persons now turning up dead all over Guatemala. Badly beaten and amputated bodies have appeared in many localities. All of them show signs of torture, some the ominous mark of strangulation.

The naked or semi-clad bodies of the five people found with the corpse of Alirio Mejía included a nine-year-old boy and other juveniles, all of whom were brutally disfigured. The murder of all six victims was an abominable act, especially the butchering of the nine-year-old who, in addition to being knifed in the face, also had his tongue cut out. When reporters arrived in Cuilapa seeking information, the gravediggers had begun to bury the five juveniles. Because no family members were there to identify them, they were laid to rest in an unmarked common grave. Several locals offered prayers to the Almighty for the eternal rest of their souls.

Alirio Mejía "reappeared" and, despite the mutilated condition of his corpse, was identified by his wife. The sorrow of relatives and friends of other victims who vanish but do *not* reappear is prolonged indefinitely. Such is the case of the journalist Rodrigo Ramírez Morales. According to a July 16 report in *El Gráfico,* Ramírez had still not "reappeared" following his abduction one month earlier by a group of armed men. He had been driving his car one day in June, accompanied by his wife. She, like many others, placed a notice in the newspapers beseeching his captors to spare his life and to allow him to return home, in this case to five young children. The pleas of distraught next of kin appear, with photos of disappeared loved ones, in the personal columns, not too far from notices of bereavement. The following is an example:

DISAPPEARED: The family of Licenciado Oswaldo René Cifuentes de León once again appeals, in the name of God, to those who have it in their power to release him. Already his absence has brought much pain and suffering to his home, especially to his mother Marta de Cifuentes and to his wife Elvia de Cifuentes, who are in great distress at not knowing his whereabouts. His infant son cries to have his father back with him. The family begs those who hold him to respect his person and to let him return home, for he is a man dedicated to his family and to his profession. He has never been involved in any kind of political activity. At the same time his family begs the Supreme Creator that those responsible for his captivity never have to suffer what they are going through, but that He forgives them and makes them see the error of their ways. Any information will be gratefully appreciated. God will pay you back.

Into such cases few official inquiries are made. Seldom is anyone brought to trial. This is hardly surprising, for while a criminal element undoubtedly exploits the situation, most acts of violence can be attributed to government security forces. If the government were to pursue the cause of justice, its own soldiers and police officers would be the ones brought before the courts.

This is not to deny that acts of violence are also perpetrated by guerrilla insurgents. The guerrillas, however, tend to strike swiftly—at army convoys, at retired or off-duty soldiers and policemen. The work of the death squads, by contrast, is often sadistically prolonged—designed, so it seems, to inflict maximum physical suffering on the victim and maximum psychological anguish on next of kin. Terror is sown with cold and calculated precision.

At times, though, the national armed forces move into action with draconian speed. This was apparent on July 9 and 10 when, on two separate occasions, guerrilla "safe houses" in different neighborhoods of Guatemala

City were located, surrounded, and attacked, resulting in over thirty deaths. Perhaps the most harrowing aspect of these two episodes is that when the bodies of the deceased, including eight women, were displayed in La Verbena morgue, a number of them—judging, said *El Gráfico* of July 12, from the reaction of people looking for missing relatives—were obviously recognized and could therefore have been identified. But because people feared that reprisals would accompany any known association with the dead, no one spoke up. The corpses were interred, marked with an anonymous double X, in yet another common grave.

The heavy-handedness of these two operations (artillery and tanks were brought in) is somewhat unusual, for they occurred in fairly well-to-do districts of Guatemala City, in Colonia El Carmen and in Vista Hermosa. The countryside, not the capital city, is more commonly the scene of the heaviest fighting, particularly the departments of Huehuetenango and El Quiché. So great is the strife in these two departments—remote, mountainous, the ideal terrain in which to wage a guerrilla war—that the government is careful not to allow news of all that happens there to reach the press. Such is the case with events that took place in early June in San Mateo Ixtatán, a community of Chuj-speaking Mayas in the northern reaches of Huehuetenango.

On June 4 the front page of *El Gráfico* showed two young boys in the local hospital. The caption beneath their photos reads:

> Juan Domingo Martín is one of four survivors of the actions of a heavily armed group of men who invaded the homes of the townspeople of San Mateo Ixtatán, murdering thirty-six men, women, and children. The young boy does not speak Spanish and has no serious injuries, but is now an orphan, for his mother and father were killed. The other young boy, named Andrés Gómez Diego, gravely wounded, tries to tell reporters, in poor Spanish, some of his impressions of what took place.

At this point the newspaper story fizzles out. Perhaps the editor of *El Gráfico* considered it unwise to print the information he received. He may even have been advised *not* to print it. What I heard was that the guerrillas, as they do often, took over San Mateo briefly at dusk. Speaking to residents in *lengua,* the native tongue, they held a meeting and explained their goals and motives in an attempt to win local sympathy and support. After the speechmaking was over, the guerrillas withdrew to the safety of the hills. Night fell and the townspeople went to bed.

Alerted to the presence of guerrillas, by what means never made clear, the army arrived shortly after midnight. Their search proved fruitless. Frustrated, the soldiers turned on the townspeople themselves, but not before they had been ordered by their commanding officer to take off their uniforms and put on civilian clothes.

Massacres like the one at San Mateo are calculated to terrorize survivors and make them shun all contact with the guerrilla insurgency, which the government chooses to view as an external, not domestic, reaction to decades of neglect and exploitation. Vinicio Cerezo Arévalo, the leader of the Christian Democracy Party, puts it succinctly: "My government would have you believe that communism is the enemy of democracy in Guatemala, when in reality the government itself is freedom's greatest foe."

Meanwhile, in an attempt to improve its image at home and abroad, the government of General Romeo Lucas García has launched a propaganda campaign. It portrays itself as pushing ahead on all social fronts: health, education, land reform, housing, installation of water and electricity, and the creation of new jobs. Along the Pan-American Highway, carved into thick walls of volcanic ash, above fresh asphalt and a widened road surface, a message declares: IN PUBLIC WORKS LIKE THIS THE GOVERNMENT OF GENERAL LUCAS INVESTS YOUR TAXES. Ironically, but not surprisingly, the tourists expected to make use of the improved highway system grow fewer and fewer. A hard-hitting editorial in *El Gráfico* of June 10 addresses the related issues of political violence, foreign image, and the collapse of the tourist industry:

GUATEMALA, A TOURIST PARADISE
— BUT WITHOUT ANY TOURISTS

The hotel business in this country, upon which the livelihoods of thousands of Guatemalans depend, is in a state of crisis, a crisis brought on by the understandable decline of foreign tourism, principally from North America and Europe. This decline affects not only the hotel business but also many other related activities, such as tours organized by travel agencies and the handicraft industry, which are directly linked to the inflow of visitors.

In Quetzaltenango, a recent convention had as its main focus the hard times that have fallen on hoteliers not just in the capital but throughout the country, on account of the drastic decrease in tourism, which has already forced the closure of one important hotel, the Cortijo de las Flores in Sacatepéquez, and threatens the closure of others. Guatemala is an open book of Latin American history: the richness of our pre-Columbian and colonial heritage is well recognized, set in landscapes of dreamlike beauty and in one of the most agreeable climates in the world. All this means nothing, however, when viewed alongside the violence that afflicts our country today. This image, projected abroad, is the main reason behind the decline in tourism, a business that thrived here not long ago.

Conservative estimates place the drop in foreign visitors over the past year at 20 percent. But we believe this figure to be an optimistic one. We must confront the reality of our situation and not bury our heads in the sand.

What is said about Guatemala in other countries exerts a powerful influence over the well-being of tourism. Violence prevails in our country today, violence we see escalating each day in the number of kidnappings, murders, and attempts on human life. A recent bulletin released by the Associated Press lists Guatemala, along with El Salvador, as being among parts of the world currently in a state of war. Violence is something that has spilled beyond our borders to the notice of the outside world, and this is something we cannot hide. The decline of tourism is damaging, particularly because its vibrancy over the past few years assisted our economy and helped us withstand the effects of the collapse of coffee on the international market. Until a short time ago, Guatemala showed to the rest of humankind a friendly, cheerful face. Today we are a sad and preoccupied people. And the splendor of our landscapes, the kindliness of our weather, the richness of our culture can do nothing to change that demeanor.

Like most foreigners who visit Guatemala, I have fond memories of time spent there. The temples of Tikal under a full solstice moon. Walking the streets of Antigua at dusk. Jacarandas and flame trees. The blaze of bougainvillaea on an old church wall. Early morning sounds at Lake Atitlán. Mist in a cornfield at dawn. The smell of burning *pom* at Chichicastenango. Cutting open a *pitaya*. Smiles and grins on market day. Driving through the countryside, offering people lifts, then listening to their stories. After rain, watching the sky clear and the light fall on Volcán Agua.

To the voice inside that asks, "How can you marvel at beauty in the midst of so much pain?" I have yet to find an answer.

NINE

PEACE OF THE DEAD (1982–1983)

I missed the visit of Pope John Paul II by only a few days. He was in Guatemala on March 7, 1983, during one of his whirlwind pastoral engagements. Part of his address to an assembly of indigenous Mayas was delivered in K'iche'. "The Church is aware of the discrimination you suffer and the injustices you must put up with," the Pope told his audience. "It raises its voice in condemnation when your dignity as human beings and children of God is violated."

Pope John Paul's words were spoken exactly one year after General Angel Aníbal Guevara was declared to have won an election even the most blinkered of Guatemalans knew to be rigged. Discontent with the election outcome so troubled junior officers in the armed forces that they closed ranks and plotted a coup that led to the overthrow, on March 23, 1982, of the government headed by General Romeo Lucas García. Guevara never got to serve as president because the removal of Lucas García brought about the political resurrection of the man denied the presidency in the fraudulent elections of 1974, General Efraín Ríos Montt.

From their days in military college the junior officers responsible for the coup remembered Ríos Montt as a soldier of impeccable integrity, an honest, moral, consummate professional. They asked him to head a military *junta* that also included General Horacio Maldonado Schaad and Colonel Francisco Luis Gordillo.

Ríos Montt re-entered national politics at a time of widespread public disgust with the Lucas García administration. There was also growing concern among the armed forces that the war against guerrilla insurgents was not yielding satisfactory results. Ríos Montt, it was hoped, would turn things around. Three stages can be distinguished that allow an assessment to be made of the consequences of the junior officers' coup, consequences that can be attributed in large measure to the return of Ríos Montt.

Stage one lasted a little over five months, from March through August 1982. It represented, in essence, the declaration of war on any individual or group suspected of assisting, or even sympathizing with, the guerrilla insurgency. This phase of counterinsurgency was especially harmful to Maya communities within whose territory the Guerrilla Army of the Poor and the Organization of People in Arms had established a strategic, insurgent base. Having realized, to paraphrase Mao Tse-Tung, that the native settlements were the water in which the fish to be caught swam freely, the armed forces unleashed a fearful repression on them—worse than anything experienced even under Lucas García, whose soldiers were responsible for an estimated twenty-seven thousand killings between 1978 and 1982.

One of the first public notices of renewed and even intensified atrocities came on May 12, 1982. Following a peaceful occupation of the Brazilian Embassy in Guatemala City, members of the peasant organization known as the Committee for Campesino Unity (CUC) issued a statement later circulated among the national and international press. The CUC declared:

> We wish to denounce before our people and the peoples of the world the brutal repression that the indigenous communities of Guatemala are suffering at the hands of the military *junta's* army. We wish it to be known that this *junta* of generals and colonels, since March 23, has not only continued the policy of massacres and destruction practised by the previous military government, but in some regions has intensified the massacres to levels never before experienced. Since March 23, far from seeing an end to the massacres, we have seen the *junta* continue and intensify them.

The CUC's claim was reiterated, only five days later, in an editorial that appeared in *El Gráfico*. Signed by the newspaper's general director, Jorge Carpio Nicolle, the editorial observed:

> Massacres have become commonplace, massacres in which no respect or mercy is shown for grandparents, children, or grandchildren. Shortly before the coup we published an editorial entitled "At least spare our children." The cases discussed in that article are very similar to the current one: excessive use of force, unrestrained sadism, psychotic mercilessness. It would be difficult for any person in his right mind to imagine this kind of extermination. How is it possible to decapitate an eight- or nine-year-old child? How is it possible for a human adult to murder, in cold blood, a baby of less than a year-and-a-half? In war, one cannot hope for mercy on

the field of battle. That is understandable, but not the actions of someone who kills defenseless non-combatants, children and old people who are not involved in anything. Nor is it acceptable to murder pregnant women, for these acts of bestiality only serve to sink the nation deeper into the most degenerate immorality.

On May 20, 1982, another editorial ran:

To anyone who has any sympathy with their fellow human beings, the kind of genocidal annihilation taking place in the indigenous areas of the country is truly horrific. There has been much talk of improving our image abroad, but this image will continue to darken more and more with this new resurgence of blind and absurd violence. This new resurgence of mass murders sends the message that Guatemala is very far from peace, or even experiencing a decrease in violence. The outside world will once again close its doors to us, because in fact we do not deserve any kind of foreign assistance as long as these episodes continue.

The *junta* headed by Ríos Montt denounced such allegations as a smear campaign organized by the international Marxist press, pointing to a fall in the body count in major towns and cities as evidence of its good intentions. Shortly thereafter the *junta* attempted to improve its image by offering, from June 1 on, an amnesty to all those who had fought against it. The guerrillas ignored the amnesty. On June 9 General Maldonado and Colonel Gordillo were removed from their posts as members of the *junta*, leaving Ríos Montt to be named President of the Republic.

One of Ríos Montt's first acts as president was to impose press censorship, a measure taken "to avoid publications that spread confusion, cause panic, or aggravate the situation." He also decreed, effective July 1, a state of siege, which allowed secret tribunals to operate—tribunals invested with the power to impose the death penalty. Declaring a state of siege in effect allowed the government to legalize repression and to grant security forces an even freer hand in their operations.

Throughout the month of July the slaughter of indigenous Mayas continued. In one incident involving the remote community of San Francisco, near Nentón in the Department of Huehuetenango, the army entered the village, gutted houses, burned crops, slayed livestock, and killed over three hundred men, women, and children. One eyewitness, whose account was corroborated by fellow survivors who fled to Mexico, recalls the scene:

The soldiers took our wives out of the church in groups of ten or twenty. Then twelve or so soldiers went into our houses to rape our wives. When they were finished raping them, they shot our wives and burned the houses down.

All our children had been left locked up in the church. They were crying, our poor children were screaming. They were calling us. Some of the older ones were aware that their mothers were being killed and were shouting and calling out to us.

They took the children outside. The soldiers killed them with knife stabs. We could see them. They killed them in the house in front of the church. They yanked them by the hair and stabbed them in the bellies; then they disembowelled our poor little children. Still they cried. When they finished disembowelling them, they threw them into the house and then brought out more.

Then they started with the old people.

"What fault is it of ours," the old people said.

"OUTSIDE!" a soldier said. They took the poor old people out and stabbed them as if they were animals. It made the soldiers laugh. Poor old people, they were crying and suffering. They killed them with dull *machetes*. They took them outside and put them on top of a board; then they started to hack at them with a rusty *machete*. It was pitiful how they broke the poor old people's necks.

They began to take out the adults, the grown men of working age. They took us out in groups of ten. Soldiers were standing there waiting to throw the prisoners down in the patio of the courthouse. Then they shot them. When they finished shooting, they piled them up and other soldiers came and carried the bodies into the church.

A survivor of an earlier massacre, who also fled to Mexico from neighboring Huehuetenango, depicted the desperate plight of his people in a painting with the caption: "This is the village of Acal, where the army massacred the people on Wednesday, May 26, 1982, when they were all in church. When they realized what was happening the soldiers had already surrounded the village. That is why we see many people dead and hanging and lying on the ground." According to Amnesty International, between March and July of 1982 over two thousand Mayas were slaughtered in sixty separate acts of violence. The Mexican Christian movement Justice and Peace suggests that the human toll was considerably higher: nine thousand killings in the five months following the coup.

In an attempt to escape the carnage, thousands of Maya families abandoned their communities. They sought refuge in the mountains, in the squatter settlements of Guatemala City, in the plantations of the Pacific coast, and in refugee camps across the border in the Mexican state of Chiapas. Even to people for whom conquest and subjugation have been a way of life for centuries, Ríos Montt's first five months in office rank among the bloodiest of times the Maya have known.

A second stage of counterinsurgency lasted from September through December 1982. These four months saw a reversal of tactics, best described as a shift from physical to psychological war.

Having terrorized rural communities and prompted the retreat of an estimated four thousand guerrilla combatants, the armed forces scaled down their search-and-destroy missions, replacing them with a program called the Plan of Assistance to Areas of Conflict, better known as *frijoles y fusiles,* "beans and rifles." Aware that its scorched-earth forays had created a large number of hungry as well as dead people, the army demanded that in return for the provision of food, towns and villages set up civil defense patrols to keep future guerrilla encroachment at bay.

The message was clear: comply and be fed, equivocate and be killed. Since it was by now evident that the guerrillas were no match for the army, that alliance with the insurgents (real or perceived) spelled death and destruction, Maya communities across the highlands realized the imperative of cooperating with their aggressors. By year's end hundreds of towns and villages had formed civil defense patrols in which local residents, under army directives, maintained guard against guerrilla penetration.

Ríos Montt claimed personal responsibility for the success of the "beans and rifles" campaign. Speaking in Honduras during President Ronald Reagan's visit to Central America in December 1982, the general explained:

> In response to subversive activity we have developed a combined security and development program known as our "beans and rifles" policy, to provide for the needs of the peasant farmers in the war zone. Farmers who have been prevented by threat of terrorist attacks from working their fields are being furnished with food by the government, and in return they provide the labor to repair the physical devastation caused by the terrorists. At the same time, the very real threat they now face from the terrorists has not been overlooked. We have granted the farmers the right to defend them-

selves militarily. In 850 largely isolated and previously helpless villages, 300,000 Indians have now been organized into civilian self-defense units which, armed with homemade rifles, patrol their towns and fields and can fend off terrorist attacks when necessary.

The overall success of the program has been striking. Vast areas have been recovered from terrorist control, allowing local officials to be re-instated. We have reopened schools and health centers. Social service teams travelling in the wake of the army have provided food, shelter, work, and medical attention to Indian peasants left destitute by the strife around them.

The general also claimed responsibility for a twelve-point code of conduct supposed to govern the behavior of his troops when they dealt with civilians, especially in rural areas. The code states:

1. I will not take so much as a pin from the villagers.

2. I will not make romantic overtures toward the women of the district, nor take advantage of them.

3. I will protect and take care not to harm the crops growing in the fields through which we travel.

4. I will pay a fair price for what I buy. In case of doubt, I will offer to pay more.

5. I will return anything I borrow and pay for anything that is damaged.

6. I will be courteous, treating the elderly and children with special affection and respect.

7. I will receive anyone who wishes to speak to me pleasantly and courteously.

8. I will respect the customs and traditions of the villagers, and be respectful also of their civilian and religious authorities.

9. On the highways and roads I will yield the right-of-way any time this does not jeopardize the security of the troops.

10. I will not accept gifts or exaggerated compliments from the rich or powerful.

11. I will not take unfair advantage of the inhabitants' hospitality in the countryside.

12. I will observe respect for graves, sepulchres, churches, and other structures that are respected by the community.

Like Spanish conquistadors, whose actions centuries earlier were also cloaked in high-sounding rhetoric, Ríos Montt's soldiers conformed to only one code of conduct: *"Obedezco, pero no cumplo. . . . I* obey, but I do not act accordingly."

Stage three of Ríos Montt's offensive began in December 1982 and was still under way when I was in Guatemala during the months of February and March 1983. Known as *techo, trabajo y tortilla*—shelter, work, and food—this stage was alluded to by the general when he addressed President Reagan in Honduras, informing him: "The underlying philosophy of 'beans and rifles' is that permanent security ultimately comes only through economic development, social justice, and technological progress. Thus the initiative known as 'beans and rifles' will gradually be expanded into an ambitious and comprehensive development program to improve the *campesino's* life permanently." President Reagan was said to be impressed.

A striking characteristic of Ríos Montt's strategy of food for allegiance was that many of the groups sanctioned by the government to organize community development were Protestant evangelical sects based in the United States. Ríos Montt is himself a devout, born-again Christian, belonging to a California fundamentalist group called Church of the Word. His presidency coincided, not by accident, with the presence of hundreds of American missionaries conducting "spiritual work" throughout the countryside. A booklet written by a member of one of these groups declared that, with the coming to power of Ríos Montt, a miracle had occurred. It depicted the general as "the saviour of Guatemala." A strong evangelical bond had thus formed to unite Guatemala and the United States, a bond that had a far greater impact on the lives of ordinary Guatemalans than more formal aspects of U.S. foreign policy.

Another feature of Ríos Montt's presidency was a massive confidence-raising campaign to convince citizens long accustomed to graft and corruption that such things belonged to the past and had no place in a Guatemala governed by him. The government required state employees, from post-office clerks to treasury officials, from high-ranking generals to village policemen, to swear an oath of honesty in which they publicly declared: "I do not steal. I do not lie. I do not abuse my office." Beneath a poster announcing "this government has a commitment to change"—a series of pro-government posters appeared in public agencies throughout Guatemala on January 3, 1983—a legend proclaimed:

> For years dishonest authorities, as their own property, have taken money, goods, and resources that do not belong to them. For years the rule has been that the government and authorities distort the truth, tell lies, and do not fulfill their duties. For years officials have believed that their position gives them rights over the rest of the citizenry and that the law is something they need not abide by. All this constitutes stealing, lying, and abuse of office. It must not continue. Our government has pledged a commitment to change. Respect this commitment yourself. Change!

Another poster forming part of the same campaign depicted a smiling Maya boy with the caption: "For me, you have a commitment to change." Yet another, of a well-groomed brother and sister dressed not in indigenous but in Ladino clothes, declared: "For your family and for Guatemala, you have a commitment to change." The change that Ríos Montt championed most, it seems, was a change of heart, which he espoused with unbridled passion during Sunday evening television broadcasts.

Watching and listening to him, I found myself bombarded by questions. Is this man evil? If so, on what grounds? Because he himself directly sanctioned the slaughter of his fellow Guatemalans? How could he? Is he not a Christian? Isn't he a son, a husband, a father who appreciates the value of life? He must surely know about the massacres that his troops commit. Can such awful deeds be done without him, as commander in chief of the armed forces, sanctioning them? Has the bloodbath been planned from above, or is it the work of soldiers in the field, deranged killers gone completely out of control? With whom does responsibility and the burden of truth ultimately rest?

I am still unable to answer these questions. I can, however, volunteer a few points of information about Ríos Montt's presidency with some degree of confidence. By the early part of 1983 violence had decreased, not just in towns and cities but also in the countryside. A drop in the number of killings, however, was interpreted by Washington, far too prematurely, as further evidence that the United States was now dealing with a more responsible government. The Reagan administration went so far as to recommend to Congress that Guatemala be taken off the human rights "black list" imposed by President Carter, thus enabling military and economic assistance to be resumed.

If, in relative terms, peace prevailed, it was an uneasy, unsettling peace—the peace of the dead. When this peace was shattered it was often difficult to determine the identity and motives of those involved. Rural confrontations were especially murky. Was the cause of an incident the army taking action against a community that would not cooperate and set up civil defense patrols? Could it perhaps be attributed to guerrillas returning to teach a lesson to communities that *had* set up civil defense patrols? Or was the source of conflict one in which old scores were settled—say, over ownership of land, access to a tract of forest, or the right to draw water from a certain stream—under cover of insurgency or the dutiful execution of army orders?

Like all countries in turmoil, Guatemala does not inspire easy answers, except, perhaps, to the chosen likes of Efraín Ríos Montt. In the flux of the moment, however, not even a God-fearing general could have known how long his presidency would last.

TEN

FUTILITY AT THE POLLS (1984)

My two weeks passed quickly. Visiting Guatemala for such a short time is by no means ideal, but at least it affords me some opportunity to take stock *in situ*. Ríos Montt is gone, ousted in August 1983 by a coup that saw General Oscar Humberto Mejía Víctores assume the presidency. But the violence continues. To the twenty-seven thousand killings under the Lucas García regime, and an estimated ten thousand under Ríos Montt, must now be added thousands more under Mejía Víctores.

An editorial in the February 23 issue of *El Gráfico* has this to say:

THE VIOLENCE HAS TO END

There is fear among the people over the increase in violence that has been manifest the past several weeks. It is feared that a resurgence of violence may influence the process of democratization, a process that will pass through a crucial stage in the form of an election, called for July 1, to designate members for a National Constituent Assembly. Fear reigns because no one knows what will be the consequences of this new wave of violence, one that has claimed many lives in a short space of time.

Several people have been kidnapped or killed in the last few days alone. The image invoked by General Ríos Montt during his spell in the presidency—"no more bodies on the roadside"—has lost all meaning. Many are the bodies found along highways and thrown down ravines. Many are the Guatemalans—professionals, students, workers, farmers—who are kidnapped in broad daylight in the middle of the street, in full public view of a helpless and terrorized citizenry. Many are the Guatemalans who are abducted from their homes under cover of darkness. Many are the wives, many are the mothers, many are the children who appear in court with the personal effects of their missing relatives, demanding to know their whereabouts. And many also are the people who visit the morgues in an attempt to identify, in the features of the dead, the face of a loved one who has vanished.

This editorial was followed, on March 2, by another equally as frank:

THE KIDNAPPINGS MUST CEASE

Kidnapping as a political weapon or as a means of attaining financial reward is deplorable from any point of view. Many Guatemalans, among them university professors and students, have been kidnapped during the past few weeks in a renewed outbreak of violence that is sweeping the country. The number of these victims has multiplied at an alarming rate. Of the victims, very few have been fortunate enough to show up alive; many have yet to reappear alive or dead. Anguish spreads through the homes of the disappeared, inflicting pain on an impotent citizenry that witnesses the spectacle of violence without being able to do anything about it.

The incidence of these kidnappings, which occur with an elaborate display of force in broad daylight, indicates the degree to which violence has escalated. The citizenry is frightened. It feels insecure and has lost all trust. Guatemala has been afflicted for many years by a lack of security and by a feeling of defenselessness on the part of its population. If these kidnappings and murders persist, peacemaking will be impossible and we will continue to represent, in the eyes of the world, a country where human rights are violated and where the lives of ordinary people are simply not respected.

As well as outspoken editorial opinion, *El Gráfico* ran stories in February and March that highlight the situation. In one episode a group of armed men disguised as doctors abducted the victim of an assassination attempt from a hospital. A single page in the February 23 issue of *El Gráfico* documented the kidnapping of thirty-eight Mayas from communities in the highlands, reported the discovery of the beaten and bullet-ridden body of a university professor, and described a shoot-out in downtown Guatemala City. On March 2 *El Gráfico* also reported that the man in charge of overseeing the July 1 elections, Arturo Herbruger Asturias, had received threats against his life for assuming the presidency of the Supreme Electoral Tribunal.

Back in Canada a report prepared by the Inter-Church Committee on Human Rights in Latin America (ICCHRLA) revealed the gravity of the situation. Presented on June 12 to External Affairs Minister Allan MacEachen, the ICCHRLA report states:

In the case of Guatemala, the internal human rights situation remains the most serious in Central America. Through recent ICCHRLA visits and through the testimony of refugees, including an escapee from a clandestine prison now resident in Canada, details of torture, kidnappings, detentions, and disappearances in the thousands during the early part of 1984 have been recorded. Continued massacres in the countryside, and of the responsibility of the armed forces themselves for these violations, have been documented by ICCHRLA in conversations with religious personnel working in several areas of Guatemala. The refugee flow and the weight upon Mexico in particular continue to be matters of priority humanitarian concern. The more than seventy documented incursions by Guatemalan military forces into Mexico, including the April 30 attack on a refugee camp several kilometres inside Mexico resulting in grotesque tortures and deaths, should provoke strong international reaction.

Under such circumstances, I ask myself, what difference could an election make? How many people are likely to cast ballots, and who will they be voting for? Is a National Constituent Assembly likely to improve the situation after the election is over?

The July 1 vote turns out to be Guatemala's first major electoral event since the abortive presidential campaign of March 7, 1982. Rampant fraud in the course of that election precipitated a military coup two weeks later, bringing Ríos Montt to power. No elections were held during his fourteen-month presidency. Now some 2.5 million registered voters are being asked to choose among 1,179 candidates representing no fewer than seventeen political parties.

On first inspection, such figures suggest a healthy degree of involvement, but this impression is misleading: no left-of-center parties are represented. Right-wing groups predominate, among them the Anti-Communist Unification Party and the Authentic Nationalist Party. One contender is General Angel Aníbal Guevara, declared the "winner" of the fraudulent presidential election of 1982. (Although he was president-elect, Guevara never assumed office because of the junior officers' coup of March 23 that same year.) Another contender is General Carlos Manuel Arana, a former president known as the "Butcher of Zacapa" because of his handling of an insurgency threat in eastern Guatemala in the 1960s. An election is irrelevant, for all options represent a continuation of the status quo, not an attempt to change it.

The greatest danger in the July 1 election lies in the possibility of it being perceived as an opportunity for the United States to integrate Guatemala more fully into its plans for Central America as a whole. If the White House greets the election results with approval, if Mejía Víctores then responds to Washington's call for Guatemala to assume a more central regional role in the U.S. isthmian agenda, the only guarantee for the Guatemalan people is even greater repression than they already experience. In this regard, the response of the Reagan administration is crucial.

As for Canada, Ottawa's position toward Guatemala has been one of increasing detachment and censure, beginning in 1982 with the suspension of bilateral aid. With respect to Central America in general, Canada has moved to distance itself from the ahistorical stance of the United States, even if, in the words of analyst Tim Draimin, Ottawa's policy in the region is "cautious, confused, contradictory, and ineffectual." Canadians concerned about their country's views of Central America can derive some encouragement from a speech delivered in Washington by Maurice Dupras, chairman of the Parliamentary Subcommittee for Canada's Relations with Latin America and the Caribbean.

I testified before the subcommittee in April 1982, and afterward Dupras solicited my services as a research consultant. Our contract called for me to furnish the veteran politician with two "position papers," one on whether or not Canada should seek full membership in the Organization of American States, another on policy options toward Central America. I found him to be genuinely affected by the human rights issues that his chairmanship exposed him to, a principled man not at all disposed to mince his words. In Washington straight talking was very much in evidence when Dupras told his U.S. audience:

> It hardly needs to be said that it is Washington, not Moscow, that has been for many decades the dominant outside power south of the Río Grande, and nowhere more so than in Central America. Washington's policies in the region closest to it have produced a bloody shambles rather than the intended result of social stability and political acquiescence. There is no area of the world riper for revolutionary change. This is the case despite decades during which the United States has not hesitated to employ its immense military, economic, and political influence in the region. Yet, when challenged, President Reagan's stock response is to resort to ideological formulas. History notwithstanding, he reaffirms his simple belief that "the Soviet Union underlies all the unrest that is going on." Progress toward needed reforms will be very difficult without a fundamental change in the attitude of the U.S. government. That means putting faith in the people rather than in military oligarchs with blood on their hands.

In stressing the need for the United States to assist, not subvert, the process of change, Dupras strikes at the heart of the problem. Discontent in Central America arises from generations of poverty and injustice, not a bogey Soviet presence. Nowhere is this more apparent than in Guatemala. Not until the United States understands that what people in Guatemala struggle for is the same cause Americans themselves fought for two centuries ago will peace and stability be possible.

ELEVEN

CIVILIAN RULE (1985–1986)

I arrived in Guatemala well ahead of the date set for the runoff election, December 8, 1985. Victory at the polls that day belonged to Vinicio Cerezo Arévalo, who won comfortably with 68 percent of the popular vote. There was a fiesta feel to election day, at least in Antigua. People swarmed the central plaza even more than they do normally. Bands played. Rockets soared. Firecrackers snapped. The returning officers I spoke with were cordial and relaxed, answering questions and even posing for photographs. When it was announced the next day that Cerezo had won, people expressed hope that the coming of a civilian president, not a military one, would signal a new beginning.

I was not so sure. On my flight to Guatemala I had read an interview with Cerezo in *Time* magazine. Cerezo himself appeared to have no illusion about the task at hand. "If I win," he said, "during the first six months I'll have 30 percent of the power. In the first two years I'll have 50 percent, and I'll never have more than 70 percent of the power during my five-year term." How he arrived at these figures was not made clear, but Cerezo's presumably well-informed reckoning was echoed by the archbishop of Guatemala City, Próspero Penados del Barrio, who remarked: "Whoever becomes president is going to have to move with great caution. You cannot have a dialogue with the armed forces."

The pragmatism of the heads of both church and state is revealing. It comes, in large part, from their awareness of a structure put in place in Guatemala called the National System of Inter-Institutional Coordination. Set up by the army as a means by which to monitor political decision making, this framework ensures continued military involvement in running the country, from mundane local affairs to issues that affect Guatemala on the national and international stage. The hold on political life that the armed forces have exerted for decades will not be relinquished. Instead, certain powers will be entrusted to a civilian administration allowed only to operate within a clearly defined governmental space.

The process of democratization, moreover, is unlikely to unfold in Guatemala in the same way as it has elsewhere in Latin America. Those responsible for past deeds, from plunder of the national treasury to the willful practice of terror and intimidation, are unlikely to be held accountable. Unlike, say, General Viela or General Galtieri in Argentina, former presidents Lucas García, Ríos Montt, and Mejía Víctores, all military rulers, will be safe from prosecution as the individuals ultimately responsible for horrific acts of war and gross violation of human rights. One of the last decrees passed by Mejía Víctores before he left office was to grant members of the armed forces immunity from civilian trial for their role in counterinsurgency operations.

Cerezo's star, for the moment, is on the rise. He enjoys immense popularity, ran a well-organized campaign, and won an election that, by Guatemalan standards, was honest and free of fraud. A brave and lucky man who has survived numerous attempts on his life, Cerezo is well aware of the danger of moderate politics in a land where extremes are the norm. He advocates peace talks with the Unidad Revolucionaria Nacional Guatemalteca (URNG), an umbrella organization representing various factions of the insurgent left. During a brief visit to Washington after his election, Cerezo claimed that his government would delay requests from the United States for up to $10 million in military aid already budgeted for Guatemala.

Economic aid is likely to be a different matter. Counterinsurgency war has had a disastrous effect on an economy that, hitherto, was reasonably healthy and well managed, if massively subsidized by underpaid local labor. Capital flight, an increase in joblessness and underemployment, rising inflation, falling productivity, and decreases in the value of traditional export crops have meant severe economic contraction that only a resumption of full-scale assistance from the United States can alleviate. While a $2.3 billion foreign debt appears minuscule in comparison to what Mexico or Brazil owes to international bankers, unless terms are renegotiated, interest payments alone will absorb 40 percent of Guatemala's annual export earnings.

Repayment of the national debt, however, remains a concept alien to the concerns of most poor Guatemalan families. For indigenous Mayas in particular, there is primarily the hope that, after years of destruction, life in the highlands may return to its ancient seasonal rhythm.

It had been years since I had felt it was safe enough to travel in the country-side, but after the election I took advantage of the opportunity to do so, visiting towns and villages I knew and remembered well from the days before repression. I rented a pickup truck in Guatemala City and headed west and north across the highlands as far as San Mateo Ixtatán. One of my graduate students travelled with me. North of Huehuetenango we were stopped several times at roadblocks and questioned either by civil defense patrols or by the army. None of these checks caused any problems, but they reminded us to be careful. We had to show our passports and prove who we were. We also had to say where we were going and why we wanted to go there.

Along the way I stopped the pickup once in a while to offer people a ride. Our passengers were predominantly Mayas, who climbed in the back with chickens, pigs, an occasional goat, and assorted bundles and baskets. When we dropped them off, they were grateful at not having to pay, which allowed us the possibility of conversation. The men did most of the talking; the women as a rule were taciturn and wary. The children who accompanied them were invariably silent, save for the odd infant wanting to be fed. Most of the people we spoke with commented repeatedly that, *"primero a Dios,"* thanks be to God, their situation had improved considerably since the early 1980s. They told us they enjoyed freer access to their fields and that both government forces and guerrilla units swept through their communities less and less frequently.

While these people are disposed always to make the best of what life has to offer, around them hang impenetrable memories of suffering and loss. The army bears the most responsibility for the slaughter unleashed on them, but guerrilla insurgents are not without blame. Especially in the Sierra de Chua-cús and across the northern reaches of the Sierra de los Cuchumatanes, native communities suffered terribly when the Guerrilla Army of the Poor retreated in the face of sustained army offensives, leaving behind unarmed villagers to bear savage reprisal for having provided food, shelter, or moral support for the insurgent cause.

The Saturday before Christmas found us walking around Sacapulas, a town in the Department of El Quiché. We had earlier noticed a huge bill-board at the entrance to the department capital, Santa Cruz del Quiché:

WELCOME TO EL QUICHÉ!
LAND OF COURAGEOUS MEN
WHERE THE PEOPLE AND THE ARMY
HAVE SAID "NO!"
TO COMMUNIST SUBVERSION

In Sacapulas it was the army barracks overlooking the town square that caught our attention. The soldiers on guard duty couldn't have been more than sixteen or seventeen years of age. A slogan painted on the side of the watchtower declared:

> ONLY THOSE WHO FIGHT
> HAVE THE RIGHT TO CONQUER
> ONLY THOSE WHO CONQUER
> HAVE THE RIGHT TO LIVE

At a time of alleged peace and goodwill — a time when not just Christmas but "democracy," in the form of a civilian president, were supposed to be celebrated — the words on the watchtower invoked quite contrary sentiments.

When I passed through Sacapulas again some months later, the declaration was still prominently displayed, even if the soldiers stationed there looked distinctly off guard playing basketball with some local schoolgirls. A few weeks earlier, in Verapaz, the land of "true peace," a soldier had opened fire across my path when the car in which two friends and I were travelling attempted to pass his slow-moving jeep.

Like the slogan at Sacapulas, that single shot said it all. The army, not a civilian president, rules Guatemala. The army remains in the driving seat, and its finger is still on the trigger.

TWELVE

A MILITARIZED SOCIETY
(1987–1990)

A number of people told me they had heard the bombs being dropped. I didn't know whether to believe them or not. "Not *that* close to Antigua," I remember thinking. I remained skeptical until I read about it afterward, the accounts confirmed by official military sources.

On Sunday, February 25, 1990—the day the Sandinistas lost the Nicaraguan election—four fighters belonging to the Quetzal Squadron of the Guatemalan Air Force bombed hilly locations in the Guatemalan township of Magdalena Milpas Altas, where the Organization of People in Arms had earlier engaged an army patrol in combat. The bombing did not take place in some remote, mountain stronghold but in a small community near the old colonial capital, these days a tourist town where Sunday visitors normally fill the central plaza and keep Maya vendors and local merchants busy.

I found Antigua the Sunday following the air raid to be a lot quieter than usual. Visitors stayed away not just because of what had happened in Magdalena Milpas Altas, but because the army and guerrillas had clashed again two days later, in Santa María de Jesús, a township only half-an-hour's bus ride from Antigua and less than fifty kilometers from Guatemala City.

Almost unnoticed by the rest of the world, the war in Guatemala drags dishearteningly on. The army claims that incidents such as those at Magdalena Milpas Altas and Santa María de Jesús (just two of a growing number of confrontations largely unreported outside the country) involve only a small group of "terrorists" left over from the counterinsurgency war of the 1980s. If resistance is so slight, why, one wonders, does the army feel compelled to maintain such a conspicuous presence, not just in and around Antigua but throughout the western highlands? The visibility of the national armed forces, in the countryside most of all, underscores its hold on virtually every aspect of Guatemalan life. At the army barracks in Sololá, the military has imprinted its mark on the landscape, literally as well as figuratively, by constructing its entranceway in the shape of a helmet placed on top of a pair of combat boots. The role of the army in civil society, its self-stated vision of what kind of a country Guatemala should be, is worth examining in some detail.

In August 1987, less than a week before the presidents of Central America convened to sign the peace accord known as Esquipulas II, a group known in Guatemala as the Private Enterprise Council organized a "National Forum" that it called "Twenty-Seven Years of Struggle for Liberty." Part of this forum consisted of official presentations by military personnel, with several representatives outlining the army's blueprint for the Guatemala of the future. Counterinsurgency in the 1980s was justified, one official said, "to rescue the nation from subversion and terrorism, a situation that has arisen due to the incompetence of previous governments." The army felt itself, in the words of Colonel Terraza Pinot, "compelled to assume control of the government, so that national dignity could be restored and people's faith in their institutions renewed."

In another speech, General Héctor Gramajo, President Cerezo's minister of defense, spelled out how the army views its role as guardian of both democracy and nationhood:

> At this time we consider ourselves to be the institution that gives impetus to democracy. We defend the interests of the nation in its totality, not the interests of a political party, group, or institution. We protect the interests of the nation through political and military action that encompasses all the nation. This action has reciprocal consequences throughout Guatemala.

What General Gramajo means by "reciprocal consequences" is unclear. It may simply be military jargon for fear, harm, and harassment should any priest, lawyer, union representative, or university professor dare to speak out against the army's way of doing things.

One of Gramajo's colleagues, General Manuel Callejas, summed up army objectives:

> We seek to create a framework of security that permits integrated development in the best of conditions, supporting in all our greatness the different sectors of the nation, especially the most needy, focusing the discharge of our duty on achieving both the supreme national goal and the common good.

The "discharge of duty" Callejas refers to can only be exercised by commanding not just the apparatus of government but all that makes the country function, socially and economically as well as politically and psychologically. The army, "the supreme expression of the state," could not forge a "national destiny" without first wielding "national power."

Brigadier General Juan Bolaños elaborates on the military's concept of power:

> Power signifies survival, the ability to impose on others the methods and procedures of life appropriate for their welfare and mutual understanding. It is the capacity to enforce the law on those who lack it, and the ability to extract concessions from the opponent whom one has defeated.

The "concessions" the brigadier general speaks of have been extracted at a criminally high price.

What all this rhetoric amounts to, after heartbreak and misery, is proper recognition that it is the national armed forces, not the Christian Democracy Party of President Cerezo, who are the effective brokers of power in Guatemala. Cerezo has shied away from any attempt to dismantle the national security state devised and maintained by the army. To be fair, assuming presidential office in Guatemala under the circumstances that Cerezo did allowed for little political maneuvering, but few Guatemalans could have imagined when they voted for them that the Christian Democrats would achieve so very little. Rather than create its own ideas and pave the way for meaningful social change, Cerezo's government has absorbed, or has been absorbed by, the military's agenda.

This should not surprise us. As long ago as the 1970s, the Christian Democrats drew closer to the military in a move that, the following decade, resulted in the emergence of a "strategic alliance." Cerezo himself, then the secretary general of the Christian Democracy Party, helped forge this marriage of convenience, the outcome of which is politics as the continuation of war. In 1975 Cerezo declared:

> Instead of regarding the army as an enemy of the democratic parties, we ought to consider accepting it as an ally of these parties. What I am suggesting is that progressive politicians and military officers have a common responsibility and that both sectors ought to share in the making of national decisions.

Cerezo now speaks of "national reorganization" and the need "to bury the past" in order to attain "national reconciliation." Overall, his tenure as president has been lamentable; in his last year in office, human rights violations again made Guatemala an international pariah. How can people "forget the past" when its horrors are part of the present, when the nightmare still haunts them?

Criticism of the Cerezo government's record came in January 1990 from bishops of the Catholic Church when they met in Quetzaltenango, Guatemala's second largest city. The bishops published a communiqué that expressed alarm over recent political violence "that has struck at leaders, students, workers, and members of popular organizations." Their statement read: "Human rights, such as the right to dignity and equality, do not exist." They pointed to the injustice inherent in "the traditional structure of a minority that accumulates wealth and privilege while the impoverished majority lacks food, good health, education, and reasonably paid labor."

Episcopal concerns were later reinforced by the United Nations Commission for Human Rights at its 46th session held in Geneva in March 1990. After reviewing the evidence, compiled by both national and international experts, the commission declared itself "profoundly disturbed that the [Guatemalan] government has been unable to control an ongoing climate of violence." It urged Cerezo's government "to initiate or intensify investigations that will allow identification and judicial prosecution of those responsible for acts of torture, disappearances, assassinations, and extra-legal executions." The commission also called for the apprehension of members of acknowledged death squads. It was particularly concerned with what it termed the "grave situation that has affected native peoples from time immemorial." Indigenous Mayas, the commission said, were "the object of discrimination and exploitation, as well as suffering serious violation of their human rights and fundamental liberties."

The disapproval of the Catholic bishops and the United Nations Commission on Human Rights were damning enough, but an even more embarrassing censure came from the U.S. ambassador to Guatemala, Thomas F. Stroock. Addressing the Rotary Club of Guatemala, Ambassador Stroock commented that he found it extraordinary that none of those guilty of kidnapping and killing had yet been brought to justice.

The ambassador's remarks were followed by the release of a hard-hitting report compiled not by Amnesty International or Americas Watch but by the U.S. Department of State. In it the United States (which has furnished Cerezo's government with $800 million in aid) observed that a deteriorating human rights situation in 1989 had taken the lives of over two thousand Guatemalans. Their deaths were attributed, among other causes, to the activities of "ultra-right groups" and "military personnel" involved in "extra-judicial killing." President Cerezo dismissed the report, which considers

Guatemala to be among a handful of countries across the world "plagued by insurgency, civil unrest, and terrorism," as "false press information." His comment, in turn, prompted the release of another State Department bulletin, which noted "the disturbing increase in what appears to be politically related violence."

There is no small, tragic irony in this exchange of words, for the architects of U.S. foreign policy in the 1990s only have their colleagues of forty years ago to thank for cultivating a military caste that has brought so much suffering and grief to the people of Guatemala.

THIRTEEN

THE DAILY NEWS (1990)

I make my way to my favorite table, in the corner of the patio where the light is good, and start to read. The waitress brings me coffee. She hovers, nods at the papers, and asks, "Don't you ever get tired of all that news?"

It is the summer of 1990, the time of year they call winter in Guatemala on account of the rains. I am here for several months, working with a translator on turning the English text of a book of mine into a Spanish-language edition. It is a slow, tedious process; sometimes progress is made not even sentence by sentence, but word by word. Reading the newspapers constitutes something of a break.

"Not really," I reply. "I like to know what's going on."

"Nobody I know reads the newspapers as much as you do," she says. "They find them too upsetting. Besides, they don't have the time."

She leaves me to ponder our exchange. For better or worse, I *do* have the time. By summer's end I have accumulated a larger pile of newspaper clippings than usual.

Two items from *El Gráfico* of June 11 help put the country in social, economic, and political context. The first, with the headline "Guatemala: 6.4 Million Impoverished People," states:

> With nine million inhabitants, Guatemala reflects conditions of poverty that embrace 71 percent of its population, a statistic that classifies the country as the worst off in this regard in all of Central America, according to a report released by the Instituto de Nutrición de Centroamérica y Panamá (INCAP). Data from INCAP reveal that poverty most seriously afflicts people living in rural areas, where the index pertains to 83.7 percent of

residents, the index for urban areas being 47 percent. INCAP's figures lend support to the findings of the latest national survey of socio-demographic conditions, in which it was found that 83 percent of Guatemalan families live in poverty.

Further analysis, specifically of families considered in dire need, shows that 64 percent of them earn 251 *quetzales* [at the time, $59 U.S.] or less each year. Poverty is most chronic, according to the national survey, in the northwestern departments of Huehuetenango and El Quiché, where 91.5 percent of families are affected.

The second item, under the headline "Guatemala: 40,000 disappeared," summarizes the proceedings of the "First National Seminar on the Effectiveness of Habeas Corpus." Held in the civilized ambience of the Sheraton Conquistador Hotel, the seminar was reported by *El Gráfico* as revealing that "more than half of the 90,000 political disappearances that have occurred in Latin America in recent years relate to Central America." The reporter covering the seminar further notes that most of the Central American cases involve Guatemala, "where more than 40,000 disappearances have been recorded and where no explanation has been given to the thousands of families who suffer on account of this phenomenon." What the reporter failed to note is that no member of the government who had earlier promised to attend the seminar—representatives of the Supreme Court, the Ministry of Justice, and the Human Rights Office—actually showed up to discuss matters with members of non-governmental and international agencies who did.

A couple of weeks later, on June 27, a story on the human rights situation appeared in the *Prensa Libre*, a Guatemalan newspaper whose official motto advocates journalism that is "independent, honorable, and dignified." Careful to attribute what it states to the wire services of the Mexican daily *El Excelsior*, the story in the *Prensa Libre* runs:

> According to the [UN] Commissioner for Human Rights in Central America, Guatemala heads the list of countries in that region in violation of human rights. With the coming to power of President [Vinicio] Cerezo, expectations were raised that an end would be put to the wave of terrorism unleashed by the military and death squads. But the [Cerezo] regime has been unable to distinguish itself in any way, or to leave behind a human rights record different from that of [military] dictatorships.

Prensa Libre continues:

According to statistics provided by the Guatemalan Human Rights Commission, during the time that President Cerezo has held office extralegal executions have taken the lives of two thousand people, while another two thousand have disappeared. Death squads, human rights groups allege, are once again in action, intimidating and informing on people, killing them or carrying them off to clandestine prisons where they are subjected to physical and psychological torture. Guatemala is considered the worst violator of human rights in Latin America, for in this country between 1966 and 1990 more than 40,000 people have disappeared, 100,000 have been killed, 75,000 have been widowed, 125,000 have been orphaned, 150,000 have been displaced outside the country, and over one million displaced internally.

A good way of gaining perspective on any situation is to compare the present with the past or to contrast what is going on somewhere today with what currently prevails elsewhere. This is the strategy adopted by Carlos Rafael Soto in a biting op-ed piece published by *Siglo Veintiuno* on June 22. Soto takes as his point of departure the spirited performance in the World Cup of one of Guatemala's neighbors, Costa Rica, whose soccer players disposed of both Scotland and Sweden en route not only to the second round of *mundial* competition but also to a hallowed place in Central American sports history. Costa Rica's success, in other endeavors besides soccer, moves Soto to the following reflections:

> The victories of Costa Rica in World Cup action make all of us, as Central Americans, feel proud. At the same time, however, they cause to stir within us feelings of jealousy and sadness, not just because of a fine sporting performance but because that fine sporting performance reflects Costa Rican reality, in contrast to the reality in which Guatemalans find themselves.
>
> Back in the 1950s, Guatemala reigned supreme in Central America. In the soccer match that inaugurated Mateo Flores stadium, Guatemala played Colombia as part of the Central American and Caribbean Games. Guatemala won 1–0, thanks to a wonderful goal by Pepino Toledo and some spectacular attacking play by Gabriel Urriola. Students would come from all over Central America to our university. We were then still the undisputed leader of the region, a country where President Arbenz had begun to enact policies which—even his closest rivals would today concede—sought to promote capitalist development, dismantling U.S. monopolies

and taking control for ourselves of means of transportation by land and by sea. But that happened forty years ago. Since then all we have to show is four decades of blood-letting, kidnapping, corruption, greed, foreign domination, and a shameful quality of life, which relegate us to a position among the poorest, most backward nations on earth.

Soto goes on to list an array of statistics that show how much better off Costa Ricans are than Guatemalans, whether the difference is measured in terms of food consumption, rates of infant mortality, or access to education. He attributes Costa Rica's advances in social welfare, as well as its ability to compete at soccer with the best of the world, to imaginative and responsible leadership. Soto elaborates:

A case in point is the peace process in Central America. The original idea was Vinicio Cerezo's, but the Nobel Peace Prize went to [Oscar] Arias [president of Costa Rica]. Why? Because Arias understood better his role as political and moral leader of his country, because Arias was sufficiently patriotic to resist the temptation to fill his government with personal friends, because Arias knew how to construct a respectable image. In Guatemala the opposite occurred. What happened to Costa Rica during the World Cup in Italy, therefore, is not an isolated incident. It is the natural outcome of a people who live in relative calm, who know that their institutions are functioning more or less adequately, who have confidence that their social services as well as their health and education facilities are properly run. These people know that when they are born opportunity awaits them, that it will be possible for them to go to school, that it will be possible for them to eat well enough so as not to fall victim to the malnutrition that plagues Guatemalan school children in second and third grade. These people know, furthermore, that the rules of politics have been established and respected for some time, that they need not live in fear of a fraudulent election, a military coup, or crippling pillage of public funds.

Soto's disgust at the corrupt, self-serving ways of Guatemalan politics, and his disappointment that civilian president Vinicio Cerezo has done no better in this regard than the colonels and generals who preceded him, are sentiments commonly shared and expressed. Cerezo's presidency is destined to be remembered as one of opportunity lost. To be sure, his options were limited from the start. If, as most observers acknowledge, radical change was not part of the Christian Democrat agenda, the opportunity at least existed for the president to set a respectful personal example. This might have been achieved by exercising what Soto identifies as "moral" leadership, making sound decisions not only in public but in private life as well, decisions that would perhaps restore some faith to Guatemalans long accustomed to broken promises that civilian presidents conduct themselves differently than military ones.

Cerezo's reputation has suffered badly as a result of several tactless actions, including the purchase of a Mediterranean island also sought by singer Julio Iglesias. It was the singer's ire at the sale not going his way that moved him to investigate and later disclose the name of his competitor.

Whether or not Cerezo will retire to his private island after serving out his term, he will be able to set sail for the Mediterranean in his private yacht, as he did in July, following his return from meetings in Mexico with President Carlos Salinas de Gortari. *Siglo Veintiuno* noted on July 21 that Cerezo, rather than returning and facing any number of domestic crises, "went down to the Pacific to embark on a pleasure trip aboard his yacht *Odyssey,* with the likelihood of sailing beyond Central American territory." In a thinly veiled reference to the president's notorious womanizing, *Siglo Veintiuno* also noted: "It is not known who is accompanying him." His wife, apparently, was not aboard.

Cerezo had gone to Mexico to discuss with President Salinas the fate of thousands of Guatemalans, most of them indigenous Mayas, who fled to Mexico in the early 1980s to escape political violence in their homeland. Living in Mexico for up to ten years, these families built homes, saw children born, and forged new ties. They have refused government offers of repatriation and resettlement, maintaining that those who return to Guatemala live there in fear of persecution. The "solution" to the "problem" now being proposed is to grant refugees and their offspring status as Mexican residents or citizens.

An editorial in *La Hora* of July 18 addresses the plight of the refugees:

> One has to understand that the trauma caused by violence to these thousands of Guatemalans will not disappear overnight but will, in many cases, leave scars that never can heal. We must remember that Guatemalan Indians found themselves, literally, in the crossfire between the guerrillas and the army, caught in a national conflict in which the innocent and the anonymous were the principal victims. The most extreme action to which these people sought recourse was in the long march overland to Mexico, where they settled in search of peace and security. The existence of these refugees serves as a permanent reminder to our national conscience, telling

us that we must never again allow events to happen that cause people to abandon the land of their ancestors.

We must comprehend, furthermore, that Indian customs and traditions are rooted in the land of their forefathers. That the pressures to leave were so great that they swept aside such attachments and values is made only more extreme by the fact that most of those who left have no desire to return, doubtless fearful that if they did come back they might relive the nightmare they have already experienced.

Any refugee who fled Guatemala in the early 1980s and is pondering government appeals to return and resume normal life will find good reason to stay away in the body counts reported daily. It is simply not possible to document all incidents of assassination or disappearance. It is equally impossible to ascribe plausible motives to many of the atrocities brought to public notice by the press. If details concerning the reasons behind acts of violence are absent or vague, not so are some of the circumstances that reporters encounter when they are sent to investigate wrongdoing. What they discover or are told is often written up in cold, alienating prose, as if the victim's sole purpose in life was to be, in death, so casually and unsympathetically described.

The gory weekly *Extra* specializes in this sort of horror, but neither are the mainstream dailies above depicting a violent end to human life in language devoid of all semblance of dignity. The glib detachment of the following items, from *El Gráfico* of June 28, is not easy to render, but translated from bland, eviscerated Spanish, the notices run something like this:

A CRIME IN ATITLÁN

Violence in Santiago Atitlán has intensified of late. Now it is reported that a crime has been perpetrated against Sebastián Baltasar Vásquez, eighteen years of age. He was cut down by delinquents who opened fire on him with automatic weapons. His body was taken to the morgue at the national hospital in Sololá.

THIS TIME IN ZONE 2

An unknown man was killed by five gunshots when he was walking down Second Street in Zone 2, so it was revealed when law officers arrived at the scene of the crime. The victim carried no identification but it was explained that the five gunshots his body received were of varying calibers, indicating that he was attacked by more than one person.

ONE MORE IN EL CAMPANERO

A man yet to be identified was shot to death by the occupants of three vehicles, who dumped his body in the district of Guatemala City known as El Campanero. Someone who observed the killing disclosed to the authorities that the assassins numbered at least eight and that they arrived and left in three different vehicles.

A WOMAN

A change of gender, but the act is the same. A woman was strangled to death at the corner of 22nd Avenue and 27th Street in Zone 5, after she was assaulted by a gang of thugs. As of yesterday she had not been identified. Her body may be found in the Autopsy Hall in Zone 3.

Guatemala's land is rich and fertile, yet its people are hungry and poor. The country whose first agriculturalists domesticated and harvested corn now has to import it from the United States. The paradox is disconcerting.

Perhaps the greatest irony of all is that in Guatemala a group of scientists laid claim to medical history with their successful experiments in finding a substitute for human blood, one they maintain can be used in any transfusion without the complications created by the age of AIDS. A country in which blood is routinely spilled hopes to become known as a country where life can be saved, not brutally taken. A feature from *Siglo Veintiuno* on June 8 reports:

> Guatemalan researchers have made a major breakthrough that will allow transfusions of animal blood to be used to save human lives. Doctors from our country will soon become famous for their sensational discovery of a substitute for human blood, a compound consisting of blood extracted from calves mixed with other clinical ingredients. Known as *Hemopure,* the compound can be used on human beings. Its discovery marks an important step in the history of medicine, one of benefit to all humankind.
>
> Guatemalan scientists Rodolfo Herrera Llerandi, Rodolfo García-Gallont, Erika von der Goltz, Ruediger von der Goltz, Edgar López, and the American doctor William Trainor carried out a series of tests in laboratories at the Herrera Llerandi private hospital to determine the precise extent to which the special compound works on human patients. The most essential feature of the discovery is that animal blood taken from calves contains no RH elements and is not group specific, meaning that it is a

common blood, one that can be put into any living person, no matter what that person's blood type happens to be.

A hospital spokesman, Dr. Dagoberto Sosa Montalvo, expressed his enthusiasm at the discovery, pointing out that transfusions henceforth could be done without exposing patients to hepatitis or AIDS. The first person to receive the calf-blood compound was in fact Dr. Rodolfo García-Gallont, who was subjected to intensive scrutiny for twenty-four hours after the transfusion was undertaken. During observation his organism showed no sign of complications. Laboratory tests also proved positive and normal. Nine other volunteer doctors were similarly treated and tested.

As well as being suitable for all blood groups, the substitute is easily manufactured and can be kept in refrigeration until needed. In the future it will be possible to carry out transfusions without beforehand testing for blood type, thus saving valuable time during an emergency.

Hemopure, the substitute for human blood, is the outcome of cooperation between Guatemalan doctors supported by the Biopure Corporation of Boston, Massachusetts, the Guatemalan company Laboratorios Biopur, and its parent company Hemo-Innovations. This historic landmark in the annals of Guatemalan and world medicine will be made public in a special ceremony at the United Nations.

June 30 is Army Day in Guatemala, complete with a parade passing through the downtown streets of the capital. The armed forces consider themselves the guardians of the nation, the only institution that can be relied upon to keep at bay the virulent cancer of communism. No better spectacle exists to showcase just how militarized Guatemalan society has become than the Army Day parade. If a trip to Ixil country and a tour of "model villages" there do not convince the foreign visitor of the army's pervasive authority, then observing the extent to which civil defense patrols figured in the 1990 commemoration certainly does. Watching seasoned counterinsurgency units march past in full combat regalia or contemplating the manipulation involved in getting Maya recruits to turn out in traditional community attire also imparts a sense of the obstacles that guerrilla forces are up against. *El Gráfico* of July 1 captures the scene:

> With the presence of historic battalions and a dense column of civil defense members, the parade commemorating Army Day filed past the army high command and its chief officer, President Cerezo. From the executive balcony of the national palace, protected by three darkened screens of

bulletproof glass, President Cerezo watched in the company of Juan Leonel Bolaños, Minister of Defense and Head of Division, and generals Juan José Marroquín Silezár, Roberto Mata Gálvez, and Raúl Molina Bedoya. The army chose yesterday only to put on display small components of its manpower and weaponry, giving greater emphasis to the participation of reserves and civil defense patrols. The loudest cheers were for the Army Corps of Engineers, in recognition of its work in rural areas of the country. Also applauded were the *kaibiles* [counterinsurgency veterans] and the parachute brigade. The Guard of Honor had in its ranks two children, a boy and a girl, both dressed in army fatigues and marching behind flag-carrying escorts. The children attracted a lot of attention.

One general not watching the parade from the "executive balcony" was ex-president Efraín Ríos Montt. Driven from the political limelight by a rival faction during the military coup of August 1983, Ríos Montt is once again in the news. His intention is to run for the presidency in the November elections, even though clause 186(a) of the Guatemalan constitution prohibits anyone involved in a military coup, as Ríos Montt was in March 1982, from campaigning for office. He claims that this clause became law after 1982 and therefore does not apply to his case. The Supreme Electoral Tribunal disagrees and has declared him ineligible. It has also responded negatively to an appeal that its decision be reversed. None of this has deterred the general, whose counterinsurgency operations during his fourteen months as president have led human rights activists to suggest that it would be more appropriate for Ríos Montt to be put on trial for crimes against humanity than be considered a candidate for the presidency.

Ríos Montt's high profile has also drawn concern from Archbishop Próspero Penados del Barrio, who fears a serious confrontation over religious matters if the general participates in the election, for his evangelical ways (and those of his fanatical hangers-on) undermine popular support for the Catholic Church. When, on the evening of July 12, Congress began to debate Ríos Montt's case, the session had to be suspended after repeated interruptions from the public in attendance. Most civilians present backed Ríos Montt's candidacy and heckled constantly during the proceedings, which were chaired by Guatemalan Vice President Roberto Carpio Nicolle. At one point two congressmen, Oliverio García Rodas and Victor Hugo Godoy, beseeched the crowd for order, only to have chili peppers thrown in their eyes. Godoy also had his spectacles seized and trampled on.

According to *Siglo Veintiuno*, when Ríos Montt was asked to comment on the disturbances, he denounced the congressional forum as a charade organized by "sick, mistaken, dirty old fools of men who rape their own daughters." He also warned congressmen, "They can be sure that when I win the elections I will judge them one by one, and will order meticulous investigations to be made into how they managed to spend so much money so quickly." When he was asked, "What else would you do if elected?" Ríos Montt replied, "Perhaps I would talk less and do more. I cannot be bought. I am a soldier. I have always been faithful. I have always been honest."

One morning a heavy, persistent rain catches me without an umbrella and keeps me away from the chores of translation longer than I had anticipated. At the café I have finished my second cup of coffee—and reading the news-papers—some time ago. I listen to the downpour and watch it transform the street outside into a flash-flood aqueduct. As I wait for the rain to end, I notice the waitress concentrating on an issue of *Prensa Libre*.

"Well," I say. "You've found time after all to catch up on the news."

"No," she answers. "I'm just checking the lottery numbers."

FOURTEEN

THE FICTION OF DEMOCRACY (1991)

At Chimaltenango, fifty-five kilometers west of Guatemala City, the Pan-American Highway becomes a desolate strip of bars, nightclubs, gambling joints, and brothels. Branching off the highway, the road to Antigua is lined on both sides by towering stands of eucalyptus. Night is falling as we approach the army base on the outskirts of town. The speed bumps in front of it slow us down to a crawl. A soldier stares at the pickup as it passes the garrison entrance. I glance behind where he stands to a building beside the parade ground. The light is dim, but I can still make out the words emblazoned on the wall:

SOME PEOPLE THINK ABOUT PEACE: OUR JOB IS TO WORK FOR IT.

The notion of an army that most observers consider a perpetual violator of human rights touting itself as an agent of peace may seem absurd, but Guatemala abounds in such sick manipulation. Jorge Serrano Elías, who won the presidential election on January 6, 1991, shows himself no more capable of controlling the national armed forces than his predecessor, Vinicio Cerezo. Political killings and intimidations continue at an alarming rate, reflecting the civilian government's inability or fear to get to the bottom of things, especially if the army is implicated. Failure to investigate crimes and lay charges in a court of law is the norm.

Cerezo's last year in office saw human rights violations in Guatemala continue to be monitored by the U.S. Department of State, a source even the most hard-line of generals could hardly link to "communist subversion." The State Department issued a report on July 28, 1991, indicating that, in 1990, six thousand people were assassinated in Guatemala: five hundred a month, fifteen persons a day. Most controversial was the report's willingness to categorize 304 killings as political assassinations. The report attributed blame for these killings directly to the national armed forces or to individuals associated with the national armed forces and therefore protected by them. The report emphasized that the army and also the police are exempt from prosecution in cases of human rights violations, which effectively means that the rule of law operates with serious restriction, if at all.

A week before the distribution of the State Department report, Guatemala's own human rights ombudsman, Ramiro de León Carpio, drew public attention to more than three hundred "extrajudicial killings" between January 1 and June 30, 1991, the first six months of Serrano's presidency. De León also pointed out that two of every three depositions brought to his attention fell beyond his terms of reference. This made him unwilling to designate Serrano's presidency as one in which, thus far, an improvement could be observed in human rights. Hundreds of killings reported by the local press went without any kind of official inquiry.

De León's statement did not please members of Serrano's administration. Nor did remarks he made about "unconstitutional" recruitment go over well with the army high command, many of whose rank and file are abducted into service. The outspokenness of someone in de León's position is rare, for far more than most state bureaucrats, he knows the price paid by Guatemalans who dare to challenge the system.

One particularly repugnant assassination was that of agronomist Julio Quevedo Quezada, murdered in front of his wife and children by two gunmen while on his way to visit his parents in Santa Cruz del Quiché. Quevedo was a prominent member of the Catholic relief agency CARITAS. His shooting provoked strong condemnation from both Bishop Julio Cabrera of El Quiché and Monseñor Próspero Penados del Barrio, archbishop of Guatemala City. Penados lashed out at the impunity that the culprits of the deed would enjoy.

"Crimes such as this are never resolved," he said. "The authorities always tell us they will investigate and everything ends right there, which means the identity of the killers is never determined nor is anyone apprehended."

Having the will to prosecute means taking enormous risks, as lawyer Roberto Arturo Lemus can attest. He, like Quevedo, also worked in El Quiché, where he represented indigenous Mayas who wished to bring to trial members of a civil defense patrol accused of the murder and harassment of fellow community residents. Shortly after overseeing the necessary legal proceedings, Lemus and his family received multiple death threats. On July 15, 1991, Lemus left Guatemala for exile in Canada.

Human rights violations have become so serious that the United States has once again decided to suspend military aid and to impose conditions on programs of economic assistance. These actions were taken after Serrano refused to have disbursements of military aid tied to improvements in human rights. Thus a nonmilitary package amounting to $56.5 million in 1990 was cut to $30 million for 1991. This reduction has served to cool relations between the two countries considerably and has worsened the already dismal plight of the Guatemalan economy. Surveys of working conditions by local and international agencies reckon that 65 percent of the economically active population is underemployed, that three out of every four workers earn wages of only $2.00 (U.S.) daily. These starvation incomes mean mass poverty.

Mass poverty assumed the specter of a medical nightmare with the arrival in Guatemala of cholera. In an odd geographical diffusion, the disease entered Guatemala not, as expected, from the south but from the north, moving "down" from Mexico as opposed to "up" through Central America from Peru (the country of origin), Ecuador, and Colombia. The first confirmed case was that of Gabriel Zacarias Méndez, a resident of San Marcos who had returned to Guatemala after a period of work on a farm in the Mexican state of Chiapas.

Zacarias was admitted to a hospital in Guatemala City on July 21. He was taken off the critical list four days later, following an intensive course of treatment that turned the migrant worker into a temporary celebrity. His expensive, high-tech recovery will not be a fate shared by other Guatemalans. By August 4, sixteen more cases had been confirmed and were being attended to in Coatepeque. A medical alert was raised, not just in Guatemala but throughout Central America, where doctors estimated six hundred thousand people might eventually be infected, about four thousand of them fatally. The Suchiate River, which forms part of Guatemala's western border with Mexico, was found to be contaminated, and health officials were clamping down on public eating facilities following a survey reporting that nine of every ten plates of food sold by street vendors contained fecal matter—and there are reportedly thirteen thousand street vendors alone in and around Guatemala City. Cholera thrives under such conditions and could become endemic in Guatemala for the remainder of the century.

Serrano, then, presides over Guatemala during a time of ongoing crisis. He deserves some recognition for promoting face-to-face discussions in Mexico with representatives of the guerrilla insurgency, whose combatants have now been waging war against the army for over thirty years. An agreement signed in Querétaro on July 25, under the auspices of the United Nations, delineated a common platform relating to issues of "democratization" that many onlookers hope is a prelude to peace talks and a negotiated settlement. Significantly, four signatories for the Guatemalan government were members of the national armed forces. Only if their institution truly decides to work for peace will any prospect of it be possible.

FIFTEEN

SEARCHING FOR PEACE (1993–1994)

The tense days between May 25 and June 5, 1993, saw Ramiro de León Carpio, the country's human rights ombudsman, replace Jorge Serrano Elías as the president of Guatemala. I was working in Spain at the time, but I managed to follow events hour by hour by tuning in to that most dedicated of correspondents, the BBC World Service. The Spanish daily *El País* also kept me informed. An attempt on Serrano's part to seize dictatorial powers appeared at first to have military approval, but senior members of the armed forces distanced themselves from Serrano's maneuvers and his "constitutional coup" soon aborted. Like Vinicio Cerezo in 1986, de León enjoyed widespread public support when he assumed the presidency, for as human rights ombudsman he was sharply critical of both the government and the army. As president, however, de León has seen his popularity drop sharply, and so far his policies have had mixed results.

The most impressive achievement of de León's first year in office was the signing of the Comprehensive Human Rights Accord on March 29, 1994, during peace negotiations in Mexico City with rebel insurgents of the Unidad Revolucionaria Nacional Guatemalteca (URNG). The discussions had begun with some promise under Serrano in April 1991, but they had turned sour and acrimonious by March 1993, with the government claiming positive outcomes that neither the URNG nor Monseñor Rodolfo Quezada Toruño, president of the Committee for National Reconciliation, could confirm. The URNG was especially troubled by the attitude of Serrano's defense minister, General Domingo García Samayoa. It accused García Samayoa of making statements that "put in serious risk the continuation of further dialogue." De León managed to restore faith in the stalled peace talks, culminating in the Human Rights Accord, which in principle represents a major breakthrough.

Several clauses of the accord are noteworthy. Both the government and the URNG acknowledge that "all agreements must be accompanied by appropriate national and international verification." This means, among other things, that the United Nations will be invited "to establish itself and to move freely" throughout Guatemala. A UN delegation led by Leonardo Franco arrived in Guatemala on April 25, 1994, to lay the groundwork for the verification process.

The presence of the United Nations is crucial not only to the implementation of the accord but also as a potential deterrent to Guatemala's heavy-handed security forces, which for years have operated with impunity. The accord explicitly recognizes "the need for firm action against impunity," with the government agreeing not to permit "the adoption of legislative or other kinds of measures designed to prevent the prosecution and punishment of persons responsible for human rights violations." This clause suggests that amnesty legislation favored by the Guatemalan military will not be pursued. Holding the national armed forces accountable for past actions—they, not the URNG, have committed the worst of atrocities—will be a decisive test of de León's credibility.

The president himself is in favor of establishing a truth commission as a necessary step in forging national reconciliation. The URNG supports him in this view, and both parties are mindful that such investigations helped heal the wounds of war in El Salvador, Chile, and Argentina. The national armed forces are less enthusiastic. De León's minister of defense, General Mario René Enríquez Morales, has made it clear that the Guatemalan military would only tolerate a truth commission that did not identify human rights abusers by name.

In addition to the Human Rights Accord, the government and the URNG signed an agreement outlining a timetable for subsequent negotiations. Its goals are worthy but formidable. Each month between May and November 1994, talks are to address such key issues as the repatriation and resettlement of displaced families, native rights, social and economic improvement, the role of the army in civil society, the transformation of the URNG from a fighting force to a political party, and constitutional and electoral reform. Successful negotiation of these issues commits both parties to signing a peace agreement meant to be "firm and lasting."

But even if consensus can be struck, the issues themselves will continue to be thorny. The high-profile return of about 2,500 refugees from Mexico in January 1993 was to have been followed, between May and August that same year, by another 1,600 families—some 8,000 people. Official statistics indicate that by January 1994 less than half that number had moved back to Guatemala from camps in the Mexican states of Chiapas, Campeche, and Quintana Roo. Those who were repatriated often found themselves in a difficult situation, stigmatized by the army and even government officials as guerrilla sympathizers and consequently treated with suspicion or outright hostility by residents of the communities to which they returned or in which they were resettled. Statements by de León himself linked refugee families to the URNG, an unwarranted association that only serves to perpetuate fear, distrust, and uncertainty.

Native rights are similarly intractable. Any number of social indicators puts Guatemala's six to seven million indigenous Mayas among the most disadvantaged of its citizens. Statistics concerning access to education are particularly acute. Only one in four elementary school pupils is Maya, with the ratio for secondary participation dropping to one in ten. University-level attendance is even lower: one in twenty. Six of every ten women in Guatemala cannot read or write. Some three-quarters of nonliterate women are Maya, whose schooling in rural areas is often basic or nonexistent, with only one girl in eight advancing beyond sixth grade. To his credit, de León named one Maya, Celestino Tay Coyoy, as minister of education, but the resources he has to work with are limited and the prejudices of the system he heads entrenched.

Equally entrenched are elite positions with respect to land and landholding. Skewed patterns of land distribution lie at the heart of Guatemala's woes. The country is strikingly agrarian, with the lives of thousands of peasant families and the existence of a privileged elite connected by the politics of land ownership. In Guatemala, 90 percent of the total number of farms account for 16 percent of total farm area, while 2 percent of the total number of farms occupy 65 percent of total farm area. The best land is used to grow coffee, cotton, bananas, and sugar cane for export, not to feed malnourished local populations. Recent UN statistics indicate that 85 percent of Guatemalans live in poverty, 70 percent of them in a state of deprivation described as extreme. Only 15 percent are considered to live well. They live well not only because they enjoy the fruits of the land but also because lenient taxation laws mean that their contribution to state revenues, in percentage terms, is among the lowest in Latin America. Elite benefits would be enhanced if the government assumes private sector debts, a move that the president of Congress, Vinicio Villar, defended against public outcry.

One of President de León's most contradictory stands involves the continued existence of civil defense patrols, which exemplify the extent to which Guatemala has become, and remains, a militarized society. Some five hundred thousand men currently perform civil defense duty, a number that the army says it can raise to nine hundred thousand should the need arise. As human rights ombudsman, de León was a fierce critic of civil defense patrols and advocated that they be dismantled. As president he asserts the need for them to be retained, despite evidence that links the patrols directly with assaults, intimidation, illegal detentions, and assassination, especially in the countryside. Positive steps that saw military personnel purged from the ranks of the police force are therefore offset by the president's reversal on the issue of civil defense patrols. His reversal, not surprisingly, has drawn him closer in allegiance to the army high command that he once spoke out against. The army continues to be the most powerful and best-organized institution in Guatemala. Its control of civil defense patrols allows it to exert its influence at the local level in towns and villages throughout the country.

Major obstacles surround the dissolution of the URNG as an armed force and seem certain to retard its emergence as a viable political player on the national scene. Understandably, the URNG is reluctant to demobilize its ranks until all aspects of the Human Rights Accord are operative and guarantees for personal safety are in place. Then begins the delicate business of turning clandestine backing into open support, followed by the mammoth task of convincing voters in a future election to cast their ballots for whatever party the URNG evolves into. If neighboring El Salvador offers any basis for comparison, the URNG faces an uphill struggle. In El Salvador, the insurgent groups making up the Farabundo Martí National Liberation Front (FMLN) waged a war that ended in stalemate, not in defeat. There, on election day, the FMLN could count on greater public sympathy than the URNG enjoys in Guatemala. If electoral defeat, followed by bitter internal feuding, was the fate of the FMLN, it is difficult to imagine a more encouraging outcome for the URNG.

Also difficult to imagine is politics in Guatemala without some kind of military involvement. The national armed forces, at forty-seven thousand men the largest and most professional military force in Central America, are headed by a corps of officers whose training cultivates politics as a legitimate military preoccupation. For any president of Guatemala, the greatest challenge is to convince the army that civil society, as in the case of Costa Rica, can function reasonably well without the involvement of the military. Peace in Guatemala hinges on defining a very different role for the national armed forces than they have assumed and enacted up to now.

SIXTEEN

SCARRED BY WAR (1995)

The caption on the calendar at a friend's house catches my eye: "1995 — The Year of Peace." It is only my first week back in Guatemala, but nothing I have heard or read warrants such an assertion. In Guatemala, declaring peace does not mean the end of war.

A special "Peace Supplement" in the April 30 issue of *Prensa Libre* shares the calendar's optimism. "When the guns fall silent and peace breaks out," *Prensa Libre* states, "Guatemalans will say goodbye to thirty-four years of armed conflict. The task, then, will be to look to the future, determined to avoid a new struggle between brother and brother."

How, I ask myself, can a "new struggle" be avoided if the root causes of civil war are talked about, year after year, administration after administration, only to be addressed in theory, not in practice? The "firm and lasting" peace agreement scheduled to be signed in December 1994 never materialized. Instead, the government and guerrilla representatives agreed on another round of talks. Talking about peace may be the closest Guatemala ever gets to it.

President Ramiro de León Carpio epitomizes the gulf between rhetoric and reality. In an interview published in the news magazine *Crónica*, the president expressed his belief that, when 1995 ends, he will have passed on to his successor "an entirely different scenario" than the one he inherited when he took office. A public relations campaign mounted in the Guatemalan press is meant to portray de León's government in a positive light. Four well-intentioned announcements in several newspapers serve equally well as a form of self-indictment. They run:

CONDEMNED TO IGNORANCE: Lack of education in our country impedes our social and economic development. An estimated 54 percent of our population is illiterate.

CONDEMNED TO FEAR: Each day our country experiences a high number of assassinations, the result of common delinquency. For every one thousand inhabitants we have only one police officer.

CONDEMNED TO ISOLATION: The absence of roads and bridges marginalizes many of our communities, restricting their commercial and economic development. We lose as much as 20 percent of what small farmers produce each year because of inadequate infrastructure.

CONDEMNED TO DEATH: A shortage of health services causes us to have one of the highest rates of infant mortality in Latin America. Only one in three Guatemalans has access to medical facilities.

All four announcements appear alongside related images—a tired teenager at work in the fields; a street urchin huddled anxiously on a bench; a young girl carrying corn in a basket on her head; a crying, malnourished child—and they all impart the same simplistic, remedial message: "In order for the Value Added Tax you pay to be channelled into works that benefit everyone, ask for a receipt or a record of payment, because whoever defrauds Guatemala defrauds and condemns you."

As worthy as this initiative may be, far more deserving of government attention is nonpayment of property taxes or failure to ensure that workers receive a legally established minimum daily wage. Insisting that an intransigent elite assume some measure of fiscal and financial responsibility does not constitute an excessive demand, given the taboo status of land reform, but de León dodges these issues as resolutely as any of his predecessors.

If Guatemala's economic elite continues to evade the moral obligation to pay taxes and disburse fair wages, a flicker of hope now exists that members of another powerful group—the military—may at last be brought to account for past crimes. Revelations in March 1995 that Colonel Julio Roberto Alpírez, a senior officer in the Guatemalan armed forces, was involved in the June 1990 murder of a U.S. citizen, Michael DeVine, shocked senators and members of Congress in Washington but caused little commotion in Guatemala. American indignation grew when it was further revealed that Alpírez, a graduate of the U.S. Army's School of the Americas in Fort Benning, Georgia, was on the payroll of the Central Intelligence Agency at the time of DeVine's murder, which took place near Poptún, where DeVine owned an inn. The CIA relieved Alpírez of his duties in July 1992—the colonel received a severance payment of $44,000—only after he was implicated in a second murder, that of the Guatemalan guerrilla leader Efraín Bámaca. Bámaca is alleged to have died under torture, if not at Alpírez's hands then under the colonel's direct supervision as commanding officer of the army base in San Marcos. Bámaca was detained there following his capture in March 1992.

Bámaca was married to Jennifer Harbury, a U.S. lawyer whose pursuit of justice has brought to light multiple irregularities. One is that the CIA continued to finance army intelligence units in Guatemala even though President George H. Bush ordered a halt to all military assistance to Guatemala because of a lack of cooperation in investigation of the DeVine case. On March 23, 1995, Harbury issued the following statement:

> I am saddened but not at all surprised to hear of the direct link with the CIA in the assassination of my husband. I have lived in Guatemala for two years, and have been closely involved with that country for a decade now. Over and over again, I have seen the direct linkage with an obvious support for the Guatemalan army, which has long been labelled the worst human rights violator in the western hemisphere. Our Department of State has long sheltered, supported, and trained this army, and helped to cover up for its terrible and criminal acts. As a result, its impunity has grown stronger and stronger, and 150,000 civilians lie dead. We, the citizens of the United States, must now insist that our tax dollars be better spent.

Harbury gives her personal loss an all-important collective dimension:

> I ask that all of us, here in the United States, recognize that I am but one of hundreds of thousands of women across Latin America who have suffered the grim experience of searching for a loved one who has been "disappeared" by the authorities. Many such women in Guatemala are in fact my close friends. Unlike them, I have been given the privilege of at last knowing the truth, and being freed from the constant nightmare that my husband is being tortured. Others have received no such relief. . . . I must now learn where my husband is buried, and return to Guatemala to reclaim his body. I cannot leave him tossed like so much trash into an unmarked grave. His bones belong to me.

Alpírez, who denies both charges of murder and any remunerative association with the CIA, was suspended from duty on April 27, 1995, along with fellow colonel Mario García Catalán, also implicated in the DeVine affair. Robert Torricelli, the U.S. congressman responsible for exposing Alpírez's connections, has called for the colonel's extradition and prosecution in a U.S. court of law. President de León's advice to Alpírez prior to his suspension was to sue Torricelli for defamation of character.

Whether or not Alpírez is eventually put on trial, it is clear that the courage found to lodge a case against him will also be drawn upon to press charges against other members of the Guatemalan military. The Grupo de Apoyo Mutuo, a human rights association, intends to bring a suit against Alpírez because of his involvement in a series of abductions in 1984. Another human rights group, the Asociación de Familiares de Detenidos-Desaparecidos (FAMDEGUA), plans to charge army officers with responsibility for the massacre committed in 1982 in the Petén district of La Libertad, where thirteen sets of bones were exhumed from a village well in July 1994. Aura Elena Farfán, a FAMDEGUA spokesperson, says that "the soldiers were most astute, for after they killed some villagers, they stripped them of their clothes, and put them on." The soldiers apparently did this in a deliberate attempt to conceal their identity as they set about killing other village residents.

"But the soldiers forgot to change their boots," Farfán observes, and this gave them away. The soldiers in question were stationed at the army base in Las Cruces under the command of Captain Carlos Carías. Farfán, quoted in the *Prensa Libre* of May 6, adds: "We intend to keep going until we find our loved ones, even if all we find are their remains. We seek justice, not revenge. Without justice it is impossible to speak of peace and reconciliation."

Farfán's stance is supported by Archbishop Próspero Penados del Barrio, who has committed the Catholic Church to a social project called the Recovery of Historical Memory, designed to put on record details of atrocities carried out in Guatemala in the 1980s. The Church's project will benefit enormously from the work of the Equipo de Antropología Forense de Guatemala (EAFG), a forensic science team that in 1994 exhumed eighty-four bodies from a clandestine cemetery in Plan de Sánchez, a small rural community nine kilometers southwest of Rabinal. If the evidence from Plan de Sánchez is anything to judge by—*Prensa Libre* carried a full-page account on April 30—eyewitness testimony is available to corroborate clinical findings. Stefan Schmitt, a member of EAFG and the person in charge of the exhumation, had this to say:

> Our investigation reveals that death was brought about by a violent attack, which involved the use of grenades, firearms, and hand weapons such as blades and bayonets. Most bodies were also badly burned. In the course of excavation we found splinters from grenades as well as the cartridge shells of 5.56 caliber bullets, the kind used in Galil and M-16 rifles. In addition, some bones exhibited marks characteristically made by the thrust of a

knife. Others showed signs of sustained beating. Of the eighty-four sets of remains, five belonged to persons three years of age or less, seventeen belonged to persons between four and twelve years of age, seventeen belonged to persons between thirteen and twenty-two years of age, forty belonged to persons between twenty-three and forty-nine years of age, and five belonged to persons fifty years of age or more.

After exhumation, twenty-five people were identified by name and their age at death established. They ranged from seven to eighty-eight years of age. Many of them, judging by the high incidence of common surnames, were members of the same family or closely related. These people, and over 150 of their neighbors, were massacred on Sunday, July 18, 1982, having been snared by the army on the outskirts of Plan de Sánchez as they returned home from market in Rabinal. Salvador García Sánchez, aged fifteen at the time, was there:

> The women were all dressed up in their best clothes and people from all around had brought in their corn to sell at market. An army patrol, twenty-five soldiers in all, left the barracks in Rabinal about three o'clock in the afternoon and headed toward Plan de Sánchez. There they laid a trap, surrounding the community, so that no one who entered it could leave. They locked people up—old people, men, women, and children—in the house of my cousin, Rosa Manuel Jerónimo, right in the heart of the community. They took twelve young girls to a place where no one lived, raped them, tortured them, and then killed them.

The house in which people were locked up, according to Adrián Cajbón Jerónimo, who also saw what happened, was then struck by grenades, strafed by gunfire, and set alight. "When the house was engulfed by flames, the soldiers threw in more people," Cajbón says. "That night 180 people died. The fire didn't go out until six o'clock the following morning."

On April 29, 1995, almost thirteen years after they died, eighty-four victims of the massacre at Plan de Sánchez were laid side by side in rustic wooden coffins before the main altar of the Church of San Mateo Apóstol in Salamá. The bishop of Baja Verapaz, Oscar García Urízar, presided over a special mass in which Catholic and Maya rites were both observed. Monseñor García looked down on the eighty-four coffins in front of him.

"I am ashamed and feel the sorrow that the relatives of the dead must feel," he said. "It is degrading to behold the savagery resorted to by men who would govern us."

The man who governed Guatemala when the people of Plan de Sánchez were slaughtered was General Efraín Ríos Montt. According to a survey published in *La República* the day before Monseñor García said mass, Ríos Montt was the first-choice candidate of 38 percent of all those polled, ten percentage points ahead of his closest rival, for the 1995 presidential election.

SEVENTEEN

HOW WAS GUATEMALA?

I miss my morning chats with Joselino very much. Even on days when the news he delivers is particularly grim, he has something to say about soccer, the rains, his girlfriends, Antigua gossip, or world affairs that cheers me up. I miss his quirky human touch. The anonymous manner by which *The Globe and Mail* arrives on my front porch in Canada does not compare. When I make my way through its pages the trace of Guatemala is as faint as the trace of Canada is there.

Guatemala, I have learned to accept, unfolds in a trajectory of its own elaboration. It has become for me a peculiar habit of mind, a metaphor of life and death. The only thing I'm sure of is that its citizens deserve better than they get. I think of Isaías, a gardener who lost his job in an organizational reshuffle, and wonder if he's found some other employment. I think of José, who shines shoes for a living, and wonder if the money I left with him secured him a place to live. I think of Beto, a tramp who sits outside the Hotel Aurora acknowledging alms with the smile of an angel. I think of the woman in Antigua who sells *arroz*, a delicious hot drink made of rice and milk, and wonder if inflation will cause her to raise the price of a glass another fifty *centavos*. I think of the nuns I visit at San Cristóbal Totonicapán, and wonder how the medicine they distribute is holding up.

How was Guatemala? I'll know better next time I visit.

PART THREE

SPANIARDS, LADINOS, AND THE ENDURING MAYA

EIGHTEEN

THE COLONIAL EXPERIENCE

Unlike native peoples elsewhere in the Americas, whose memory belongs to history, whose trace on the earth is faint, the Maya of Guatemala are very much a living culture. They sustain a presence no visitor to the country can fail to notice, can avoid being struck by. I recall how unusual I felt the first time I realized that I was the odd one out, a foreigner travelling alone in a busload of Mayas north of Huehuetenango.

Even modern government censuses, which enumerate fewer indigenous inhabitants than there actually are, record sizeable native populations: 1 million in 1893, 1.6 million in 1950, and 3 million in 1973. Today, between six and seven million strong, Mayas are challenging the Guatemalan state as never before, pressing for community autonomy, lobbying for land and language rights, and articulating the cause of self-determination with canny, characteristic persistence. Commentators and protagonists alike speak of a Maya nationalist movement in Guatemala, a development that has given a decidedly ethnic dimension to political struggle.

Who are these native peoples? How, through the centuries, have they managed to survive? What sorts of lives have they lived? Why should their lot concern us? These questions have charged my research interests for some time: I am inspired by the stand made by Spaniards like Bartolomé de las Casas, a Dominican friar who championed native rights in the sixteenth century; I am moved by the courage of Rigoberta Menchú, the Maya woman whose award of the Nobel Peace Prize in 1992 focused international attention on more recent burdens, more recent iniquities, more recent threats to survival.

Survival itself is the fundamental issue, but one we must tackle with caution. I try my best as a geographer not to romanticize or oversimplify what happened in history, but the tendency to do the opposite is common practice. *National Geographic,* for instance, is apt to portray the Maya as an assortment of relics, timeless throwbacks to a golden age before the Spanish conquest. Marxist texts often cultivate another image, one in which the Maya emerge as inert victims forged and preserved by colonial exploitation. Neither representation fits satisfactorily what we now know to have been a variable experience, for the confrontation in Guatemala between natives and newcomers was something that differed quite markedly from region to region, if not from place to place within a region. If we view Mayas as subjects and not as objects, if we look at the particulars of the historical record and do not make do with myths and stereotypes, we can see them instead as social actors, as human agents who responded to invasion and domination in order to shape, at least in part, key elements of their culture. Viewing Mayas in this light, I believe, allows a more active emphasis to be placed in depicting their fate under Spanish rule.

When, in 1524, Spaniards first arrived in Guatemala, they found themselves in a challenging situation: wars of conquest would have to be waged not against a cohesive, hierarchical state, as had been largely the case in Mexico, but against quarrelsome, disparate polities long accustomed to harboring grudge and grievance amongst themselves. Under these circumstances, conquest would neither be sudden nor sure.

It began with an incursion led by Pedro de Alvarado, whose forces entered Guatemala from Mexico three years after the fall of the Aztec capital, Tenochtitlán, to Hernán Cortés. The Spaniards and their Mexican allies encountered no appreciable Maya resistance along the Pacific coast, but following an ascent into the highlands a number of battles ensued. Alvarado's main opponents were the K'iche', but after their defeat other Maya peoples had to be dealt with, one by one by one: the Mam, the Ixil, and the Ch'orti', only three among many. On several occasions Kaqchikel warriors fought alongside the Spaniards, as in the conquest of the Tz'utujiles of Atitlán. Kaqchikel allegiance, however, withered after barely six months, when excessive demands for tribute caused them to stage a rebellion that lasted almost four years. Maya scribes wrote down their version of events in an account known as the *Annals of the Cakchiquels:*

> Ten days after we fled from the city [Yximché], Tunatiuh [Alvarado] began to make war upon us. On the day 4 Camey [September 5, 1524] they began to make us suffer. We scattered ourselves under the trees, under the vines. . . . All our tribes joined in the fight against Tunatiuh. The Spaniards began to leave at once. They went out of the city, leaving it deserted.

Then the Cakchiquels began hostilities against the Spaniards. They dug holes and pits for the horses and scattered sharp stakes so that they should be killed. At the same time the people made war on them. Many Spaniards perished and the horses also. . . . Only thus did the Spaniards give them a breathing spell, [only thus] our hearts had some rest.

On the day 1 Caok [March 27, 1527] our slaughter by the Spaniards began. The people fought them, and they continued to fight a prolonged war. Death struck us anew, but none of the people paid the tribute.

Some Mayas, the Q'eqchi's and the Uspantekos among them, inflicted temporary defeat on the invaders before succumbing to later, better organized acts of aggression. In one meandering foray, Pedro de Portocarrero, responsible for Spanish gains against the Kaqchikeles in 1527, pushed west across Guatemala and on into Chiapas, where he met up with fellow conquistador Diego de Mazariegos. This meeting most likely occurred in 1528, by which time Mazariegos may have got the better of Maya groups in Chiapas; the followers of Alvarado, however, were then still hard pressed in Guatemala. Not until some ten years later, in certain areas even longer, did Spaniards bring Maya groups in Guatemala to heel. Their resistance made the task of subjugation a savage, protracted affair.

The ability of Maya peoples to raise armies to thwart Spanish ambitions is an important indication that Guatemala supported sizeable, well-organized populations when the Spaniards first invaded; the invaders, it is now increasingly recognized, were assisted in their goals of conquest by large contingents of native auxiliaries, who marched under their own banners as well as those of imperial Spain. One of my primary research interests is in the field of historical demography. A colleague and I reckon that two million Mayas inhabited Guatemala on the eve of conquest, a number that fell precipitously to 427,850 by 1550 and 197,260 by 1575, before reaching a nadir level of 131,250 by the years between 1624 and 1628.

Population collapse can be attributed to many factors; foremost of all, however, is the role of disease. As with other Native American peoples, the Maya had no natural immunity to Old World maladies such as smallpox, measles, typhus, mumps, and plague, diseases that entered a "virgin soil" environment along with the Europeans, with disastrous consequences for native welfare. Between 1519 and 1632 eight epidemics lashed Guatemala, with more localized episodes occurring over the same period. Quite often bouts of sickness triggered other crisis scenarios, for poor health resulted in failure to plant fields, which in turn led to food shortages and the onset of famine. Once again, the Kaqchikel furnish us with a vivid eyewitness account, which tells of disease actually preceding the arrival of Alvarado by three or four years:

> It happened that during the twenty-fifth year [August 1519–October 1520] the plague began, oh, my sons! First they became ill of a cough, they suffered from nosebleeds and illness of the bladder. It was truly terrible, the number of dead there were in that period. The prince Vakaki Ahmak died then. Little by little heavy shadows and black night enveloped our fathers and grandfathers and us also, oh, my sons! when the plague raged.
>
> It was in truth terrible, the number of dead among the people. The people could not in any way control the sickness.
>
> Great was the stench of the dead. After our fathers and grandfathers succumbed, half of the people fled to the fields. The dogs and the vultures devoured the bodies. The mortality was terrible. Your grandfathers died, and with them died the son of the king and his brothers and kinsmen. So it was that we became orphans, oh, my sons! So we became when we were young. All of us were thus. We were born to die!

The immediate results of Spanish intrusion, then, were warfare, outbreaks of disease, and the beginning of native depopulation. After the trauma of these disruptions came the onerous responsibility of being Maya in the Spanish scheme of empire, a status that demanded expressions of loyalty and terms of commitment far different from those adhered to before. The Spaniards introduced various institutions to implement and meet their imperial expectations. Two institutions that figured prominently in the apparatus of conquest were *encomienda* and *congregación*.

The history of *encomienda* is complex, but throughout the sixteenth and seventeenth centuries it remained a device whereby privileged Spaniards and their American-born *criollo* offspring received tribute in labor, goods, or cash from the natives entrusted to their charge. *Encomiendas* were not grants of land but rather awards to enjoy the fruits of what the land and its people could provide, whether prized items such as gold, silver, salt, or cacao, or less spectacular produce such as corn, cloth, or chickens. The entitlement carried with it certain obligations, among them arranging that wards held in *encomienda* receive proper instruction in the tenets and practice of Christian faith, an obligation that few Spaniards ever met.

Grants of *encomienda* made shortly after conquest, assigned primarily to Spaniards who had fought for the Crown with distinction, frequently entailed the allocation of impressive amounts of tribute. *Encomenderos,* individuals who held and shared *encomiendas,* wielded considerable power early on as recipients of Indian tribute, but the Crown's role with respect to *encomienda* was one of strategic curtailment. It eventually took measures to dismantle privileges—placing restrictions on labor provisions and limiting inheritance beyond one or two generations—so that even the most enterprising of *encomenderos* would be stopped from becoming the equivalent of a feudal lord. Of particular importance in this regard were reforms carried out between 1548 and 1555, when Alonso López de Cerrato served as president of the Audiencia de Guatemala, a court whose members were appointed by the Crown and charged with the day-to-day government of far-flung territories from Chiapas to Costa Rica. When it was abolished in the eighteenth century, *encomienda* represented little more than a modest form of pension.

Encomiendas encompassed, in varying spatial degree, one or more communities that Spaniards referred to as *pueblos de indios*, "Indian towns" in the municipal sense of central place and surrounding countryside, segregated areas where nonnatives in theory were not supposed to settle. Upon arrival Spaniards observed that Maya settlements were customarily more dispersed than nucleated. What little urbanization that had developed was restricted to defensive, hilltop sites not in the least conducive to proper and efficient administration. The policy of *congregación* was designed to deal with this situation, and *pueblos de indios* were the result of its zealous implementation.

As promulgated by Spanish law, *congregación* was a means whereby Mayas found dwelling in scattered rural groups would be brought together, converted to Christianity, and moulded into harmonious, resourceful communities that reflected imperial notions of orderly, civilized life. To the Church, especially members of the Dominican and Franciscan orders, fell the difficult job of getting Indian families down from the mountains and resettled in towns built around a Catholic place of worship. A royal order issued on March 21, 1551, spells out the mandate to missionize, and the rationale behind it:

> With great care and particular attention we have always attempted to impose the most convenient means of instructing the Indians in the Holy Catholic Faith and evangelical law, causing them to forget their ancient erroneous rites and ceremonies and to live in concert and order; and, so that this might be brought about, those of our Council of [the] Indies have met together several times with other religious persons . . . and they, with the desire of promoting the service of God, and ours, resolved that the Indians should be reduced to villages and not be allowed to live divided and separated in the mountains and wildernesses, where they are deprived of all spiritual and temporal comforts, the aid of our ministers, and those

other things which human necessities oblige men to give one to another; therefore . . . the viceroys, presidents, and governors [are] charged and ordered to execute the reduction, settlement, and indoctrination of the Indians.

The rhetoric of *congregación* belongs to what Carlos Fuentes has called the "legal country," a colonial fiction distinctly at odds with the "real country" that came into being. In the overall vision of empire, few endeavors differed in outcome so markedly from original intent as did *congregación*, prompting contemporary observers to express outrage, astonishment, and despair that such a grand plan could amount to so little. *Congregación* did make its mark on the landscape at an early date: *pueblos de indios* created by regular and secular clergy in the course of the sixteenth century persist today as *municipios*, or townships, that generations of anthropologists have considered the key unit in defining Maya community life. But no sooner had the Spaniards resettled native families where they deemed suitable than the Maya drifted back to the mountains from which they had been moved. Why did this happen? What caused the grip of *congregación* to become undone?

For one thing, *congregación* was carried out not by persuasion but by force. Because entire families were shifted against their will from one location to another, it was unlikely that people who found the experience disagreeable, if not hateful, would stay put. To escape the exploitation they suffered while residing in town or nearby, Mayas repeatedly fled to outlying rural areas. There they could be free of compulsory demands to furnish tribute, provide labor, work on local roads or the parish church, and serve as human carriers. They also sought the refuge of the mountains when disease struck, the impact of sickness on *pueblos de indios* correctly perceived as being more destructive than arm's-length subsistence in the hills. Furthermore, the labor-intensive manner in which Maya farmers tended their fields was best undertaken by living close to them in small, dispersed groups, not far removed in large, nucleated settlements.

Next, there is the issue of denominational friction and the deployment of spiritual resources. Along with the Mercedarians, a less-dominant third party in the missionary enterprise, Dominicans and Franciscans waged a territorial war while being simultaneously driven by the higher calling of *congregación*. The two largest, most powerful orders each carved out a sphere of influence relative to the colonial capital of Santiago de Guatemala. Dominicans moved into the far north and west, responsible for a vast, daunting expanse that stretched from Verapaz to Chiapas. Franciscans opted for a more manageable central zone within a fifty-kilometer radius of Lake Atitlán. Both orders jealously guarded against rival encroachment the *pueblos de indios* established in the confines of their jurisdictions. Bickering between them diverted energy from the pressing concern of native conversion and became so tiresome that the Crown issued a royal order on January 22, 1556, accusing the friars of "petty ambition" and "name calling," and commanding them to resolve their differences in a more seemly, Christian fashion.

In the eyes of the Crown, such behavior set a bad example and made little practical sense, given that friars were few and their responsibilities many. Indeed, throughout three hundred years of colonial rule less than one thousand missionaries arrived in Guatemala to propagate the faith. Civil authorities well recognized the uphill battle that their religious associates faced; two Crown officers, Antonio Rodríguez de Quesada and Pedro Ramírez de Quiñones, openly acknowledged that "in these parts there is a great lack of missionaries." By the mid-sixteenth century the Dominicans were so overextended that they ceded a large part of their domain to the Mercedarians, a more acceptable choice to the Dominicans than their Franciscan adversaries. For their part, as early as 1552 the Franciscans requested permission from the Crown to assume responsibility for establishing missions in Dominican territory, "because the fathers of Santo Domingo are just not up to it."

At the other end of the Maya realm, to the south and east of Santiago, none of the three orders established a notable presence, leaving the Oriente in the proselytizing hands of the less-experienced secular clergy. The divide in missionary jurisdiction between a "secular" east and a "regular" west is an important one to recognize. Ecclesiastical divisions, however, serve only to underscore another more profound process, one best articulated by Murdo MacLeod in his landmark work on the colonial experience in Central America.

MacLeod argues that exploitation of the isthmian resource base operated in such a way that Spanish attention was drawn primarily to the cacao-rich Pacific coast or to the rolling, temperate lands to the south and east of the capital, where indigo could be grown, cattle grazed, and two or even three corn crops harvested each year. Spaniards viewed the *tierra fría,* or cold land, to the north and west of Santiago—more difficult to reach and with fewer entrepreneurial options—as far less attractive. Their interest in the north and west, therefore, was never as intense as their interest in the south and east. When Spanish attitudes concerning the worth of the land were translated into thousands of individual actions, they resulted in a notably different colonial experience.

South and east of Santiago de Guatemala, the Spaniards encroached upon Maya communities to a greater degree, and cultural and biological assimilation proceeded at a brisker pace. There, as in El Salvador, Honduras, and Nicaragua, Spaniards mixed not only with the natives but also with black slaves imported from Africa, creating a predominantly *mestizo* or Ladino milieu. To the north and west of the capital, where possibilities for enrichment were less and fewer Spaniards were inclined to settle, Maya peoples withstood the onslaught of acculturation more resiliently, holding onto much of their land, retaining traditional principles of community organization, and guarding a sense of identity that was resolutely their own. Maya languages were kept alive, as were Maya ways of worshipping the gods. Daily chores and the seasonal round followed a Maya, not Spanish, rhythm. Even time itself, the days and months that make up a year, ticked on with a Maya pulse. When, existentially, *congregación* is situated within this larger panorama, Maya reaction to it takes on a vital, formative dynamic.

Condemned by geography to inhabit a backwater region in the Spanish scheme of empire, Maya peoples in Guatemala shaped for themselves a culture of refuge in which Hispanic traits and institutions were absorbed and intertwined with indigenous ones, often in elaborate ways that baffled, mocked, and in the end eroded imperial authority. Periodization is somewhat difficult. Certainly by the early seventeenth century, patterns of hybrid mores were much in evidence, but the trend had set in earlier. Recognition that all was far from well, that *congregación* was not unfolding according to plan, prompted the following remarks by Pedro Ramírez de Quiñones, uttered in frustration on May 20, 1556:

> There is great disorder among the Indians in matters that relate to their government and administration. Things are chaotic, lacking direction. Grave public sins abound. What is most of concern is that Indian actions go unpunished, without redress, because they are not brought to the attention of the court. In most *pueblos de indios* people live much as they wish to, or can, and since the court cannot arrange for visitations to be made, we, its officers, cannot vouch for one-tenth of the district we are in charge of.

Even when Indians displaced by *congregación* chose to remain within its spatial embrace, they frequently regrouped in town or close by along preconquest domestic lines that Spaniards called *parcialidades*. These were social units of great antiquity, organized as patrilineal clans or localized kin affiliates, and usually associated with particular tracts of land.

Unfamiliarity on the part of missionaries as to the discrete nature of *parcialidades* often resulted in several of them being thrown together to form, in theory, a single community. Once gathered around a new center, however,

parcialidades would preserve their aboriginal identity by continuing to operate socially and economically as separate components rather than merging to
form a corporate body. Far from being the placid, homogeneous entities that
colonial legislation conjures up, many *pueblos de indios* turned out to be a mo-
saic of *parcialidades* that touched but did not interpenetrate, that coexisted
but did not always cooperate. In the Province of Totonicapán, for instance,
nine *pueblos de indios* alone comprised over thirty *parcialidades,* each of them
assessed individually for tribute-paying purposes in the late seventeenth century. At least one of these towns, Sacapulas, also arranged that land be held
and farmed by *parcialidad,* as did other *pueblos de indios. Parcialidades* might
also be associated with specific *cofradías,* religious sodalities originally introduced for the worship of a favored saint but which, over time, came to serve
as useful Christian cover for more suspect forms of worship.

If residential commitment to *congregación* resulted in a certain degree of improvisation, town abandonment led to manifest aberrations. Resistance to
the Spanish master plan, once again, set in early. Sacapulas, for example,
may not have crystallized quite as its Dominican founders first imagined, but
once their convent had been established, a well-defined community did form
around it. Another matter entirely was the outlying countryside.

Archival work can be a tedious, monotonous grind, a ritual of days spent
sifting through documents for marginal, inconsequential returns. Occasionally something out of the ordinary turns up, like the letter I found in the
Archive of the Indies in Seville that deals "hands on" with conducting God's
work among the Maya of Sacapulas.

The letter was penned in the convent at Sacapulas on December 6, 1555, by
Tomás de Cárdenas and Juan de Torres, who wrote to King Charles V, Holy
Roman Emperor, about the tremendous obstacles working against effective
congregación. They mention, first, the difficulties imposed by the environment, stating not unreasonably that "this part of the sierra is the most rugged
and broken to be found in these lands." Making their way across it, Cárdenas
and Torres had stumbled upon groups "of eight, six, and even four houses or
huts, tucked and hidden away in gullies where, until the arrival of one of us,
no other Spaniard had reached." The friars lament that during their trek they
discovered "idols in abundance, not just concealed but placed in people's
houses more or less as they had them before they were baptized."

Indians, they tell the king, populate such desolate, faraway places so that
"no one could reach there who might disturb or destroy their evil living."
The people they had found living that way, the Dominicans state with some

relief, "now that they are housed together will have less opportunity to practice idolatry and, ourselves, more opportunity to watch over them." Thus resettled, Indians "can more readily be instructed not only in matters that concern our Holy Faith but also in proper human conduct."

To those who might protest that *congregación* is carried out involuntarily, that it shifts families from one place to another against their will, Cárdenas and Torres declare that "there is no sick person who does not find the taste of medicine unpleasant." In this sense Indians are held to be "like children," and so "one must do not what most pleases them but what is best for them."

If, at times, the tone of the friars is sober and paternalistic, so also is it poignant and insightful. Nowhere do the two Dominicans capture more perceptively why Maya families might resist and resent resettlement than when they remark: "Among all these Indians there is not one who wishes to leave behind the hut passed on to him by his father, nor to abandon a pestilential ravine or desert some inaccessible craggy rocks, for that is where the bones of his forefathers rest."

Solemn words, but voiced with a sense of foreboding that soon proved well founded. Five years after Cárdenas and Torres addressed the Crown, the native leaders of Santiago Atítlán also wrote to complain that in the outlying settlements they were responsible for lived "rebellious Indians who wish to remain outside our authority and who disobey our orders concerning what tribute should be paid." Even near the capital city desertion was rife; the years between 1575 and 1578 witnessed "many Indians" in the environs of Santiago "moving about, in hiding, from one place to another" rather than be forced to furnish their own tribute as well as pay that part deemed still to be owed by deceased relatives. Around this same time, farther north in Verapaz, it was reported that "*parcialidades* and entire families leave to live idolatrously in the mountains." Two sizeable *pueblos de indios,* Santa Catalina and Zulbén, had been abandoned almost completely by 1579, only five years after the bishop of Verapaz himself had supervised the process of *congregación.* At Santa María Cahabón, baptized Mayas allegedly gave up civilized life to join unconquered Lacandón and Chol-Manché tribes in pre-Christian barbarism on the other side of the frontier.

A century or so later, after the bishop of Guatemala, Andrés de las Navas, had twice toured his jurisdiction and heard disturbing reports from parish priests about fugitivism, lawlessness, idolatry, and tax evasion, he prepared a dossier that leaves little doubt about how widespread "civil disobedience" had become. Outside San Juan Sacatepéquez, Indians "who neither hear mass nor confess their sins" had lived "for upward of twenty years, dwelling there under the pretext of growing corn." Other centrally located *pueblos de indios*—Chimaltenango, Parramos, Patzicía, Patzún, San Andrés Itzapa, San Martín Jilotepeque, Sumpango, and Tecpán among them—also drew the bishop's wrath. Religious backsliding was only one element of waywardness that concerned him. At Comalapa the parish priest told of "daykeepers and witchdoctors," informing de las Navas, "After we preach to them, warning them that they must cease their ancient superstitions, they leave church and are heard to ask: 'Why should we abandon the ways of our grandfathers and ancestors?'"

Such attitudes among Mayas living reasonably close to Santiago were, if anything, magnified farther away from the capital, nowhere more blatantly than at San Mateo Ixtatán. There, high up in the Sierra de los Cuchumatanes, Fray Alonso de León records that he had recently been informed "that some eighty families do not figure on the tribute list," which meant not only that "His Majesty is losing revenue" but also that "all these fugitives do not attend mass or go to confession." The relationship between father and son, the priest declared, was one in which "nothing is passed on save for how to take care of the cornfields and how to live all day long like savages in the hills." De León feared that proper codes of behavior would never take root, for the people of San Mateo "are at each other's throats, all year long."

What distressed Fray Alonso most was that native leaders had decided "to build a shrine, on no authority but their own, up in the hills some distance from town, at precisely the same spot where the sacrificial altar of pagan times used to be." The shrine was located "on a hill top, between the remains of ancient temples, which they call *cues,* where on any given day may be found charcoal and incense and other signs of burnt offerings." De León disclosed that "further transgressions against the Holy Church include the sacrifice of turkeys, taken up to the hills to be dispatched with the blood of other animals." Each March, at a place two leagues distant from town, wood was piled at the foot of crosses that were later set on fire. The "indios diabólicos" of San Mateo, it was alleged, "with their nasty habits and evil deeds have contaminated the entire town in such a way that it remains Christian in name only."

Life in the "real country," then, jarred dramatically with the blueprint legislated in the "legal country." It would be a mistake to imagine, however, that even though the Maya made unworthy converts, nothing could be gained from exploiting them, that Spaniards somehow were disposed to shrugging off their quest for power and enrichment so easily. Officials of both the Church and the Crown from time to time did very well at native expense, legally or otherwise.

In terms of illegality, perhaps the most obnoxious demand placed on native communities came in the form of *repartimientos*. Under this practice, *corregidores* and *alcaldes mayores,* district governors who actually bought public office with a view to making money from it, supplied Maya families with various commodities, insisting that they be purchased at prices favorable to the seller, regardless of whether or not the recipients desired the merchandise in the first place. A reverse strategy was to force a sale at rock-bottom prices in one area, then resell at higher prices in another.

Repartimientos appear on the scene in the sixteenth century, and feature in the seventeenth also, but they seem to have been most prolific in the eighteenth century. One item that figured prominently in these dealings was cotton, which district governors distributed in raw, bulk form among Maya women, compelling them to spin it into thread and then weave it into lengths of cloth, or *mantas*. The finished article fetched a tidy profit—for the *corregidor* or *alcalde mayor,* not the worker—when sold at market. Raw wool was also circulated, among male weavers, with the same end in mind. Other items peddled to the natives included axes, clothes, hats, iron tools and implements, mules, and (on occasion) money. Although community leaders petitioned against these transactions, stating that *repartimientos* caused parents to neglect their families and to slight their fields, directives ordering government officials to cease their odious racket were repeatedly ignored.

Just as the Maya were vulnerable to exploitation by government officials, so also did they fall prey to exactions by clergymen. An order issued as early as 1561 stipulated what goods and services priests could legitimately request from their parishioners. Theoretical limits, however, were not always adhered to, and so while many Spaniards did work selflessly toward spiritual goals, others concerned themselves more with personal gain than with native salvation. Abuses again seem to have been especially prevalent in the eighteenth century, with priests and friars accused of various excesses, including failure to reimburse for personal services, selling livestock without the owner's consent, overzealous collection of funds to celebrate Mass or to hear confession, and embezzlement of *cofradía* assets.

Three centuries of colonial rule cast a long and oppressive shadow, creating deep and enduring fissures in the nature of Guatemalan social, economic, and political life. No one has summed it all up more succinctly than historian Severo Martínez Peláez. "Colonial reality," he wrote in his magnum opus, *La Patria del Criollo*, "is our everyday reality," emphasizing that "we do not need to venture far from Guatemala City to see it everywhere." Certainly by the time of independence, which took place in 1821, little had changed (or was about to) in the fundamental way that Spaniards and *criollos* from all walks of life related to the indigenous presence. For them, Maya subordination was not an issue of polemic or debate: it was simply taken for granted, something that was regarded as a natural right, an accepted fixture in how Guatemala was and would remain. Coexistence under these terms fostered neither compassion nor respect. What it *did* breed were mutual feelings of suspicion, distrust, hatred, and fear.

In comprehending how subordination was maintained, anthropologist Michael Taussig offers some trenchant remarks. "We would be most unwise," he cautions, "to overlook or underestimate the role of terror." Terror, asserts Taussig, is not only "a physiological state" but also "a social fact and a cultural construction whose baroque dimensions allow it to serve as the mediator *par excellence* of colonial hegemony." Like many features created by Spanish conquest, the specter of terror—pervading "spaces of death" in which "Indian, African, and White gave birth to the New World"—haunted Maya life to scar and disfigure succeeding centuries.

NINETEEN

THE CENTURY AFTER
INDEPENDENCE

It's ironic to think that we often know more about the history of Guatemala under Spanish rule than we do about postcolonial times, especially the nineteenth century. Bit by bit, however, a more grounded appreciation of the events and circumstances of nineteenth-century life is emerging. Much of the credit for this belongs to the historian Ralph Lee Woodward, Jr. His research, while focussing primarily on the political career of Rafael Carrera, in effect sketches the lineaments of culture and society during the first half-century of Guatemala's existence as an independent republic. The years between 1821 and 1871 have also attracted the attention of another distinguished American historian, E. Bradford Burns.

What Burns and Woodward tell us about the conditions of rural life in Guatemala contrasts vividly with portrayals of what took place in the countryside after 1871, when the rule of liberal, not conservative, governments prevailed. Our knowledge of rural life from 1871 on has been advanced considerably by the findings of several scholars, among them Shelton H. Davis, David McCreery, David Stoll, and John Watanabe. The research of these individuals affords us a glimpse of the changes that occurred in Guatemala during the century after independence. Contemplation of historical forces operating at the national or regional level can be fleshed out by more detailed scrutiny of the impact they had in distinct local settings. Of particular interest to me are the communities of Santiago Chimaltenango, Nebaj, Santa Eulalia, and San Juan Ixcoy, Maya strongholds in the Sierra de los Cuchumatanes, the area of Guatemala I perhaps know best.

The political scene in Guatemala following independence from Spain was marked by prolonged internal conflict between conservatives and liberals for control of government office. Differences between the two camps were many, but centered on the conservative preference for maintaining Hispanic-derived institutions that sought to preserve the colonial status quo, in contrast to the liberal preference for creating an entirely new social and economic order, one that viewed progress as attainable by promoting capitalist links with the outside world. In terms of the impact of ideology on Maya ways, conservatism represented a continuation of the culture of refuge shaped during colonial times. Liberalism signified Maya assimilation into a modern, outward-looking state that Severo Martínez Peláez ([1970] 2009) famously called "la patria del criollo": the criollo homeland, an elite national project. Conservatism meant minimal cultural change at the community level, liberalism intense, outside interference that would alter irrevocably long-established ways of living with the land.

Liberals dominated political office between 1823 and 1839, but their plans for radical reform were stalled, if not reversed, for three decades thereafter when Rafael Carrera led the conservatives to power following a popular uprising. A wily, pragmatic leader who came to be known as "protector of the people," Carrera undid the work of his liberal predecessor, Mariano Gálvez, and championed a stable, paternalist state founded on restored Hispanic institutions. The extent to which Maya communities benefited directly from Carrera's political agenda is unclear. Although Woodward (1990) maintains that "Carrera's pro-Indian policy did indeed protect the Indians from further encroachment on their land and labor during the 1840s," he concedes that "after 1850 that protection began to lessen as Carrera became more clearly attached to the Guatemalan elite." McCreery is more convinced by the reasoning of the late Oliver La Farge (1940), who suggested some time ago that Maya life under Carrera "becomes a smooth blend; well stabilized, it has the individuality and roundness that mark any culture, and its continued evolution is in the form of growth out of itself, rather than in response to alien pressures." McCreery (1990) argues that his research findings tend to support the views of La Farge. He depicts Carrera's program as one in which a "fragile and beleaguered state issued laws and decrees but could visit little effective attention on a rural population that resisted paying taxes and for whose land and labor the ladino elites had little use." Maya communities, McCreery concludes, were "more neglected than protected" by Carrera, a claim that diminishes or makes less relevant the role of the state in native life.

Liberals regained political office in 1871, six years after Carrera's death, and under the stewardship of Justo Rufino Barrios began to implement with fervor what they had been frustrated from doing four decades earlier. Burns (1980) describes the liberal agenda as signalling "a return to monoculture, declining food production for local consumption, rising foreign debt, forced labor, debt peonage, the growth of latifundia, and the greater impoverishment of the majority." Attacks on Maya land and assaults on Maya labor were inevitable consequences of the liberal vision of progress.

McCreery argues that Barrios and his successors did not entirely eradicate the notion of community property. What liberal legislation demanded was for land to be formally declared and, if possible, registered not by collective but by individual title. The option of registering land communally was not ruled out; it was simply more acceptable—the preferred, ideologically correct choice—to register land as individual property. McCreery (1988) makes a crucial point: "Because the process of conversion to private property rested on a number of individual, positive acts, it progressed at very different rates from village to village, depending on external conditions and on the dictates of community traditions and circumstances." While "positive acts" on the part of Maya communities by no means guaranteed lawful title to land, failure to lay claim to title exposed them to risks of seizure and encroachment.

Land was most certainly lost; exactly how much has yet to be ascertained. Scholarly opinion ranges from Robert Naylor's (1967) vague impression of there being "little discernible change" in Maya life, of its continuing "much the same as before," to Carol Smith's (1984) more realistic but undocumented assertion that Maya communities "lost about half of the lands they traditionally claimed during the colonial period." More systematic research is clearly in order.

Land was transformed from a cultural into an economic resource, wrested from community and spun into commodity, by liberal desires to capitalize on Guatemala's untapped potential as a producer of coffee. The Pacific piedmont and the Verapaz highlands in particular offered ideal growing conditions. Both these regions had been relatively untouched by the search for a successful cash crop during colonial times, which had seen cacao, cochineal, and indigo go through short-lived cycles of boom and bust. Investment by domestic and foreign capital resulted in coffee emerging during the second half of the nineteenth century as Guatemala's principal export crop, a position it has maintained in the national economy from the time of President Barrios on. Martínez Peláez asserts that "the coffee dictatorships were the full and radical realization of criollo notions of the patria," creating not just interconnected modes of privilege and exclusion but notions of "the Guatemalan nation and Guatemalan identity" that are still dominant today.

Organized on a *finca* or plantation basis, coffee production demands intensive labor input, mostly at harvest time. What suits the requirements of coffee planters best, therefore, is a seasonal workforce, one that provides labor when needed and that can be dispensed with when not. Outright coercion in the form of a draft known as *mandamiento,* authorized by President Barrios in 1876, reinforced the long-standing practice of legalized debt peonage, which endured well into the twentieth century in Guatemala, when it was eventually replaced by a vagrancy law requiring individuals holding less than a stipulated amount of land to work part of each year as wage laborers for others: anyone farming ten or more *cuerdas,* but less than the three or four *manzanas* that qualified them for an exemption, was expected to work one hundred days; anyone farming less than ten *cuerdas* was expected to work one hundred and fifty days.* A *libreto de jornaleros,* an account and identification booklet, had to be carried at all times and was best inspected with the requisite number of work days fulfilled.

With the advent of liberal rule, then, Maya communities throughout Guatemala were exposed to a double threat, one that targeted labor as well as land as desirable economic assets. The degree to which liberal prerogatives made their mark on native life, however, varied considerably from community to community, as the following case studies demonstrate.

SANTIAGO CHIMALTENANGO

Santiago Chimaltenango, known to local residents simply as Chimbal, is a Mam community lying along the southern flanks of the Sierra de los Cuchumatanes at elevations ranging from around 1,400 to over 2,700 meters. While growing conditions in lower-elevation *tierra templada* are favorable, the cultivation of coffee as a cash crop in Chimbal dates only to the middle of the twentieth century, primarily as an activity of small-scale producers. Chimbal was studied in the 1930s by Charles Wagley, who produced two benchmark accounts (1941, 1949). Forty years after Wagley first visited, Chimbal attracted the attention of another anthropologist, John Watanabe (1990, 1992), whose work provides insight into land-related incidents in the late nineteenth century.

Chimbal is an interesting case. In terms of the overall impact of the liberal reforms, it cannot be said to have suffered the worst of transformations. What Chimbal's experience illustrates, however, is that moves to lay claim to title triggered counterclaims on the part of neighboring communities, often with detrimental consequences.

Watanabe informs us that on May 19, 1879, representatives from Chimbal lodged a petition with the district governor of Huehuetenango for legal title

---

*A *cuerda* is a variable unit of land, measuring either 0.11 acres or 0.27 aces. A *manzana* equals approximately 1.7 acres.

to community land. Chimbal's petition was submitted two years after the Barrios administration issued Decree 170, which terminated the colonial system of land rental known as *censo enfiteusis*. Under *censo enfiteusis*, community residents could acquire usufruct rights to specific plots of land, rights that could be inherited, sold, sublet, or exchanged but did not allow for the legal transfer of land itself. These were precisely the arrangements Decree 170 was designed to eliminate.

Chimbal's petition provoked a contrary response from three of its neighbors, all of them alleging that tracts of the land claimed by Chimbal belonged to them. San Juan Atitán was first to protest, stating on June 20, 1879, that six years previously it had claimed lands included in the Chimbal petition. San Pedro Necta followed, stating in November that a village called Niyá fell within its territory, not Chimbal's. San Martín Cuchumatán declared jurisdiction over a village called Tajumuc, which it said it had incorporated long before. Chimbal, in turn, disputed all three counterclaims and in December requested that a survey be arranged to resolve the matter.

Responsibility for the survey fell to one Juan María Ordóñez, who was charged with measuring land designated as *ejido*, a standard allotment of one square league (16.6 square kilometers) around the main township center, and *baldío*, an indeterminate amount of public or state land beyond. Ordóñez conducted the survey between June 2 and June 17, 1880, and subsequently filed a report that calculated Chimbal's *ejido* to be 17.4 square kilometers in extent, surrounded by almost 54 square kilometers of *baldío*. The land disputed with San Pedro and San Martín—San Juan, by now, had apparently withdrawn from the fray—lay exclusively in the *baldío*. Three years later a government official reviewing Ordóñez's report observed that Chimbal enjoyed access to more *ejido* land than its old colonial entitlement. He also noted that *baldío* land contested by San Pedro totalled almost 25 square kilometers. When a municipal title was finally issued on September 10, 1891, it recognized as *ejido* all 17.4 square kilometers registered in Ordóñez's survey but awarded to Chimbal little more than half the land, some 29 square kilometers, claimed as *baldío*.

Out of a total claim of 71 square kilometers, then, Chimbal ended up with legal title to 46. The 25 square kilometers forfeited in the dispute, Watanabe reckons, went in equal measure to San Pedro and San Martín, with the latter's share being absorbed by Todos Santos Cuchumatán when San Martín became part of its municipal jurisdiction.

The stakes at Chimbal, compared to what was up for grabs elsewhere in Guatemala, may have been slim, but the titling episode is instructive on three counts. First, by pitting neighbor against neighbor, Maya against Maya, the practice conformed to that most obdurate rule of conquest: divide and rule. Second, it established that a new order would indeed replace the old, for land henceforth would be owned, not merely worked. And three, it represented the beginnings of Maya accommodation to the modern state, which Watanabe (1992) expresses thus: "In seeking legal title—whether municipal or individual—to safeguard their lands, Chimaltecos in effect abdicated sovereignty over that land by appealing to state authority to validate their claims." Further accommodation would be necessary as the power of the state grew.

NEBAJ

Nebaj, one of three Ixil townships lying at the eastern edge of the Cuchumatanes Mountains, embraces municipal territory ranging from below 1,400 to upward of 3,000 meters in elevation. Nebaj and its two Ixil neighbors, Chajul and San Juan Cotzal, were studied in the early 1940s by Jackson Steward Lincoln. His untimely death while engaged in fieldwork in Guatemala cut short a promising career, if Lincoln's posthumously published notes (1945) are anything to judge by. Benjamin Colby and Pierre van den Berghe (1969), whose research activities in the 1960s focused on ethnic relations, also subjected all three Ixil townships to rewarding scrutiny. Ixil country was hard-hit by the counterinsurgency war of the early 1980s, in the wake of which David Stoll (1993) conducted a detailed examination of the community life of people who, in the words of several survivors, had been caught "between two fires." Stoll's work on the nineteenth and early twentieth centuries draws in part on archival investigation by Elaine Elliott.

Colby and van den Berghe, as well as Stoll, lean heavily on Lincoln in depicting how the coffee economy "opened up" Ixil country. Labor, not land, appears initially to have been the big attraction. The prospect of recruiting seasonal workers lured to Nebaj one Isaías Palacios, a Spaniard who arrived in the early 1890s to take up the post of town secretary. He soon became Nebaj's first labor contractor, forwarding loans in return for commitments to work on coffee plantations. Palacios and agents like him sealed contracts with the assistance of drink, proffering the natives liquor, trapping them into debt and dependency, and cultivating a pattern of behavior from which escape was difficult. Stoll invokes the words of the Irish-Canadian archaeologist Robert Burkitt, who in 1913, while staying at Nebaj, observed "an unceasing coming and going of labor contractors and plantation agents getting out gangs of Indians for the Pacific Coast." Burkitt (1930) pulled no punches and spoke frankly about what he saw:

Years ago, when I first visited Nebaj, it was a different place from now. . . .
I had struck the place at an especially bad moment. The plantation agents
were at the height of their activity, scattering money, advance pay for work,
and every Indian was able to buy rum. The rum business and the coffee
business work together in this country, automatically. The plantation advances money to the Indian and the rum seller takes it away from him and
the Indian has to go to work again. Work leads to rum and rum leads to
work. . . . I used to think that Chichicastenango was the drunkenest town
in the country, but now I think it is Nebaj. My plans at Nebaj were upset
by rum. There are two ruin places that I know of that are to be got at from
Nebaj and I did nothing at either of them, and one of them I never even
saw. The Indians I was going to take were never sober.

Lincoln also noted connections between the "rum business" and the "coffee business," acknowledging that while "Indians drank on all ceremonial
occasions," it was Ladinos who were responsible "for increasing the amount
and the strength of the liquor for the purpose of enriching themselves." Nebaj
at one juncture supported eighty watering holes, which lends some credibility
to Burkitt's claim that town inhabitants there were "drunk from morning to
night." Stoll attributes a key role to Ladinos who moved to Nebaj from Malacatán, now Malacatancito, a town near Huehuetenango. These people and
other Ladinos, Stoll claims, by "selling liquor and loaning the cash needed
to go on binges . . . separated Ixils from much of their best arable land," for
after an agreement was struck "anything less than prompt repayment meant
that the house or land put up for collateral could change hands."

To land lost in this manner was added further amounts appropriated during the titling process. When a municipal title for 388 *caballerías* was issued
in 1885 to San Juan Cotzal, 180 *caballerías* also went to private individuals, a
substantial amount of the total land available.* Chajul received title to 2,424
caballerías in 1900, an additional 157 *caballerías* being allocated to private
individuals. Nebaj was awarded 1,237 *caballerías* in 1903, with 87 *caballerías*
privately titled. Most of the land deeded to private individuals was in lower-
lying *tierra templada* at elevations suitable for raising coffee or sugar cane.

Serious loss occurred in the far north of Ixil country, especially in Sotzil
and Ilom, which retained little more than the land surrounding residential
compounds. Chel, Ixtupil, and Sacsiguan did not forfeit as much, but they
did lose their most prized units of land. The claimant whose name kept appearing on title deeds was Lisandro Gordillo Galán, a Mexican citizen re-

---

*A *caballería* of land measures about 112 acres or 45.4 hectares.

corded in 1895 as having served as the town secretary of Chajul. "Titling land may not seem the most obvious way to lose it," Stoll observes, "but such has been the experience of indigenous people, because what can be titled can be alienated." Irregularities in the way that land was owned and operated in Ixil country continued well into the twentieth century.

SANTA EULALIA

A Q'anjob'al community situated in the northern reaches of the Sierra de los Cuchumatanes, Santa Eulalia incorporates territory that stretches from *tierra caliente,* around 800 meters in elevation, to *tierra fría,* well above the township center at 2,600 meters. Oliver La Farge visited Santa Eulalia in 1932, and his study (1947) of an array of Maya cultural expressions there remains one of the landmark contributions to Mesoamerican anthropology. Another anthropologist, Shelton H. Davis, studied the community in the 1960s. His doctoral dissertation (1970) is a model of historically informed ethnography, certainly one of the best inquiries we have to date of how national-level politics shaped local-level landholding in Guatemala in the late nineteenth century.

Assessing the impact of the Barrios reforms was not the primary reason that La Farge or Davis studied Santa Eulalia. Neither of them, however, could address his research questions without looking into land and labor relations. What La Farge considered the "happy isolation" of the Cuchumatanes "was shattered in the last half of the nineteenth century when the development of the coffee *fincas* on the Pacific slopes of the Sierra Madre produced a demand for labor which could be filled only by drawing upon the population reservoirs of the highlands." Labor may have been plentiful, but in the case of Santa Eulalia land itself was also a major consideration. The community estate traditionally encompassed fertile land at elevations ideal for raising coffee, which did not escape entrepreneurial curiosity. La Farge had earlier established the validity of Stoll's observation, recording that a "survey" of Santa Eulalia "resulted in the passing of much valuable land into the hands of Ladinos and a considerable reduction in the extent of the *ejidos,* or common lands." Not until Davis arrived on the scene was the magnitude of loss more fully discerned.

Davis begins by noting that, although the Laws of the Indies in colonial times and republican legislation under Carrera in theory protected Maya rights to communal land, in practice "they never clearly defined the actual limits of these Indian estates." Reluctance to do so was clearly a matter of exercising power, for "giving Indian *municipios* the legal right to ancient estates, especially those in the hot country areas distant from pueblo centers, meant that political control and ecclesiastical conversion would be impossible." Tenure arrangements that were "chaotic and unstructured" led to bitter disputes about land rights, which set one Maya community against another and allowed opportunistic intervention on the part of Ladino interests.

Davis reckons that, over the forty-year period covered by his data, roughly 70 percent of Santa Eulalia's land fell into Ladino hands, including land in Barillas and the Ixcán, "zones of greatest ecological and economic potential." Of fifty-five lots titled in these areas, Maya recipients were allocated only nine; of the 1,520 *caballerías* involved in the titling process, Q'anjob'ales were awarded 183. Ladinos titled land, as the government wished, individually, not as a corporate body, the customary Maya way of laying claim. Titles issued to Ladinos were frequently in excess of thirty *caballerías*. As Ladinos carved up the *tierra caliente* in latifundia fashion, the Maya of Santa Eulalia concentrated on acquiring legal hold of the *tierra fría* around the town center. A classic Latin American dichotomy emerged of large, Ladino-owned estates in the lowlands and a patchwork of small, Indian-tilled fields in the highlands.

Davis records that the first land lost was around the village of Santa Cruz Yalmux, where a group of Ladinos from Huehuetenango claimed some two hundred *caballerías*. The claimants, members of the local militia, made their case on May 22, 1888, appearing in person before General Manuel Lisandro Barillas, then president of Guatemala. They laid claim on the grounds that: (1) the *ejidos* of Santa Eulalia in *tierra fría* "were large and sufficient" for the number of indigenous families who lived there; (2) the petitioners would deploy the lands to which they sought title "for the development of capitalistic agriculture"; (3) during "the rise to power of Justo Rufino Barrios" Huehuetenango had played a "military role," which the government was obliged to recognize; and (4) issuing title to land would allow for the creation of a new *municipio*, which would function "as a military outpost for the protection of the frontier between Mexico and Guatemala" along the Usumacinta River. Despite protests that the claimants "only wished to gain title to this land so as to later resell it to Indian residents," the Barillas government awarded two hundred *caballerías* of Yalmux land to the Ladinos of Huehuetenango in July 1888. On October 17 that same year the *municipio* of Barillas came into being. The choice of place name directly linked government action with the erosion of the Maya estate.

Despite lobbying for land in order to stimulate "capitalistic agriculture," Ladinos who received title did not develop their property. What did develop was small-scale cattle ranching, with the new owners more commonly renting out land as absentee landlords to native occupants. Other Maya families, however, paid no formal rent and simply continued to subsist as "illegal squatters" on land that they still considered as belonging to them. Not until much later was the agricultural potential of the Ixcán systematically exploited, resulting in an inevitable clash of interests.

SAN JUAN IXCOY

San Juan Ixcoy is a Q'anjob'al township located in the heart of the Cuchumatán highlands, mostly in *tierra fría* upward of 1,500 meters in elevation. The town center lies at around 2,200 meters, in a narrow valley drained by the San Juan River. San Juan has yet to receive the scholarly attention afforded other Maya communities. It is a gloomy, unwelcoming place that keeps outsiders at bay, as if the memory of the carnage that occurred there in 1898 still lingers, giving it a grim reputation even by the standards of contemporary Guatemalan violence.

David McCreery (1988) has written with admirable attention to detail about what happened in 1898 in San Juan. Disputes over land, he observes, were nothing new to the township, which during the colonial period had been involved in such litigation with two of its neighbors, Nebaj and Soloma. Problems were exacerbated, however, with the advent of the liberal reforms. McCreery notes, like Stoll and Davis, that because of "often shaky bases for claims," titling was not only elaborate and costly but also extremely risky, a legal process "into which the villages, in the absence of any immediate threat, entered reluctantly."

San Juan was forced into legal proceedings by a claim laid in 1893 by Ladino members of the army reserve at Chiantla. Represented by one Mariano García, the Chiantla *milicianos* were listened to favorably. They couched their application in liberal parlance, stressing "progress" and "private property," key words that fell on government ears with more sympathy than San Juan's petition, lodged on the basis of "ancient titles" and exploitation of land "since time immemorial." As with Santa Eulalia, the claimants from Chiantla counted on government recognition that it was militia like themselves that functioned "as the state's chief instrument of coercion and control in the countryside." At stake in San Juan was land that lay south of the town center toward Chiantla, part of an allotment of 250 *caballerías* that San Juan claimed exclusively as its own.

San Juan's claim drew a storm of protest not just from Chiantla but also from Soloma and Nebaj. To advance their case the leaders of San Juan sought the services of an engineer, whom they recruited to conduct a survey that was to be paid for by selling community labor. Using the agent Friedrich Koch, they arranged a contract for men from San Juan to work on a *finca* called Buenos Aires "in return for the finca paying the costs of the land survey," giving Koch as collateral what land titles San Juan already possessed, as well as other relevant documentation. When it appeared that the results of the survey were not to San Juan's advantage, the community refused to take part in any further deliberation. Tempers flared—Ladino *milicianos* from Soloma, it was alleged, laid hands on San Juan's leaders—and discontent grew.

Discontent burst into bloodshed on the evening of July 18, 1898. Failing to acknowledge that the titling process had not been resolved, agents from Finca Buenos Aires arrived in San Juan and began harassing for labor. The people of San Juan believed that the condition upon which their toil had been pledged had yet to be met; there was thus no possibility of their leaving for the coast. Still the agents pressed. Natives from outlying parts of San Juan arrived in town, adding their resentment to the anger of those already assembled. After the agents had retired to their sleeping quarters in the town hall, the building was set on fire. As they fled the blaze the agents were attacked and killed. Thinking, in McCreery's words, "to eliminate hostile witnesses and conceal their crime," the crowd then "spread through the village, killing ladino men, women, and children" in addition to "abusing and threatening" those native residents who had cooperated with the agents. When, by morning, it became clear that some agents or their associates had escaped, San Juan steeled itself for retaliation.

It came swiftly from both north and south. Soloma and Chiantla sent in their militia, which according to McCreery caused "an unknown number" of indigenous deaths. Some sixty individuals were sent to stand trial in Huehuetenango. While McCreery finds "no evidence that the government specifically stripped San Juan of its land as punishment," he notes that "in the aftermath of the violence the inhabitants were in a weak position to defend their rights." The *milicianos* of Chiantla eventually received 113 *caballerías* near Tocal. Others from Soloma did equally well. As with Ladino successes in Barillas and the Ixcán, those residents of Chiantla and Soloma who were awarded title "did little to develop their new properties," preferring instead to convince "existing residents to stay," recruit "new ones where possible," and simply live off rents "while waiting for the land to appreciate in value."

They did not have long to wait. Within a few years the successful claimants resold land to plantation owners on the Pacific slope. The new owners required rent to be paid not in cash or in kind but in labor, thus creating a situation in which "workers' estates" in the highlands supplied lowland plantations with a seasonal supply of hired hands. San Juan never ceased to dispute the legitimacy of the grip plantation owners exerted over community land: "We don't know how it came into the hands of the *fincas*," townspeople lamented in one communication. Over the course of the next thirty years, McCreery writes, San Juan sustained "a steady and largely non-violent, but certainly not passive resistance to the *finca* properties in their midst." Not until the late 1940s were the "workers' estates" dismantled and formerly native land delivered back to Maya owners.

What, in sum, can be said to have occurred in Guatemala during the century after independence? Despite their physical and psychological seclusion, Maya communities between 1821 and 1920 were exposed to the same historical forces that prevailed in Spanish America as a whole.

The first half-century after independence, especially under the conservative regime of Rafael Carrera, saw Maya life continue to unfold for the most part within the culture of refuge that had crystallized during colonial times. Whether neglected or protected by the policies of Carrera, Maya communities could not help but be affected by the radical change in how Guatemala was governed after 1871, when liberals held power. The presidency of Justo Rufino Barrios in particular signalled dramatic and unprecedented change as Guatemala was transformed from a colonial backwater into a modern capitalist nation, primarily on the basis of the commercial production of coffee. To the state, coffee represented progress, civilization, and advancement, the epitome of "la patria del criollo"; to Maya communities, it meant loss of land and forced or indentured labor.

The four Cuchumatán case studies indicate that, at the local or community level, the outcome of the liberal reforms was nuanced and variable. Santiago Chimaltenango appears to have been affected only minimally, Nebaj significantly more. Santa Eulalia and San Juan Ixcoy both suffered considerably— San Juan with the additional consequences of state retribution after a bloody uprising. Differences in the degree of impact and opposition characterize other parts of Guatemala as well. Inequalities that began to emerge at the national level in the nineteenth century have yet to be redressed, especially in the Maya countryside. There land is life. To deprive native communities of land is to deprive them of life itself.

TWENTY

ARBENZ AND THE FRUIT COMPANY

The struggle for justice in Guatemala is inseparable from the struggle for land rights on the part of its impoverished majority, Ladinos as well as Mayas. No chapter in the country's history revolves so pivotally around the land question as the presidency of Jacobo Arbenz Guzmán in the early 1950s. To understand the importance of the Arbenz period, however, it is necessary to go back a few years, to 1944, when a ten-year period of change began.

In June of that year public unrest and a revolt by junior officers in the armed forces led to the overthrow of General Jorge Ubico, the last of the liberal dictators who had ruled Guatemala since the time of Justo Rufino Barrios. Four months later popular sentiments gave rise to what in Guatemala is known as the October Revolution. Elections held the following year saw Juan José Arévalo, a schoolteacher in his early forties, sweep into power with more than 85 percent of the vote. During his six-year term of office, from March 1945 until March 1951, Arévalo was guided by concerns for agrarian reform, protection of labor, a better educational system, and consolidation of Guatemala's fragile democracy. Commitment to the last goal in particular called for repeated vigilance against numerous *coup d'états*. Arévalo, however, survived numerous plots by dissident factions to dislodge him. An election held in November 1950 was won comfortably by Arbenz, a colonel in the armed forces who assumed the presidency by gaining some 65 percent of all votes cast. Three years Arévalo's junior, Arbenz was in his late thirties when he became Guatemala's second president in a row to be elected democratically.

Central to Arbenz's designs for a new Guatemala was an agrarian reform that sought to redress chronic landholding disparities and the appalling social and economic inequalities that accompany them. In 1950 agricultural workers could expect to earn an annual income of around $87. According to a census taken that same year, 2.2 percent of the nation's landowners managed 70 percent of Guatemala's total arable land. Of about four million acres in the hands of plantation owners, less than one-quarter was actually under cultivation. U.S. corporations invested heavily at the time in Guatemalan agribusiness, to the tune of some $120 million. The largest and most powerful U.S. corporation was the United Fruit Company of Boston, known in Guatemala either as *La Frutera* (The Fruit Company) or, perhaps more revealingly, *El Pulpo* (The Octopus). Its stranglehold on the country is immortalized in the "banana trilogy" of Guatemala's Nobel Laureate in Literature, Miguel Angel Asturias (1968, 1971, 1973).

In his first speech as president, delivered on March 15, 1951, Arbenz outlined his vision of the path that lay ahead:

> Our government proposes to begin the march toward the economic development of Guatemala, and proposes three fundamental objectives: (1) to convert our country from a dependent nation with a semi-colonial economy to an economically independent country; (2) to convert Guatemala from a backward country with a predominantly feudal economy into a modern capitalist state; and (3) to make this transformation in a way that will raise the standard of living of the great mass of our people.
>
> Our economic policy must of necessity be based on strengthening private initiative and developing Guatemalan capital, in whose hands rests the fundamental economic activity of the country . . . Foreign capital will always be welcome as long as it adjusts to local conditions, remains always subordinate to Guatemalan laws, cooperates with the economic development of the country, and strictly abstains from interfering in the nation's social and political life.
>
> Agrarian reform is a vital part of our program, undertaken so that we can rid ourselves of huge estates and introduce fundamental changes in our primitive work methods, undertaken so as to bring into production uncultivated land and properties where feudal customs are maintained, introducing [the benefits] of science and agricultural technology.

On June 17, 1952, the national congress approved Decree 900, legislation struck to empower the Arbenz government to secure the uncultivated portions of large plantations alluded to in his inaugural address, and thereafter turn them over to landless peasants. Arbenz considered his agrarian policies, Jim Handy (1994) tells us, as "the most precious fruit of the revolution," praising landowners like coffee planter Erwin Paul Dieseldorf "who abided by the rules of the decree and placed few obstacles in its way." Arbenz led by example, relinquishing fifteen *caballerías* of his own land. Government ministers did likewise, among them Nicolás Brol, minister of agriculture, who gave up eighty-five *caballerías,* and Guillermo Toriello, ambassador to the United States and later minister of foreign affairs, who forfeited over ten *caballerías.* Land was appropriated by the government at a price related directly to its declared taxable worth, and reimbursement for it was calculated accordingly.

The latter provision, however, was not to the liking of certain targets, particularly United Fruit, since for years its property had been deliberately undervalued in order to reduce the company's tax liability. During the following eighteen months, some one hundred thousand poor Guatemalan families received a total of 1.5 million acres of formerly uncultivated land, for which the reform authorities paid $8.3 million in government bonds. The Arbenz administration expropriated about four hundred thousand acres of land from United Fruit, offering in return $1.25 million, a figure based entirely on the company's own taxation records.

United Fruit's response, to this day, constitutes one of the most repugnant episodes in Latin American history, an episode reconstructed with nuanced attention to detail in *Bitter Fruit,* a model of investigative journalism wrought by Stephen Schlesinger and Stephen Kinzer. Taking advantage of its close connections in Washington—the company had previously received legal counsel from John Foster Dulles, then U.S. secretary of state, and his brother, Allen, then director of the Central Intelligence Agency—United Fruit was able to convince the Eisenhower administration that a "red menace" in Guatemala threatened American business and security interests. It then wooed the CIA into masterminding, at an estimated cost to U.S. taxpayers of $20 million, the overthrow of the Arbenz government, ushering into power a repressive *junta* headed by Colonel Carlos Castillo Armas, whose forces, protected by American air strikes, invaded from neighboring Honduras. Betty Jane Peurifoy, the wife of the U.S. ambassador to Guatemala, John Peurifoy, composed a Cold War ditty later published in *Time* magazine on July 26, 1954:

> Sing a song of quetzals, pockets full of peace!
> The *junta's* in the Palace, they've taken out a lease.
> The commies are in hiding, just across the street;
> To the embassy of Mexico they beat a quick retreat.
> And pistol-packing Peurifoy looks mighty optimistic
> For the land of Guatemala is no longer Communistic!

The only air strikes Arbenz could launch were on the radio. On the second day of the invasion he spoke to the nation in a tone markedly more grave than that of the nursery-rhyme parody:

Our only crime consisted of decreeing our own laws and applying them to all without exception. Our crime is having enacted an agrarian reform that affected the interests of the United Fruit Company. Our crime is our patriotic wish to advance, to progress, to win economic independence to match our political independence. We are condemned because we have given our peasant population land and rights.

In his final broadcast Arbenz spoke with valedictory bluntness:

For fifteen days a cruel war against Guatemala has been underway. The United Fruit Company, in collaboration with the governing circles of the United States, is responsible for what is happening to us. In whose name have they carried out these barbaric acts? What is their banner? We know very well. They have used the pretext of anti-communism. The truth is very different. The truth is to be found in the financial interests of the United Fruit Company and other U.S. monopolies that have invested great amounts of money in Latin America and fear that the example of Guatemala would be followed by other Latin [American] countries.

Although United Fruit has long since departed, the legacy that it and its supporters imposed on Guatemala lives on, inflicting on the hearts and minds of thousands of people wounds that never will heal. Had the United States allowed Arbenz to govern without intervention, had the democratic process he was part of been encouraged rather than violated, had the changes begun in October 1944 simply ran their course, then the carnage of the civil war might have been averted. I have been haunted by this thought ever since, in 1980, an official at the U.S. embassy lamented the impossibility of getting hard-liners in Guatemala to cooperate, declaring thirty years too late, "What we'd give to have an Arbenz now."

There is still an Arbenz around. He is the son of the deposed president, and is also named Jacobo—or Jacobito, as I heard his mother refer to the stout man in his fifties. She was once the first lady of Guatemala, María Vilanova de Arbenz, born in El Salvador on April 17, 1915, of elite landholding stock but of progressive political persuasion. I visited the Arbenz home in Costa Rica in July 2008, where they engaged my questions about the man who was husband and father as well as president of Guatemala. It was a memorable day.

"My mother is very old," Jacobito said to me before a caregiver wheeled Doña María into a salon covered floor to ceiling with Arbenz mementos. "She has good days and bad days. We must try not to tire her out." Though Jacobito and I had been conversing in Spanish, he introduced me to his mother in English. Educated abroad eighty years before, at Notre Dame College in California, Doña María addressed me with considerable verve. "How nice to be able to talk with someone in English. Tell me about yourself."

I started to do so, but didn't get very far.

"You're *Scottish!*" she exclaimed. "You're *Scottish!*"

Doña María was having a good day, and we hit it off. With the help of her cane she rose to her feet and showed me around the salon, pointing out diplomas, certificates, medals, pennants, and an array of photographs with perfect recall and manifest pride. To the left of one photograph of herself, a black and white studio image that captured a wistful young woman of striking appearance, hung the national flag of Guatemala. She stopped at one small painting, a portrait in oil, and asked me to take it off its display hook so that she could examine it more closely.

"That's my husband," she declared. "I still miss him, you know. I loved him, and he loved me. I don't know which of us loved the more, him or me."

She gifted me a memoir she had written, *Mi esposo, el presidente Arbenz* (2003), in which she narrates her version of the events that stirred, and scarred, their life together—and the lives of millions of Guatemalans too. In the book there is a photograph of her at the degree ceremony held in Guatemala City to mark the occasion of Arbenz being awarded a posthumous doctorate "Honoris Causa" by the University of San Carlos in 1995. On the page opposite the photograph are some poignant words of Arbenz. "All the riches of Guatemala," they proclaim, "are not as important as the life, the freedom, the dignity, the health, and the happiness of the most humble of its citizens."

When it came time for her to rest, Doña María bade me farewell with an invitation to return. "How lovely to have a Scotsman around the house." Into the salon and adjacent patio Jacobito brought album after album, box after box, suitcase after suitcase filled with all sorts of correspondence: official memos and personal letters, drafts of speeches, pamphlets, telegrams, photographs, and press clippings, a veritable treasure trove that is as much a historical archive as a family one. In it are documented the family's peregrinations and travails in the wake of leaving Guatemala, a nomadic exile that included spells in France, the Soviet Union, Eastern Europe, Uruguay, and Cuba before the surviving members (Arbenz himself died under mysterious circumstances in Mexico City in 1971, predeceased by a daughter who committed suicide at age twenty-five) eventually settled in Costa Rica. One item that I pored over was the book of condolences commemorating the return of Arbenz's remains to Guatemala in 1995, forty-one years after his ouster. I resolved to visit his tomb on my next visit.

In the book of condolences, the salutation of President Ramiro de León Carpio comes first. "Welcome back, Colonel Jacobo Arbenz Guzmán, former president of the republic, to your beloved homeland. I express my gratitude because the return of your remains represents an act of justice, above all else an act of reconciliation within the Guatemalan family." De León's words are followed by those of his vice president and his president of congress, after which appear the signatures and inscriptions of dignitaries representing, in order of register, the United Kingdom, France, Canada, Germany, Italy, Switzerland, Nicaragua, Peru, Belize, Ecuador, Denmark, Panama, Sweden, Colombia, Chile, the United Nations, and the Organization of American States. One country is conspicuous by its absence: the United States of America.

A seed, once tended, bears fruit. People must eat it, if given nothing else, in order to survive. The aftertaste lingers. And poisons still.

TWENTY-ONE

THE T-SHIRT PARADE

Leonardo Buch Chiroy doesn't quite *look* like the indigenous Maya he truly is, at least compared to the exotic images that greet passengers who arrive at Aurora Airport in Guatemala City. It's his clothes that do it, especially the T-shirt, which hangs loosely over a pair of jeans and gives his outward appearance a distinct, otherworldly dimension. The words on the T-shirt are familiar but a bit disorienting: BEAM ME UP, SCOTTY, they declare. How many Maya Trekkies are there in Guatemala? Beats me, but I spotted and spoke with at least one.

Leonardo is a teenager from San Jorge La Laguna, a Kaqchikel community lying off the road halfway between Sololá and Panajachel. We look down at San Jorge from the *mirador,* or viewpoint, where cars and buses stop so their passengers can behold the majesty of Lake Atitlán, still beautiful despite the ravages of modern tourism. It's from the tourist trade that Leonardo, like many Mayas, makes his living. He sells jewelry—rings, necklaces, bracelets, and earrings—to passing travellers. One of his customers negotiated a deal for the T-shirt; hence Leonardo's Star Trek apparel.

I ask Leonardo if he understands what the words on his T-shirt refer to. "Something to do with your gods," he replies. Not quite, but pretty close, I say to myself. He sees my camera. "Want me to take your photo?" He clicks the shutter like a pro. "You can take one of me if you like. Only *send* it to me. People take photos of us all the time"—he gestures to his two sisters, both younger than him and both wearing colorful Maya clothes—"but they never send anything back, even though they say they will."

The chance encounter convinces me to keep my eyes peeled, for I've noticed T-shirts, those global articles of clothing, being worn in Guatemala more and more these days, usually by Maya men, not women, as is the case with Leonardo and his sisters. When I get to Chichicastenango, where I am to attend a UN-sponsored conference on sustainable development, I put my observational skills into systematic operation.

The conference proves to be of variable quality and mixed interest. I enjoy the presentations of several participants very much, a handful of Maya delegates among them. Their inclusion in the program serves to ground discussions of culture and identity, a welcome respite from the abstract musings of other speakers. One morning I decide to spend my time not listening to papers but exploring the town instead.

A huge billboard on the way to Chichicastenango, advertising cigarettes, labels the place the "Mecca of Tourism." Each Thursday and Sunday hordes of tourists, lured by willing native accomplices, engulf Chichicastenango and give market day there a pushy, commercial air. I find Chichicastenango at its enigmatic best the day before market is held, when the locals may be readying the place for imminent invasion but when the town feels more relaxed, the hustle and hype less obvious.

I walk the few blocks from my hotel to the church, choosing not to enter by climbing up the front steps but by skirting around them to a side doorway that leads into the courtyard of the former Dominican convent. Here it was, at the turn of the eighteenth century, that Francisco Ximénez, then parish priest of Chichicastenango, was first shown the *Popol Vuh,* the "Bible of America," a K'iche' Maya account of the creation of the universe. The *Popol Vuh* records a rich multiplicity of knowledge, including myths, legends, memories of historic migrations, and tales of lineage wars, from the days of the first ancestors to the arrival in Guatemala of the first Spaniards. It is a document, and a symbol, of Maya survival. A plaque on a wall commemorates Father Ximénez and the *Popol Vuh.* After I read it I pass from the courtyard into the church through a side entrance.

It takes my eyes a few seconds to adjust to the dim, crepuscular interior. I notice a group of people gathered beneath a statue of the Virgin to the left of the main altar. A mother and her daughters are dressed in *huipiles,* dextrously woven Maya blouses, and thick wraparound skirts. They have brought armfuls of flowers to demonstrate their devotion. A man I take to be both husband and father lights candles and burns incense while mumbling a prayer in K'iche'. Smoke from his offering hovers over the huddled assembly. I move closer to get a good look at the T-shirt he's wearing. On it the flag of the United States flies above a military convoy. Beneath the stars and stripes are the words OPERATION DESERT STORM: THESE COLORS DON'T RUN. The man's facial features—the high cheek bones, the hooked nose, the flat, broad forehead—could have been lifted from a stelae at Quiriguá.

I check my watch: a quarter past eight. I leave the family to their worship and walk the short distance to the graveyard at the western edge of town. Out of nowhere a drunk appears and starts to pester me. I pay him no attention, for I've noticed two old men having a conversation across the street from the Comedor Lastor. They address each other not in Spanish but in K'iche'. One of them wears a grubby, tattered T-shirt that announces YOU'VE COME A LONG WAY BABY. The other is more smartly turned out, as one would expect, for his T-shirt reads IT'S HARD BEING SEXY, BUT SOMEONE HAS TO DO IT. I glance at my watch: eight fifty-five. Time for breakfast.

I make my way to La Fonda del Tzijolaj, named (so the waiter tells me) after the horse that leads a religious procession during the fiesta of Santo Tomás, the patron saint of Chichicastenango. The restaurant is on the upper level of a building with a commanding view of the central plaza, already showing signs, on Wednesday morning, of preparing for tomorrow's influx. I spot a young man, fifteen or sixteen years of age, starting to erect a market stall. On the front of his T-shirt are the unmistakable features of Mickey Mouse. He turns around. Guess what? That's right! Who else but Minnie on the back! Someone steps up to lend a hand with the market stall. The helper seems to prefer American superheroes to Disney cartoon mice, for it's a Batman T-shirt he's wearing.

As I'm eating breakfast, a loudspeaker starts blaring. The voice belongs not to an evangelical preacher, of whom there must be hundreds in Chichicastenango alone, but to a used clothes vendor. *"Ropa barata, ropa barata. Dos piezas por un quetzal. Ropa barata, ropa barata.* . . . Cheap clothes, cheap clothes. Two items for twenty cents. Cheap clothes, cheap clothes." I trace the sound of the sales pitch to a white Dodge van parked by El Calvario, a chapel that sits across the central plaza from the church of Santo Tomás. Curiosity takes me there after breakfast.

The vendor, about eighteen years of age, turns out to be an enterprising young Ladino from Guatemala City. He sports a long-sleeved Doobie Brothers T-shirt, from the tour whose slogan must have been TAKING IT TO THE STREETS. I ask him about his business. He tells me that used clothing enters Guatemala in bulk from the United States, flown into Guatemala City from Miami. His contacts allow him a share of the delivery, which he loads up and "takes to the streets," not only of Chichicastenango but of other towns also. *"Somos muchos.* . . . There's lots of us," he says. And lots of customers too, I comment, observing a number of people picking through the vast piles laid on the ground on sheets of plastic. Sure enough, there's plenty of T-shirts in today's batch. The vendor, who sips a 7UP even though his baseball cap declares a preference for Coca-Cola, reaches for the microphone inside his van. His sales pitch becomes somewhat more refined, broadcast with a subtle hint of solidarity: *"Para nuestra gente de pocos recursos, ropa, dos piezas por un quetzal.* . . . For those of our people with limited resources, clothing, two items for twenty cents." He smiles and waves as I leave. Out of the corner of my eye I spot someone selling ice cream, Helados Donald Duck, who wears a T-shirt saying I'M ONE OF THE PARKWAY SCHOOLKIDS.

I walk back to the church and along Gucumatz Avenue, named after a K'iche' forefather. On the steps outside the *auxiliadora*, a municipal office, I talk with a man selling honey. He identifies himself as a *maxeño,* a local term for an inhabitant of Chichicastenango. I point to his T-shirt, a plain affair on which the letters UIMC are printed. "What do these letters stand for?" I inquire. "*Saber,*" he replies. "No idea. I just wear the thing." While we talk, four Maya men saunter past in succession. All of their T-shirts relate to places far removed from Chichicastenango: CABLE CAR, SAN FRANCISCO; FLAMINGO BAR, FLORIDA; MAUI, HAWAII; and EXPO 86. Expo 86—wasn't that the one held in Vancouver?

On the way back to my hotel I watch an army patrol move through the market square. A clock strikes ten. I count thirteen soldiers, all of whom look Maya to me. What kind of T-shirts they're wearing underneath their combat fatigues, I can't make out.

I clean up and get ready to head off for the conference, which is being held in plush surroundings in a new hotel on the outskirts of town. First I have to get the pickup I'm driving, parked in a compound adjacent to my more centrally located accommodation. But the pickup is hemmed in by an enormous truck dropping off a load of firewood. There's a driver at the wheel.

"Excuse me. Could you move back a little so I can get out?" I ask him politely. He scowls, jumps down from the cabin, and barks an order to the group of men unloading the firewood. The words are uttered in quickfire K'iche'. He's wearing a marvelous Joe Cocker T-shirt. With a little help from my friends, I maneuver the pickup out to the street.

I drive to the conference wondering what and when my next T-shirt encounter will be. Just before I enter the main auditorium a waiter arrives with a tray of coffee, which he lays down on a nearby table. His name tag informs me that he is called Juan. "That's an interesting T-shirt, Juan," I remark as he pours me a coffee. "Mind if I ask where you got it?"

Juan is forthcoming. "*Es un regalo de mi tío.* . . . It's a present from my uncle. He gave it to me last year at fiesta time. He lives in California. He left Chichi when I was just a kid. He's been gone more than fifteen years now, but he always comes back home in December for the fiesta of Santo Tomás." Juan's T-shirt depicts a worried-looking dog sitting in a chair watching television. The dog's head is bandaged and one of its legs is in a sling. Strewn about the dog are guns and rifles and rounds of ammunition. The words on the T-shirt say LIVING IN L.A.: BE READY. Juan's uncle, it seems, is one of the countless Mayas who prefer a life in exile to a life in Guatemala. I hope he lives in Los Angeles under less duress than the embattled dog.

I'm talking away with Juan, who tells me he's a *maxeño*, when Demetrio Cojtí Cuxil comes out of the auditorium and asks for a coffee. We exchange greetings. Demetrio's mother is from Chichicastenango, but he was born in a Kaqchikel village near Tecpán. He was schooled by Jesuits and has the distinction of being among the first Mayas from Guatemala to earn a doctorate. An alert, quirky individual, Demetrio was one of the first Mayas to teach at the national university, the Universidad de San Carlos. He worked for one recent administration as vice minister of education. Anthropologist Carol Smith considers him a "prominent spokesperson for today's Maya nationalists." The talk I heard Demetrio give earlier in the week was direct and hard-hitting. In it he stated that Mayas in Guatemala are subjected to an internal colonialism that denigrates and marginalizes native culture. He spoke, nonetheless, of the vitality of Maya culture, of a Maya identity that (in his words) is not only "generic" but also locally articulated, given to nuance and improvisation, above all else "elastic, fluid, flexible."

I mention my T-shirt sightings to Demetrio. He marshals the evidence to make a point. "The only purpose these T-shirts have is to clothe the body. Mayas don't identify with them in any meaningful way." I bring up the gender divide. "That's just how it is," he says. "A family usually puts aside more for what women wear than for what men wear. That's an important decision. Even poor people invest in weaving or in buying woven clothing, especially *huipiles.*"

Huipiles, those dazzling Maya blouses, some specialists maintain, are texts as well as textiles, saying something about community origin or affiliation that no T-shirt can possibly capture. Demetrio also makes the point that when repression was fiercest, some men discarded Maya-style clothing in favor of Western attire, for "Indians" and "guerrillas" were often considered synonymous; the abandonment of traditional community dress was a self-protective, not an assimilationist, measure. I notice that Demetrio himself, like several Mayas at the conference, wears a shirt and a jacket tailored along Western lines but made from locally produced cloth.

I make it, eventually, to the last of the morning's presentations. None of them, however, matches the liveliness of the T-shirt parade. After the talks end I return to my hotel to put my thoughts and notes in some kind of order. I'm scribbling away when I recall a passage in Eduardo Galeano's *Book of Embraces,* which I have along with me. I look it up.

"Identity is no museum piece sitting stock-still in a display case," Galeano writes, "but rather the endlessly astonishing synthesis of the contradictions of everyday life." I think back to Leonardo Buch Chiroy and the dozen or so T-shirted Mayas I saw in the course of the morning. A theoretical proposition has survived an empirical test.

TWENTY-TWO

NATIVES IN THE BACKCOUNTRY

The backcountry north of Kingston, Ontario, is home to a mix of people who seem to have little in common save for where they happen to live. I know, or know of, lots of backcountry residents: secretaries and factory workers, sheep farmers and beekeepers, carpenters and stonemasons, prison guards and school teachers, potters and painters, weavers and writers, antique dealers and second-hand book buffs, radio producers and freelance editors, draft dodgers and retired generals, hippies from the sixties who went back to the land, and their New-Age, twenty-first-century equivalents. I figured there also had to be natives in the backcountry, but I never met and spoke with any until the day I travelled up to the village of Arden with Apolinario Chile Pixtún and Matías Quex Serech.

Apolinario and Matías arrived at my house in a state of shock. They'd flown into Toronto from Guatemala the day before, and the climatic jolt between south and north in late November was taking its toll. Apolinario in particular looked quite bewildered.

"*Ay, qué frío.* . . . I can't believe how cold it is," he said. "And how everything looks so brown and dried out. When I was here only a few months ago the place was warm and green, lush almost."

Matías, who had no past experience of Canada with which to gauge the present, simply asked: "*Va a nevar?* Do you think it might snow? I'd like to see snow, I'd like to see snow falling."

They sat down and ate breakfast without taking off their coats. Matías removed his hat. Apolinario kept his on. "That's better," he sighed midway through his second cup of coffee. It was the right moment to ask a few questions. I inquired, "Why don't you tell me a bit about yourselves, what you do, why you're here, so I'll have a better idea of what it is you'll be saying later on." Matías let Apolinario speak first.

Members of the Federation of Councils of Kaqchikel Elders, the two were engaged in what might best be described as a cultural mission. Committed to staking out an agenda that addresses Maya concerns in Guatemala, their objectives in visiting Canada were twofold: first, to make contact and establish links with native groups and associations; and, second, to seek practical relationships with nongovernmental organizations involved in community development, especially projects relating to appropriate technology and traditional medicine. Their preoccupations lay with the valorization and revitalization of Maya culture, and they took pains to distinguish themselves, if not distance themselves, from the "popular movement." Politics for them was primarily a question of creating ways in which Maya customs and practices were not simply safeguarded but allowed freedom of expression, indeed, encouraged to grow.

Spiritual as well as material considerations had to be attended to, Apolinario argued, if peace in Guatemala was to have any future. His business card, inscribed with a Maya glyph depicting a god of healing, declared him "a naturopath at the service of humanity." He lives in the countryside near Chimaltenango but holds consulting hours twice a week in an office on the outskirts of Guatemala City. His previous visit to Canada was as a guest of the Royal Ontario Museum in Toronto. There he took part in the opening ceremony of an exhibit called "Human Body, Human Spirit."

Apolinario's calling prompted me, after breakfast, to ask him if he and Matías would be prepared to conduct a ceremony of blessing on the century-and-a-half-old house I'd bought. "We'll need a glass of water and some perfume," Apolinario said. I dutifully provided the former, Matías the latter, an enormous bottle of Brut aftershave. Apolinario looked around my study and unfurled a cloth on top of my desk. On it were embroidered motifs representing the twenty days, and twenty gods, of the *tzolkin* calendar, a ritual affair that has governed and measured time for the Maya for over five millennia.

"Where's south?" he asked. I pointed out the front window as he exchanged his hat for a *tzute,* an all-purpose cloth that men tie around their heads in the style of a buccaneer's bandanna. We knelt facing south as Apolinario invoked a blessing. After he finished, we turned to face north, and Matías took over the invocation. After his turn it was back to Apolinario, facing west. Matías concluded the spoken part of the ceremony, conducted in Kaqchikel, as we knelt facing east.

Both men then stood up and splashed water and aftershave around the room and on top of the embroidered cloth. I presented each of them with a copy of a book I'd written on Guatemala that had been published in Spanish, our lingua franca. They reciprocated with a calendar in which the new year ahead had been marked out in Maya days as well as in Gregorian ones, the

year by their Choltun or Long Count reckoning being 5111. I glanced at the
dedication Apolinario had written: *"Con cariño al escritor George Lowel,"* dated
"9 Imox Año 5110."

Running parallel to the twenty days that constitute a Maya month, or
winal, is a system of numbers, one to thirteen, each of which bestows on any
given day a good or bad omen. *Imox* in Kaqchikel means "World" or "Earth
Being," usually depicted as a crocodile. Nine is a propitious number, for nine
gods are thought to rule the underworld, and nine falls before ten, which
Mayas dread, for it is associated with Death. I took *9 Imox* to be a good day,
one worthy of celebration. I fetched a prized bottle of single-malt whiskey.

"People where I'm from call this the water of life," I said. "Would you care
for a glass before we set off?" Apolinario exclaimed, *"Ay, qué bueno!"* and
dispatched his dram with alacrity.

The hour or so we spent on the road saw us travel through a landscape
gnawed to the bone by nature and season. Trees were gaunt and bare, the
fields around them stripped of growth. Lakes were still, the sky above them
emitting a washed-out pearly light. I wondered what it must be like to behold
such topography through Maya eyes, for even in the dry season the highlands
of Guatemala would seem, by comparison, verdant and inviting.

Our hosts, all members of Ardoch Algonquin First Nation and Allies,
greeted us warmly. The band consists of over two hundred registered members, and eight of them were present at Marlene Sunn's large, tin-sided house
on the lonely main street of Arden.

"You made it," Marlene said with relief. "We were starting to get worried."
She introduced us to her husband Wade, an artist, and led us into the living
room where others were waiting: Kathleen and Fred Antoine, the latter a
community elder; Bob Lovelace, aboriginal student counsellor and a professor at Queen's University; Harold Perry, community spokesperson; and
Dorothy and Frank Antoine, the latter the son of Fred, from whom he takes
his leadership qualities. I introduced the Mayas, then started translating back
and forth from English into Spanish, from Spanish into English. It was more
an intermingling than a confusion of tongues, but there were moments during the hours that followed when communication across cultures was better
served by other means than words.

Dialogue, however, proved most revealing, at times determining broad
bases of similarity, at times throwing differences into sharp relief.

"How you feel about corn is the way we feel about wild rice," Dorothy
observed. "It's a sacred food for us. The wild rice we gather we share and eat.
We don't sell it."

Harold looked almost taken aback when Apolinario mentioned how many

Maya languages were spoken by how many Maya people. "Over twenty? Languages, not dialects?" he asked. Since none of our guests had been raised speaking Algonquin, though some are now learning it, it seemed remarkable to think of five to six million people speaking their traditional languages.

A delicious meal had been prepared—wild rice and chicken—but before it was served Frank performed a smudging ceremony. A bowl on the coffee table was lit, its contents of tobacco, sage, cedar, and sweetgrass crackling to aromatic life. Frank moved his hands through the grey vapor, up to and over his face, in a slow, circular rhythm. "We smudge to connect with the Creator," he intoned, "and to be in touch with the ancestors. It also cleanses us spiritually." We all smudged in turn, then ate.

After the meal the dialogue continued, topics ranging from land rights to native education, from canoeing and fishing to the colors associated with the cardinal directions. Before we left, Apolinario said that he too, like Frank, would like to perform a smudging ceremony, one that would symbolize solidarity and express appreciation. He produced a larger bowl than Frank's, filling it with *pom*, a resinous incense, and a blend of medicinal plants and herbs. He struck a match and lit the contents of the bowl.

The pyrotechnics were spectacular. Clouds billowed up across the living room, sparks flew over the coffee table and onto the floor, Marlene's cat scampered, and the smoke detector began to wail. Once Wade had silenced the alarm, Apolinario chanted a prayer.

On the road back to Kingston, Matías's wish was granted: it snowed, thick soft flakes from a glittering sky.

EPILOGUE

We have always been surrounded by terror and by the beauty
that is an inseparable part of it.

JOSEF SKVORECKY, *THE ENGINEER OF HUMAN SOULS* (1984)

Genaro Castañeda, who fled his war-torn country as a teenager, has lived
most of his life away from Guatemala. For seventeen years the province
he calls home has been British Columbia, not his native Huehuetenango.
Genaro has a steady job as the headwaiter at a private yacht club in Vancouver.
Though I visited his birthplace, Yulá, many times in the years following his
flight, Genaro never returned until word reached him of his mother's death.
By then those he had left behind belonged to an entirely different world from
the one he had shaped for himself in Canada. He kept in touch before the
mobile phone revolution by writing an occasional letter, which a neighbor
read aloud to his mother and sister. They preferred it when he sent them a
cassette, which they listened to over and over, marveling at his voice talking
about an existence they could hardly imagine.

Genaro's mother would cry whenever I showed up in Yulá without him.
His sister, Petrona, glad to know that her brother was well, nonetheless ex-
pressed resentment that it was she alone who had to care for an ailing parent.
It was an awkward situation.

"It's so difficult for us here without him," Petrona moaned. "Do you think
we'll ever get to see him again?" The money he wired or that I dropped off
helped them out, but it never made up for his absence. At the end of one visit,
his mother jumped in the pickup truck before I drove off, beseeching me,
in tears, to take her to Genaro so that she could convince him to come back
with her to Yulá. It took an age to calm her down. As dusk turned to night
and the rain began, she was a sorry sight as she disappeared into a cornfield,
led by Petrona to their house. Genaro's eyes welled up when I told him of that
sad departure. "I'll go home one day," he always said, "but not just yet."

Genaro returns to Guatemala regularly now, to visit. Others have gone back to stay. Between 1993 and 1999, over thirty thousand people moved back to Guatemala from refugee camps in Mexico. A good many of them were children born during their parents' exile, "returning" to a country they themselves had never lived in. Despite well-meaning assurances, reentry for the formerly displaced has been fraught with tension and danger, nowhere more tragically witnessed than at the community of Xamán in Alta Verapaz. There, on October 5, 1995, a confrontation between an army patrol and refugees celebrating the first anniversary of their return left eleven dead and thirty wounded, women and children among them. Occurring only five weeks before elections that eventually saw Álvaro Arzú and the Partido de Avanzada Nacional (PAN), the National Advancement Party, win and take office, the killings at Xamán undermined Guatemala's hazardous quest for peace.

ARZÚ (1996–2000) AND THE PEACE ACCORD

After his second-round victory in January 1996, Arzú committed his party to signing the "firm and lasting" peace agreement called for by the Human Rights Accord of March 1994. That accord was followed, under UN arbitration between government and guerrilla representatives, by six others, culminating in the signing of a final accord on December 29, 1996, which brought a negotiated end to thirty-six years of war. Despite serious flaws in the terms agreed upon—the Accord on Socioeconomic Issues and the Agrarian Situation in particular fails to address the geographies of inequality responsible for the conflict—there was widespread hope that, as with Vinicio Cerezo a decade before, Arzú would make a difference. "Now is the time for reconciliation," Arzú declared. "Now is the moment to get back to development."

Development for whom? "In 1997," observes William Robinson, "the PAN government committed itself to deepening and consolidating a long-delayed program of neoliberal transformation not in order to democratize and develop Guatemala but to secure it for global capitalism." As Robinson sees it, PAN's neoliberal agenda steered clear of "policies such as agrarian reform and redistributive measures that could ameliorate current social conditions." Under Arzú, as state enterprises were sold off, an aggressive new financial sector with ties abroad entrenched and enriched itself. Meanwhile, the national currency, the *quetzal,* plummeted in a spiral of impoverishing devaluation, and the lives of most Guatemalans deteriorated even further. For them, as a slogan I saw spray-painted on a wall in downtown Guatemala City ironically expressed it, PAN = HAMBRE. It was a clever play on words, as "pan" in Spanish means "bread," not what one normally associates with "hambre," which means "hunger." Whoever saw fit to record this protest was vindicated by the quality-of-life indices of a UN human development survey that, after three years of PAN government, examined social conditions throughout Central America. In it Guatemala (at number 117, down 41 places from 1990) ranked last, well behind Costa Rica (listed at 45), but also trailing other neighbors known to be desperately poor: El Salvador and Honduras, positioned at 107 and 114, respectively.

In the eyes of Mario Monteforte Toledo, it all comes down to the one thing that nobody wants to talk about: land. The veteran statesman served as head of congress under President Arévalo in the 1940s; under President Arbenz a few years later he was one of the architects of the agrarian reform that proved Arbenz's undoing. In a visceral op-ed piece published in *El Periódico* on August 15, 1999, Monteforte had this to say about the rhetoric of the peace accords and the campaign platforms of presidential candidates:

> Land is the root cause of national backwardness, of elite economic clout, of social imbalance, of the survival of pre-capitalist structures, of the overpopulation of our cities, of criminality, of the absence of internal markets, of menacing unrest in rural areas, of ignorance, of illiteracy, of the nostalgia that was this country five centuries ago.
>
> A million or so peasants who know no other toil than to work the land, have none; two and a half million more scratch away at miserable plots on the sides of mountains and lay waste to forests in order to supplement their starvation wages; three hundred thousand others leave to work in Mexico each year between the months of October and January; half a million are bought and sold, as if they were cattle, by labor contractors who deploy them here in Guatemala on coffee and sugar plantations while their corn grows in the highlands; more than half a million, for years now, possess pieces of paper that entitle them to land, but at the same time there are more than ten thousand disputes among their communities over the rights to ownership, for which they kill one another; in the plantation zones, hundreds of peasants are murdered because they are thought to be "dangerous" or are believed to be "terrorists"; hundreds more plantation owners feel threatened by discontented Indians and so arm militias in order to defend their properties and themselves; and the countryside has given birth to its own form of justice [in the form of mob lynchings], because the state simply does not exist there and the rule of law does not apply.

Monteforte then asks:

How is it possible for people with political and economic power, as well as ordinary folk in our cities, to ignore this explosive reality? How is it possible for them to believe that all is well in our country just because, in fashionable Zone 10 of the capital, restaurants are full, shops busy, and streets jam-packed with cars? And yet it is so, just as it is that we grow accustomed to all the killings, all the people begging in the streets.

He reaches the following conclusion: "But the most pathetic of all is that NO CANDIDATE OR PARTY MENTIONS, NOT EVEN MENTIONS, AGRARIAN PROBLEMS." Monteforte's capital letters express his outrage. He continues: "There appears to be a consensus not even to raise the matter of the most flagrant deformity in our country. The only explanation I can offer for this act of concealment is the fear of sounding 'like a communist'—and so not to compromise oneself with respect to solutions should one's party afterward become the government."

Monteforte's words point to a pathological avoidance that permeates provisions of the accord signed by the Arzú government on May 6, 1996. Article 28 of the accord begins promisingly enough, with a grounded assessment of why land issues are important:

> Land is central to the problems of rural development. From the Conquest to the present, historic events, often tragic, have left deep traces in ethnic, social, and economic relations concerning property and land use. These have led to a concentration of resources that contrasts with the poverty of the majority and hinders the development of Guatemala as a whole. It is essential to redress and overcome this legacy.

The accord, among other initiatives, commits the government of Guatemala to several courses of action:

> 1. Establish a land trust fund "for the acquisition of land through government funding" in order "to enable tenant farmers who either do not have land or have insufficient land to acquire land through long-term transactions at commercial or favorable interest rates with little or no down payment";
>
> 2. Encourage conditions "that will enable small and medium-scale farmers to have access to credit";
>
> 3. Promote legislative changes to the land administration and land registry systems;

4. Put in place procedures for the peaceful settlement of land disputes;

5. Provide "advice and legal assistance to small farmers and agricultural workers with a view to the full exercise of their rights";

6. Take measures to guarantee that laws governing the use of agricultural labor "are effectively applied in rural areas," in order to curb abuses, including the adoption of "sanctions against offenders";

7. Ensure that, by the year 2000, "the tax burden, measured as a ratio of gross domestic product, increases by at least 50 percent compared with the 1995 tax burden";

8. Address what is identified as "the most serious issue relating to tax injustice and inequality," namely, "evasion and fraud, especially on the part of those who should be the largest contributors to state revenues," on whom the government pledges to impose "exemplary penalties."

While all these provisions are constructive and encouraging, totally absent from them is an agenda of genuine structural reform to tackle the "concentration of resources" referred to. By the time Monteforte died, in 2003, nothing that concerned him most had been dealt with. Status quo patterns of ownership seem destined to remain intact. A few people retain lots, and many are left, still, with next to nothing. The best hope is that wealthy landowners will be content to hold on to what they have and comply with the principle of being responsible taxpayers and fair employers. This, in truth, would be a considerable advance, but it is manifestly not enough.

If no real progress has been made on the land question, so too have events taken place since peace was decreed that make it difficult, if not impossible, to ignore that those age-old tactics of terror—threat, intimidation, and reprisal—are alive and well. Of all the killings committed during decades of war, few can compare in blatant infamy with the episode during the second year of peace that took the life of Bishop Juan Gerardi, an assassination summed up by the title of Francisco Goldman's dexterous account of it: "The Art of Political Murder."

GERARDI, REMHI, AND THE RULE OF IMPUNITY

Born of Italian immigrant heritage in Guatemala City in 1924, and ordained there in 1946 at age twenty-two, Gerardi was in his early forties when he took spiritual charge of the Diocese of Verapaz. He surely must have identified with another bishop sent there over four centuries earlier, Bartolomé de las Casas. In Verapaz, Goldman informs us, Gerardi "encouraged his priests to learn Q'eqchi' and trained and sponsored Q'eqchi'-speaking catechists and other lay teachers." Influenced by the theology of liberation emanating in 1965 from the Second Vatican Council, which was bolstered three years later in Medellín by the Latin American Episcopal Conference, Gerardi declared in one of his pastoral missives: "Our Church feels deeply challenged by the reality lived by our indigenous peoples. We find ourselves faced with a situation of exploitation, marginalization, illiteracy, endemic illnesses, poverty, and even misery; all of which amount to a state of injustice, and reveal a state of sin." In another, he drew a direct connection between the example of Jesus Christ and a pact with the poor. "The suffering of Christ is something that should cause us to reflect," he wrote, adding pointedly: "If the poor are out of our lives, then perhaps Christ, too, is out of our lives." The gospel according to Gerardi was not the Christianity subscribed to by status quo Guatemalans.

Gerardi knew well the venom of the forces he was up against. As bishop of El Quiché between 1974 and 1980, he made the unprecedented decision to close down the diocese in 1980 because of savage levels of repression. In one exchange with army leaders, Gerardi told them: "You are the ones who assassinate. You are the enemy of the people. We have to be with the people. Therefore we are on the opposite side from you. As long as you do not change, there can be no agreement between us." Before leaving Guatemala in 1980 to report on the human rights situation to Rome, Gerardi narrowly escaped assassination. On his return, the government of General Lucas García denied him entry; he spent four years in exile in Costa Rica. He returned to Guatemala in 1984, when General Mejía Víctores was in power, and took up a position as an auxiliary bishop in the Archdiocese of Guatemala. Mejía Víctores, *El Periódico* reported on August 15, 1999, once stated in a radio broadcast that he allowed Gerardi back into Guatemala because he preferred to have "his enemies nearby." In 1989 Archbishop Próspero Penados delegated to Gerardi the responsibility of setting up the Oficina de Derechos Humanos del Arzobispado (ODHA), the Archdiocesan Human Rights Office. Five years later the archbishop asked ODHA to undertake the project known as "Recuperación de la Memoria Histórica" (REMHI), the Recovery of Historical Memory. Gerardi not only headed REMHI but also inspired its three-year investigation of the violence unleashed on the people of Guatemala during the country's civil war.

REMHI's work is documented in the four-volume report *Guatemala: Nunca Más,* available in English in abridged form as *Guatemala: Never Again!* The REMHI report, on the basis of 6,500 testimonies gathered by six hundred trained researchers, furnishes horrific details of fifty-five thousand human rights violations, of which over twenty-five thousand resulted in death. Sixty percent of the testimonies—a figure, some would contend, that accurately reflects the native population majority—were given in one of fifteen Maya languages, the most represented being Q'eqchi', Ixil, and K'iche'. Almost fifty thousand of the incidents recorded are attributed to state security forces: the army, the police, civil defense patrols, military commissioners, and paramilitary death squads. Guerrilla insurgents are held accountable for the remainder, less than 10 percent of total atrocities. Volume Four of *Nunca Más*, aptly titled *Victims of the Conflict*, is a thick dossier that lists the names, dates, and places of execution of fifty-two thousand assassinated individuals. It runs to 544 pages, the longest of all four volumes. While the names of the victims are recorded, left unnamed are those responsible for their murders, whether soldiers in the field who physically undertook the killing or their commanding officers, the intellectual authors of some of the worst crimes against humanity in all of Latin America.

On April 24, 1998, a Friday, Monseñor Gerardi ceremonially presented *Nunca Más* at a special mass held in the Metropolitan Cathedral of Guatemala City. "Why does the Church get involved in this?" Gerardi asked his audience. By way of reply, he said:

> We are gathering the memories of the people because we want to contribute to the construction of a different country. This path was, and continues to be, full of risks. But the building of the Kingdom of God has risks, and only those who have the strength to confront those risks can be the builders.
>
> God is inflexibly opposed to evil in any form. The root of the downfall and disgrace of humanity comes from the deliberate opposition to truth that is the radical reality of God and of human beings. It is this reality that has been intentionally deformed in our country throughout thirty-six years of war, war against the people.
>
> To open ourselves to the truth and to bring ourselves face to face with our personal and collective reality is not an option that can be accepted or rejected. It is an undeniable requirement of every society that seeks to humanize its members and be free.
>
> REMHI's work has been an astonishing endeavor of discovery, exploration, and appropriation of our personal and collective history. It has been an open door for people to be able to breathe and speak in freedom and for the creation of communities with hope. Peace is possible—a peace that is born from the truth that comes from each one of us and from all of us. It

is a painful truth, full of memories of the deep and bloody wounds of our country. It is a liberating and humanizing truth that makes it possible for all men and women to come to terms with themselves and their life stories. It is a truth that challenges each one of us to recognize our individual and collective responsibility and commit ourselves to action so that those abominable acts never happen again.

Two days after his presentation of *Nunca Más,* late in the evening of Sunday, April 26, Gerardi was beaten to death in the garage of his house. When he entered and parked his car, assailants who lay in wait pulled him from it, knocked him unconscious, and then pounded his head with a heavy concrete block.

For some people it is the assassination of President John F. Kennedy, for others the car crash that killed Princess Diana. For me it is the murder of Bishop Gerardi that I can anchor in the nexus of time, place, and memory like no other death save my father's.

I was in Seville, on a research stint at the Archive of the Indies. On the Monday evening before the news of Gerardi's fate had shown up in the Spanish press, I went to see *Men with Guns,* a film by John Sayles in which the fictional Latin American country where the plot unfolds is unequivocally Guatemala. The film's subject matter made for a restless night, during which I was haunted by the desolate angels of Guatemalan photographer Luis González Palma, whose images of faces, flowers, thorns, and wings Sayles chose to adorn the end titles of his film.

On my way to the archive the following morning, I picked up a copy of *El País* from the newsstand in the Plaza del Duque. Glancing at it before I put it in my shoulder bag, I noticed a photograph showing a dead body, not quite fully covered, head in a pool of blood. "ETA," I thought automatically, for the Basque separatist group is always in the news. Not until I stopped for a coffee a few minutes later and read the headline—"Assassinated in Guatemala, the Bishop Who Investigated the Horrors of the Army"—did I realize I was looking at a photograph of Gerardi. His feet were crossed in a curious manner, visible at the far end of the cover thrown over him on the floor of his parish-house garage. The "men with guns" had used a different weapon on this occasion, but with the same lethal effect as countless times before, and since.

The aftermath of Gerardi's murder would test the incredulity even of Guatemala's most seasoned, skeptical, and indeed, most cynical of observers. While several early tips, and a number of subsequent leads, pointed to sleek military orchestration—retired Colonel Byron Disrael Lima Estrada and his son, Captain Byron Miguel Lima Oliva, were two prime suspects—police inquiries first resulted in the arrest of known criminal and self-confessed drunkard Carlos Enrique Vielman (motive: common delinquency) and then in the arrest of Gerardi's housemate and fellow Catholic priest, Father Mario Orantes Nájera (motive: homosexual crime of passion). Also taken into custody were the woman who served as the parish household's cook, Margarita López, and Father Mario's German shepherd dog, Baloo. Orantes was charged with first-degree murder, López with obstruction of justice. Baloo, it was alleged, attacked and bit Gerardi, leaving marks on the bishop's body that a forensic anthropologist from the University of Madrid, Dr. José Manuel Reverte Coma, later claimed matched molds taken of the dog's teeth. All three parish-house suspects, and Vielman too, were eventually released because of lack of evidence. Baloo died in September 1999. In January 2000, warrants were issued for the rearrest of Orantes and López, along with the apprehension of Lima Estrada, Lima Oliva, and José Obdulio Villanueva, a former member of the Estado Mayor Presidencial (EMP), the presidential military guard. On June 8, 2001, the three men with military connections were sentenced to thirty years of imprisonment, and Orantes to twenty years. López was released. Fifteen months later, on October 8, 2002, an appeal resulted in the verdicts being overturned. They were reimposed by the supreme court on February 12, 2003, the day Villanueva was killed during a riot in the Centro Preventino, the prison where he was being held in detention. While other material culprits may find themselves charged and prosecuted—the judges in the case ruled that it be left open—a sickening veil of impunity hovers over those officers in the army high command whom the Archdiocesan Human Rights Office believes planned and plotted the murder. As in the 1990 killing of Myrna Mack Chang, one of Guatemala's most respected social scientists, the circumstances surrounding Gerardi's murder implicate most of all a society corrupt to the core. In the Mack case, a ruling on April 24, 2004, by the Inter-American Court of Human Rights actually found the Guatemalan state itself guilty of the crime.

The blows that took the bishop's life were felt by all Guatemalans who believed, as Gerardi did himself, that *Nunca Más* could represent a new beginning. "REMHI is a legitimate and painful denunciation," he had proclaimed. "But it is also an annunciation, an alternative aimed at finding new ways for human beings to live with one another."

When, four months after Gerardi's slaying, I attended a memorial service held for him in the Metropolitan Cathedral in Guatemala City, it seemed to me that the sentiments expressed by the bishop and his flock were very much at odds with each other. "Your kingdom is peace, your kingdom is love," sang a packed congregation, the voices of Mayas and non-Mayas alike filling the vast space with words of redemption. Yet placards declared "Death to Impunity," "No More Unjust Bloodshed," and "Monseñor Gerardi: Martyr of the Truth." The most moving moment came when the four volumes of *Nunca Más* and a photograph of Gerardi were placed symbolically alongside the blood and body of Christ. Two women and two men, their arms held high for all to behold which volume of *Nunca Más* they were carrying, approached the altar slowly. The images chosen for the cover of each volume, an angelic collage created by photographer Daniel Hernández-Salazar, struck a powerful chord:

ME CALLO—I AM SILENT
NO VEO—I CANNOT SEE
NO OIGO—I DO NOT HEAR
PARA QUE TODOS LO SEPAN—SO THAT ALL SHALL KNOW

As a long line of people formed to take communion, the afternoon sun entered the cathedral in slanted beams of golden light. The yellow dome above us began to glow. As Mass drew to a close, I rose from the wooden pew I shared with a row of nuns and exited through wafts of incense and the hush of prayer. Outside, a thunderous cloudburst had paved the way for a rainbow to form, its colors arching from one of the cathedral's twin spires, over jagged city rooftops, to the Church of San Sebastián, where Gerardi had lived, preached, and died. The sky, at least, seemed to have matters elementally resolved, even if justice on earth was beyond human will.

TOMUSCHAT AND THE TRUTH COMMISSION

With the REMHI report established as a moral benchmark, attention turned to the work of the Comisión de Esclarecimiento Histórico (CEH), the truth commission created under UN auspices through an accord signed in Oslo on June 23, 1994. The main difference between the two human rights projects is that, whereas REMHI was a voluntary initiative on the part of the Catholic Church, the CEH was an undertaking mandated by the international community and agreed to by the Guatemalan government and the guerrilla forces of the Unidad Revolucionara Nacional Guatemalteca (UNRG, the National Guatemalan Revolutionary Union) as an institutional component of the peace process. While REMHI chose not to "name the names" of those responsible for the violence, the CEH had to respect terms of reference that prevented it from "individualizing responsibility." Similarly, the CEH could not subpoena witnesses it wanted to question, nor requisition state records and military archives it wanted to peruse. When the CEH began its work in 1996, confined by the nature of the Oslo accord and stymied at every turn by a reluctant government and a hostile army, few could have predicted that the report it delivered three years later, *Guatemala: Memory of Silence,* would be as frank and incriminating as it turned out to be.

Memory of Silence was made public at a well-attended ceremony held on February 25, 1999, in Guatemala City's National Theater. The CEH's chief co-ordinator, German law professor Christian Tomuschat, had, the day before, set the scene for the presentation of the report in an interview with Carlos Menocal of *El Periódico.* His answers to two questions summed up not only the enormity of the violence documented by the CEH but also his view of why it occurred:

(Q) *How does the armed conflict in Guatemala compare with other wars?*
(A) In no other country in Latin America has there been recorded as many cases of human rights violations as here. In terms of statistics, Guatemala heads the list.
(Q) *What explanation can you give to account for such brutality?*
(A) That is a difficult question to answer, for Guatemala has a history of violence that dates back centuries. Also, transformed into a doctrine of na-tional security, anticommunism carries a heavy weight. No party involved, most of all the army, felt itself bound to any rule of law.

In no other country in Latin America. Guatemala, at the height of the violence unleashed on it, had a population of some eight million. That population, then and now, is a fraction the size of such recognized human rights violators (past and present) as Argentina, Chile, Colombia, Peru, Mexico, and Brazil. How, in the early 1980s, the world could pay such scant attention to what was happening in Guatemala, given the levels of repression inflicted on its relatively small population, has yet to be satisfactorily explained.

With his two Guatemalan colleagues, Otilia Lux de Cotí and Alfredo Balsells Tojo, Tomuschat has this to say in the Prologue to the 3,600 pages of *Memory of Silence:*

When we were appointed to form the CEH, each of us, through different routes and all by life's fortune, knew in general terms the outline of events.

As Guatemalans, two of us had lived the entire tragedy on our native soil, and in one way or another, had suffered it. However, none of us could have imagined the full horror and magnitude of what actually happened.

The Commission's mandate was to provide an answer to questions that continue to be asked in peacetime: why did part of society resort to armed violence in order to achieve political power? What can explain the extreme acts of violence committed by both parties—of differing types and intensities—in the armed confrontation? Why did the violence, especially that used by the State, affect civilians and particularly Maya people, whose women were considered to be the spoils of war and who bore the full brunt of the institutionalized violence? Why did defenseless children suffer acts of savagery? Why, using the name of God, was there an attempt to erase from the face of the earth the sons and daughters of Xmukane', the grandmother of life and natural creation? Why did these acts of outrageous brutality, which showed no respect for the most basic rules of humanitarian law, Christian ethics, and the values of Maya spirituality, take place?

We received thousands of testimonies; we accompanied the survivors at such moving moments as the exhumation of their loved ones from clandestine cemeteries; we listened to former heads of State and the high command of both the Army and the guerrillas; we read thousands of pages of documents received from a full range of civil society's organizations. The Commission's Report has considered all the versions and takes into account what we have heard, seen, and read regarding the many atrocities and brutalities.

The main purpose of the Report is to place on record Guatemala's recent bloody past. Although many are aware that Guatemala's armed confrontation caused death and destruction, the gravity of the abuses suffered repeatedly by its people has yet to become part of the national consciousness. The massacres that eliminated entire Maya communities belong to the same reality as the persecution of the urban political opposition, trade union leaders, priests, and catechists. These are neither perfidious allegations, nor figments of the imagination, but an authentic chapter in Guatemala's history.

At the presentation ceremony, which President Arzú attended along with an array of foreign dignitaries and representatives, including U.S. ambassador Donald J. Planty, Tomuschat delivered a summary of the CEH's findings. Between 1962 and 1996, the war took the lives of more than two hundred thousand people, 93 percent of them killed by state security forces. To guerrilla forces could be attributed 3 percent of all recorded abuses, including thirty-two incidents that the CEH considered to be massacres, at El Aguacate and elsewhere. Massacres committed by the guerrillas, however, pale in comparison with the number committed by the army, a chilling 626. It is in its clinical analysis of army massacres that the CEH exceeded all expectations, for Tomuschat and his associates argue the case in such a way as to lay charges of genocide under the precise wording of the Geneva Conventions.

Having determined that 83.33 percent of all victims were indigenous, the CEH decided to scrutinize the evidence further in four regions of the northwest highlands. There the CEH was "able to confirm that, between 1981 and 1983, the Army identified groups of the Maya population as the internal enemy, considering them to be an actual or potential support base for the guerrillas, with respect to material substance, a source of recruits, and a place to hide their members." A review of available army documents, as opposed to others to which the CEH was denied access, allowed it to assert:

Acts committed with the intent to destroy, in whole or in part, numerous groups of Mayas were not isolated acts or excesses committed by soldiers who were out of control, nor were they the result of possible improvisation by mid-level Army command. With great consternation, the CEH concludes that many massacres and other human rights violations committed against these groups obeyed a higher, strategically planned policy, manifested in actions which had a logical and coherent sequence.

The CEH then argues:

Faced with several options to combat the insurgency, the State chose the one that caused the greatest loss of human life among non-combatant civilians. Rejecting other options, such as a political effort to reach agreements with disaffected non-combatant civilians, moving people away from the conflict areas, or the arrest of insurgents, the State opted for the annihilation of those it identified as its enemy.

Confronted by all the requisite proof, the commissioners state:

In consequence, the CEH concludes that agents of the State of Guatemala, within the framework of counterinsurgency operations carried out between 1981 and 1983, committed acts of genocide against groups of Maya people who lived in the four regions analyzed. This conclusion is based on the evidence that, in light of Article II of the Convention on the Prevention and Punishment of the Crime of Genocide, the killing of members of Maya groups occurred (Article IIa), serious bodily or mental harm was inflicted (Article IIb), and the group was deliberately subjected to living conditions calculated to bring about its physical destruction in whole or in part (Article IIIc). The conclusion is also based on the evidence that all these acts were committed "with intent to destroy, in whole or in part," groups identified by their common ethnicity, by reason thereof, whatever the cause, motive, or final objective of these acts may have been.

Tomuschat had U.S. diplomats in the audience seething when he pointed out, as *Memory of Silence* words it, that the United States "demonstrated that it was willing to provide support for strong military regimes in its strategic backyard," noting that U.S. military assistance "was directed towards reinforcing the national intelligence apparatus and for training the officer corps in counterinsurgency techniques, key factors [that] had a significant bearing on human rights violations during the armed confrontation." A disconcerted Ambassador Planty afterward insisted that "these abuses were committed by Guatemalans against other Guatemalans, the result of an internal conflict." The crowd called out to President Arzú, exhorting him to accept in his own hands delivery of the 3,600-page report prepared by the CEH — thereby acknowledging, at least symbolically, its veracity as the country's official history. Arzú's response was to make a hasty backdoor exit without comment.

When the presentation of *Memory of Silence* was over, Tomuschat's actions were prompt and decisive. Mindful of what happened to Bishop Gerardi, UN staff drove him straight to the airport. Security there, I couldn't help but notice when it was time for me to leave also, was considerably tighter than usual.

APOLOGY, DENIAL, AND THE DEATH-SQUAD DOSSIER

Two weeks after Tomuschat's departure, President Bill Clinton arrived in Guatemala for a summit meeting with his Central American counterparts. While his carefully crafted speech, to some at any rate, fell short of offering a full-fledged apology for U.S. involvement, he did acknowledge: "It is important that I state clearly that support for military forces or intelligence units which engaged in violent and widespread repression of the kind described in the [CEH] report was wrong." Clinton added: "The United States must not repeat that mistake. We must, and we will, instead continue to support the process of peace and reconciliation in Guatemala."

Clinton's words of atonement were in marked contrast to those of General

Ríos Montt, president of Guatemala during the period when human rights violations were at their peak. In an interview in *Prensa Libre* on February 28, 1999, he was asked: "What is your opinion of the findings of the Commission for Historical Clarification, that while you were in office acts of genocide were committed?" The general replied: "During my presidency, 1982 and 1983, never was I informed of any act of this nature. I was neither aware of, nor did I give orders about, such matters. We issued specific orders: every commanding officer is responsible for what happens or can happen in his area of operations." He has reiterated this claim several times since. Ríos Montt's refusal to accept, as commander in chief, any responsibility for wrongdoing on the part of the army is shared by other high-ranking officers across the upper echelon of the hierarchy.

One exception is Colonel Otto Noack, who in 1998 spoke on Radio Netherlands of "excesses" perpetrated by the army. While insisting that guerrilla forces were also to blame, Noack admitted, "The army definitely overreacted. We should recognize publicly and openly that the impact of many of our operations caused effects that today are regrettable." The response of his superiors was to place him under military arrest, then to banish him to career oblivion in lowly posts that serve not only as a reprimand for the colonel but also as a deterrent to others who dare to speak out. The minister of defense, Hector Barrios Celada, remarked of Noack's insubordination: "A man opts voluntarily to renounce certain rights upon entering the military, like, for example, making declarations without prior authorization." Barrios, according to *Prensa Libre* on July 22, 1998, would concede only that "errors were made," nothing more.

If the calculated, premeditated manner in which the Guatemalan security force conducted its evil business needed further proof beyond the revelations of the truth commission, it was soon forthcoming. On May 20, 1999, at the National Press Club in Washington, four well-respected nongovernmental organizations, among them the American Association for the Advancement of Science and the National Security Archive, joined forces to focus international attention on the existence of a death-squad dossier, the now infamous *Diario Militar.*

Purchased from a former army officer for $2,000, the dossier logs the fate of 183 abducted individuals. Over a hundred of them were executed, their deaths entered in code by either the number "300" or the phrase "taken away by Pancho." Others were released from captivity, but only after they had provided military intelligence with information leading to the seizure of associates deemed to be subversive. The dossier, with photographs of, and notes about, its targeted suspects, spans the period from August 1983 to March

1985. According to human rights analyst Patrick Ball, the entries in the *Diario Militar* conform to a counterinsurgency pattern in which the large-scale rural slaughter of 1981–1982 was replaced, in 1983 and 1984, by systematic elimination of specific people in urban areas, usually in Guatemala City.

Omar Vázquez, for instance, a twenty-three-year-old medical student, is documented as having been "picked up on Seventh Avenue, in front of the Hotel Dorado Americana." Nine days later he was assassinated, his death recorded by the sequence "06–05–84: 300." Ball asserts that the dossier establishes beyond any credible argument to the contrary that "disappearances and subsequent killings were planned at an individual case-by-case level." He asks: "Who had the power to turn off the massacres and turn on selective urban assassinations?" Ball concludes: "Only the military high command had that authority. Accountability cannot include only those who pulled the triggers, or typed up the death-squad dossier. It must also include those who envisioned hundreds of lives cut short by murder as an optimal policy outcome."

Number 73 in the dossier is Julio César Pereira. At the time of his abduction, April 22, 1984, he was a member of the Partido Guatemalteco de Trabajo (PGT), the Guatemalan Communist Party. After being tortured and threatened with death, Pereira chose to collaborate with his captors, furnishing them with the name of Sergio Saúl Linares Morales, Number 74 in the dossier. "It was the only way I could save my life," Pereira told *El Periódico* on August 13, 1999. Linares Morales was picked up and executed six days later. Pereira, according to the dossier, was himself taken hostage because his name was given by Alma Lucrecia Osorio Bobadilla, listed as Number 34. Pereira's log closes with the words "released for contacts, he sought asylum with his family at the French Embassy."

Pereira, in fact, managed to get out of Guatemala under the auspices of the Venezuelan Consulate. After a stay in Caracas, he was eventually allowed entry into Canada. A return visit to Guatemala after fifteen years in exile was an attempt on his part, in the wake of disclosures about the dossier's contents, to come to terms, in his own words, with his "sullied past and sense of guilt."

Number 135 in the dossier is Luis de Lión, the pen name of Luis de León Díaz (1939–1984), who hailed from San Juan del Obispo, a community in which Kaqchikel Mayas live side by side, often uncomfortably so, with Ladinos. Though born into a Kaqchikel family, de Lión felt that he did not comprehend the language as much as he would have liked, and so undertook later on in life to learn more about it for literary purposes. Community and language lie at the heart of his posthumously published novel, *El tiempo principia en Xibalbá* (1985), a disconcerting evocation of what it is like to be born and raised in small-town (and small-minded) Guatemala.

After graduating in 1959 with a diploma in education, de Lión dedicated himself for several years to teaching in desolate rural settings not unlike the one in which he grew up. In 1971 he moved to Guatemala City. Six years later, he was teaching not at school but at university level, in the Universidad de San Carlos (USAC). His courses in philosophy and psychology are said to have been very popular, with exceptionally high enrollments: seven hundred, one source records, during his final year of teaching. Other USAC faculty members appear alongside de Lión in the *Diario Militar*. Not all of them, however, had joined the PGT, let alone risen to a position of influence within it. He was a marked man. His abduction is recorded as having taken place, in the very heart of Guatemala City late in the afternoon, on May 15, 1984. De Lión has never been seen since.

"The ideals for which he fought are worthy and still have validity," his daughter, Mayarí, stated in an interview to mark the twentieth anniversary of her father's disappearance. "That's why they killed him." In 2004 the Guatemalan government formally acknowledged de Lión's fate. As part of this recognition, de Lión's family asked that his literary output, small but striking, be incorporated in the national educational curriculum. A museum and library in San Juan del Obispo are named after him.

When questioned about the *Diario Militar* in connection with the disappearance of student leader Carlos Cuevas and political activist Fernando de la Roca, General Mejía Víctores, president during the time of the incidents logged in the dossier, was unrepentant. "We were at war," he said. "We were not going to gamble. The people who were kidnapped were not acting for the common good but to take the government by armed force and install a communist system. There were two options: communism or democracy." Unlike Pereira's, his conscience, he told a judicial hearing, was clear.

JUSTICE AND REPRESENTATION

Guatemala's criminal justice system, riddled with corruption and plagued by such routine practices as witness intimidation and harassment of judges, is simply unable to process satisfactorily all the cases brought before it, which usually involve only the material perpetrators of a crime, not its intellectual sponsors. After a lengthy trial, for example, soldiers who took part in the Xamán massacre were found guilty of culpable homicide. The sentences passed on them, however, struck me as starkly incongruent with the gravity of the acts they committed. One lieutenant and eleven of his troops received a five-year jail sentence; another thirteen civil patrol members drew four-year jail sentences. Both sentences were commutable at a rate of five *quetzales* per day, now considerably less than one U.S. dollar. The soldiers, in effect, could buy their freedom. Since they had already spent almost four years in prison awaiting trial, their lawyer was ecstatic. "The lads," he said, "practically have one foot out the door." Four months after they were first sentenced, a court of appeal ordered that "the lads" be released from captivity and cleared of all charges laid against them.

After a ten-day review of the judicial system in August 1999, UN rapporteur Dato Param Cumaraswamy found himself appalled at the extent of its deficiencies. He went so far as to call Guatemala a "sanctuary for impunity." Cumaraswamy declared: "Impunity—let me say this categorically—is the cancer of society. If it is not halted and excised, it will slowly but surely destroy society." The UN envoy's appraisal came a year after similar remarks by his colleague Kofi Annan. A decade later, in *El País* of January 21, 2008, Guatemala's human rights prosecutor Sergio Morales revealed that only one criminal incident in a thousand makes it to trial, and that only one in every twenty cases of homicide reaches the courts.

Statistics like these have triggered an alarming increase, especially in rural areas, of the vigilante justice referred to by Mario Monteforte, in which angry mobs take the law into their own hands: *justicia a mano propria*. Punishment is meted out in the form of public beatings and burnings, "linchamientos" (lynchings) in Guatemalan parlance. Over 250 (an average of one a week) occurred between 1994 and 1999; levels have since increased markedly. Few such incidents ever come to trial; one survey, in fact, revealed that three out of four Guatemalans saw nothing wrong with the practice. Ringleaders who incite or intimidate to ensure broad community participation—those accused of a crime are commonly doused with gasoline and set on fire, left to incinerate amidst taunts and cheers—often have links to the military, having served during the war years in civil defense patrols. Noting the high occurrence of the phenomena in highland Maya communities, sociologist Angelina Snodgrass Godoy observes dishearteningly that "the most lasting legacy of state terror may be its transformation into an ongoing means of enforcing social order even among those who were formerly its victims." As homicide rates soar—government sources, in all likelihood underestimated, acknowledge sixty per one hundred thousand people each year, a statistic ten times that of the United States and twenty times that of Spain—the killing of women in particular has become noxious. In February 2007, another UN rapporteur, Philip Alston, framed the matter overtly in political terms. "There are 5,000 or more killings a year," he declared. "The responsibility for this must rest with the State." Less than a month later, in its issue of March 3, *El País* published the official homicide count for 2006: 5,885 cases, an average of 500 murders a month, 17 a day, the highest in all Latin America. "Peace," correspondent Maite Rico put it bluntly, "is turning out to be even bloodier than war." Human rights analyst Victoria Sanford concurs. "If the number of murder victims continues to rise at the current rate," she notes, "more people will die in the first 25 years of peace than died in the 36-year internal armed conflict and genocide."

A major part of the problem lies in the nature of Guatemala's venal handling of its prison population. Penitentiary facilities, Attorney General Carlos de León Argueta conceded in an interview in *El Periódico* on April 27, 2003, are so antiquated and overcrowded that "there's not even any control over the number of people put behind bars, let alone dominion over them while in detention." Horrific deeds committed outside are replicated inside as gangs settle scores, vie for authority, and buy off wardens and guards to ensure that they turn a blind eye even to the most barbarous goings-on. "Our prisons," de León noted with grim irony, "are a law unto themselves." When asked to comment on the disclosure that a prisoner was made to eat a fellow inmate, he replied: "That's exactly what happened. One band killed its enemies, cut them up as if they were bits of meat, grilled them like steaks, and ate them." And forced other captives to do likewise, or themselves be killed. De León identifies "the four horsemen of the Apocalypse" as "drug trafficking, organized crime, terrorism, and corruption," all of which plague Guatemala as a result of "parallel structures" created by state repression "not being eliminated with the signing of the peace accord." Only one person in four who is in prison is actually serving a sentence; three more are there awaiting trial. "Instead of rehabilitating and preparing prisoners to reintegrate back into society," argue criminologists Fernando López and Christina Albo, "the system permits the most violent criminals to exert power over other inmates, and rewards those who have the resources to bribe their way out of prison completely." They conclude that "the prisoner emerges as a more damaged human being than before, which has great repercussions for society as a whole."

Reform of the criminal justice system, along with other security issues such as creating a new police force and curtailing military authority, is enshrined in the Agreement on the Strengthening of Civilian Power and the Role of the Army in a Democratic Society, signed on September 19, 1996. Components of this accord, and of the Agreement on the Identity and Rights of Indigenous Peoples, signed on March 31, 1995, figured prominently in a referendum held on May 16, 1999, designed to transform negotiated rhetoric into administrative reality. The future of the entire peace process was thrown into doubt by the results of the referendum, in which proposals for constitutional amendments necessary to implement legislation were rejected by a ratio of 55 to 45 percent. Only 757,000 people, 18.5 percent of all registered voters, participated in the referendum, so absenteeism was rampant. Of the ballots cast, a revealing geographical divide was apparent. In the indigenous north and west nine departments voted "Yes," while Guatemala City, with 30 percent of the total turnout, voted "No." The population of the capital city, as it often does, determined the outcome of a pivotal event.

Though a decided setback, the results of the referendum were no surprise to some observers, especially representatives of Guatemala's indigenous movement, the "Movimiento Maya." One of them, Rosalina Tuyuc, was realistic about what the signing of the peace accord would mean for native people. "The only accomplishment is that it confirms the end of the armed conflict," she commented in January 1997. "We will still have to engage in many struggles if we are to make fundamental changes." Tuyuc belongs to the "popular" stream of the Maya Movement. She advocates tackling Maya concerns in conjunction with those of Ladinos, whether in relation to the land question, economic and social rights, trade unions, or the need to demilitarize politics. Institutions in which a "popular" Maya presence is maintained include the Committee for Peasant Unity, the National Coordinating Committee for Guatemalan Widows, the National Council of Displaced Persons, and the Ethnic Communities Council known as "Runujel Tunam."

These "popular" organizations are operationally distinct from a host of "cultural" ones in which exclusively Maya issues are the focal point of group activity. One notable association that reflects this "cultural" emphasis is the Academy of Maya Languages, part of the Confederation of Maya Organizations of Guatemala, founded in 1990. Over three hundred Maya associations have emerged, many restricted to one specific language group or defined by municipal and departmental affiliation. Because of marked differences in viewpoint and frame of reference, thirteen umbrella organizations now exist to coordinate Maya activism. The most important of them is COPMAGUA — the Consejo del Pueblo Maya de Guatemala, the Council of Maya Peoples of Guatemala. Formed in 1994, COPMAGUA is perhaps the most insistent of Maya collectives in pressing for indigenous rights, though all such groups are active lobbyists.

While the Maya Movement is inevitably maligned by its opponents — the business leader Humberto Preti, for instance, accused it of "creating two nations" — the energies of most of those involved in the movement are expended not in risky separatist endeavors but in fighting for specific strategic goals. These revolve, most notably, around efforts to make Maya languages official, to validate Maya spirituality, to promote educational reform, to confront the land situation, and to advocate indigenous law (*derecho consuetudinario*). Speaking in December 1998 to the American Anthropological Association at its annual meeting in Philadelphia, one Maya leader, Raxche', pointed out that the improvements sought by him and his colleagues could more readily be attained if the government of Guatemala disbursed its budget in conformity with the findings of the latest national census. "According to the government's own statistics," he observed wryly, "we are said to constitute 42.8 percent of the population. When will we ever receive 42.8 percent of the state's resources?" Raxche''s question is one that, in Bolivia, Evo Morales has resolved to address during his spell as president of the only country in Latin America with a higher percentage of indigenous people than Guatemala.

But Guatemala is not Bolivia. The likelihood of the State allocating its Maya population a share of resources commensurate with their growing numbers—women in Guatemala on average give birth to more children than anywhere else in Latin America—is slim indeed. Ends are now often met by involvement in transmigrant labor circuits. *Prensa Libre* reported in its issue of January 12, 2007, that an estimated 1.3 million Guatemalans, a good many of them Maya, live and work in the United States, from where they send or bring home remittances valued at 3.6 billion dollars for the year 2006. Remittances, however, will never bridge the gulf between need and sufficiency. Furthermore, in 2008, the economic downturn in the United States triggered heavy-handed policing of transmigrant circuits. Nowhere was this more excessively manifest than in the raid on a meatpacking plant in Postville, Iowa, which resulted in criminal charges being laid against some three hundred illegal workers from Guatemala prior to their imprisonment and subsequent deportation.

PORTILLO (2000–2004) AND THE CORRUPTION OF POWER

Guatemala's woes were exacerbated—quite an assertion in itself—under the presidency of Alfonso Portillo. Why did his term in office cause further deterioration in the body politic and trigger renewed concerns for human rights?

In first-round voting held on November 7, 1999, Portillo and the Frente Republicano Guatemalteco (FRG) secured 48 percent of all ballots, well ahead of Oscar Berger of the incumbent PAN, which received only 31 percent. A distant third, with 12 percent, was Álvaro Colom of the Alianza Nueva Nación, the New Nation Alliance, a coalition that included former guerrilla insurgents. Portillo, whose rightist party espoused the virtues of law and order even though he himself mouthed leftist rhetoric, and Berger, former mayor of Guatemala City and a member of the country's wealthy pro-business elite, ran off against each other seven weeks later. Portillo trounced Berger by more than two votes to one.

Victory by the FRG was disquieting for two reasons. The first had to do with Portillo's violent personal history, most of all his admission that, in Mexico in 1982, he shot and killed two men, afterward fleeing the scene to avoid prosecution, even though he claims that he acted in self-defense. While a judge cleared the case up some time ago, Portillo only publicly acknowledged his part in the incident shortly before votes were cast. Remarkably, he manipulated the event to turn it into an electoral asset, allowing one campaign ad on television to allude to the affair by pronouncing: "A man who can defend his own life can defend yours." With widespread preoccupation about public safety and a dysfunctional justice system rampant in Guatemala, Portillo's gunmanship increased his "mano fuerte" (strong man) popularity and earned him votes.

A second concern had to do with the founder and secretary general of the FRG, Efraín Ríos Montt. Banned from running for the presidency because of his role in the military coup of 1982, Ríos Montt won a seat in congress and went on to serve as the legislature's president. Referred to proudly by FRG supporters as "The General" and introduced at political rallies as "Our Maximum Leader," Ríos Montt is regarded as the real power behind the FRG. Few countries in the world can boast to have had, as their president of congress, a man charged in Spanish courts, along with seven other military associates, with crimes against humanity.

Portillo made some unexpected appointments upon first taking office, which confounded more than just a few observers. "Is Guatemala's new president," asked political analyst Ruth Taylor, "puppet, champion, or chameleon?" In his inaugural address, Portillo pledged to adopt the tenets of the peace accord as state policy. Three years later, to no one's surprise, he declared that implementation was proving impractical and that it would take up to six decades before any headway could be made. What did surprise many was his advocacy of changing Guatemalan law in order to allow a civilian to assume the post of minister of defense. Portillo also challenged military authority by moving to dismantle the presidential military guard, the nerve center of army intelligence. He further confounded his critics by offering political opponents influential posts, including Otilia Lux de Cotí of the CEH the post of minister of culture and sports, former guerrilla leader Pedro Palma Lau the directorship of the institution charged with resolving land conflicts, and Edgar Gutiérrez of REMHI, in his new capacity as secretary of strategic analysis, the job of demilitarizing state intelligence services. Gutiérrez was later asked to serve as minister of foreign affairs. What started out with some promise, however, soon turned foul.

Corruption, cronyism, contempt for all that opposition parties stood for, and inconsistency in political decision making were the hallmarks of Portillo's presidency, played out against a backdrop of escalating violence and the near collapse of Guatemala's once-booming coffee industry. Crisis in the latter was triggered by a sharp drop in the price of coffee on the world market, from $130.00 per hundred-pound sack in 2000 to $50.00 in 2002, the lowest in over half a century. ANACAFE, the National Coffee Association, anticipated that annual sales would plummet from around $600 million to $200 million. Any coffee farmer I spoke with had never experienced such hard times and was looking desperately for alternatives — or considering going out of the business altogether. Almost 1,000 estates, ANACAFE reported, were abandoned, some 250 of them taken over by banks because of unpaid loans. Coffee production in Guatemala, asserts Taylor, is based economically on "a model that generates poverty." That model, however, does offer employment, albeit onerous, if not exploitative, and miserably paid. ANACAFE estimated that the coffee crisis cost 163,000 full-time workers their jobs, and that another 206,000 were not hired on a temporary basis. A new government census, meanwhile, revealed that land is held even more unequally than before: "37% of producers," Taylor relays, "hold merely 3% of agricultural land, while the top-earning 0.15% of producers own 70% of arable land." The U.S.–Central American Free Trade Agreement, which Guatemala actively pursued under Portillo, one can hardly imagine constituting a viable economic fix.

Perhaps the most ominous revelation to surface when Portillo held office came from MINUGUA, the UN agency charged with monitoring the peace process in Guatemala. In a report covering the period July 2001 through June 2002, MINUGUA cast more light on the "parallel structures" referred to by Attorney General Carlos de León Argueta. "Clandestine structures and illegal groups used in the counter-insurgency effort have undergone a transformation in post-conflict Guatemala," it notes. "Shielded by impunity, these structures have regrouped and are pursuing illegal business interests and political influence." MINUGUA concludes: "With the State no longer committing human rights abuses as a matter of policy, these groups' relations to the Government apparatus are diffuse, although they still hold some key positions and maintain informal links to police, justice officials, and military intelligence." Even officials of the George W. Bush administration voiced alarm: archconservative Otto Reich, former assistant secretary of state for Western Hemisphere affairs, admitted before a U.S. House International Relations Committee that "there is little political will in the [Guatemalan] government to address the past, [or] any type of oversight of the military, [whose] growing budget remains completely blocked."

American censure eventually came when, on January 31, 2003, Guatemala was decertified for failing to combat drug trafficking. "Drug interdiction has dropped significantly," observed a representative of the U.S. Embassy, "even though intelligence tells us that the same amount of drugs [is] arriving in Guatemala." Narcotic experts with the U.S. State Department speak of the "Colombianization" of the country. Successful anti-trafficking initiatives in Colombia have only served to strengthen the big cartels in Mexico, and neighboring Guatemala has emerged as a key player in the international drug trade: an estimated 75 percent of the cocaine that reaches the United States passes through Guatemalan territory; Europe is also a point of destination. "It's like Colombia was twenty years ago," one intelligence source states in *El País* of March 3, 2007, with four cartels (Golfo, Luciano, Sayaxché, and Zacapa) in effect dividing up the country. "They control entire areas with their own militias, buy favors, and finance local authorities."

Having entrenched themselves in rural Guatemala, the drug mafias then set up or consolidated bases in urban centers, Guatemala City being their prime target. There they co-opted gangs of youths known as *maras*—social outcasts who terrorize neighborhoods, run protection rackets, and serve as contract killers. A logical next step was to infiltrate government institutions and national security services. "The seed of all this was sown by counter-insurgency," maintains Héctor Rosada of the Center for Strategic Studies and Central American Security. "During the war, these structures operated on parallel paths, fed by corruption and impunity. Now in peacetime they have become an integral part of organized crime." What Rosada and other analysts assert is that the decommissioning of army ranks called for under the peace accord released from duty military personnel by the thousands. On returning to civilian life, these hardened professionals were hired to participate in all manner of criminal activities, from money laundering to illicit logging, from organizing car theft rings to ensuring that "strategic corridors" are "security free" for the conduit of drugs.

Taking stock of Portillo would not be complete without mention of two UN surveys carried out during his presidency. A "poverty map" for 2003 categorized 54.1 percent of Guatemalans as "poor," 27.8 percent of these "extremely poor." One year later, a UNESCO education study placed Guatemala last among the eighteen Latin American countries whose school systems were reviewed, and deemed the situation in rural areas in particular "critical."

Two other notable episodes took place during Portillo's presidency, the first involving Ríos Montt. Even as cases were being lodged against "The General" to stand trial for crimes against humanity, on July 14, 2003, the Constitutional Court voted four-to-three in favor of allowing him to run as the FRG's candidate in the next presidential election. Having stacked the court with party allies, the FRG at last attained the outcome denied it in 1990 and 1995, when Ríos Montt was disqualified from running. The second episode relates to payments that Portillo was in favor of making to former members of civil defense patrols, for services rendered during the armed conflict. Legislation that amounts to payment for killing is but one of many sinister elements left behind by a president who, within a month of his term ending, moved to Mexico to escape prosecution for his corrupt legacy.

BERGER (2004–2008), THE ATROCITY ARCHIVE, AND A DECADE OF PEACE

A Guatemalan journalist I got to know, Luis Barillas, flew into Toronto on October 30, 2003, to receive the International Press Freedom Award from the Committee to Protect Journalists. Following the ceremony, he chose not to return home and continue his work as a newspaper reporter and radio host but to stay in Canada and seek political asylum. His experience affords us some appreciation not only of the dangers of being a journalist in Guatemala—Barillas corresponded for *Prensa Libre* and *Nuestro Diario,* and could be heard frequently on Catholic radio broadcasts—but also of local politics and their national import.

An Achí Maya, Barillas hails from Rabinal, a predominantly indigenous community some 50 kilometers north of Guatemala City. There, on November 9, as in more than one hundred municipalities throughout Guatemala, elections for the post of mayor were won by the incumbent FRG, the party headed by Ríos Montt. "The General," however, finished third in the presidential race, with only 19.31 percent of the vote, well behind Álvaro Colom of UNE (National Unity for Hope), with 26.36 percent of the vote, and Oscar Berger of GANA (Great National Alliance), with 34.33 percent of the vote. A second round of voting, held on December 28, saw Berger emerge victorious, with 54 percent, as opposed to Colom's 46 percent of ballots cast.

Though Ríos Montt was defeated, the FRG was not; it won forty-three seats in congress, only five fewer than GANA and ten more than UNE. Its power would still be flexed in places such as Rabinal, where in the months prior to voting it distributed roofing material, tiles and cement blocks, seeds and fertilizers, and cash incentives to secure votes. As well as these enticements, the FRG also resorted to harassment and intimidation to sway the election in its favor.

Barillas, in newspaper articles and on his radio slots, disclosed these irregularities. His actions incensed FRG supporters, several of whom Barillas had identified, by name, as the perpetrators of crimes carried out in Rabinal at the height of the civil war in the early 1980s, when Ríos Montt was president of Guatemala. Barillas argued that, as commander in chief when repression was most rampant, Ríos Montt was ultimately responsible for the conduct of his rank and file. All participants, he maintained, but especially Ríos Montt, should be held accountable and brought to trial. For bringing civil war atrocities to the attention of his readers and listeners, and by calling for justice, Barillas started to receive death threats.

His predicament worsened following an incident that took place on June 14, five months before the elections. Arrangements had been made in Rabinal to bury the remains of seventy people recently exhumed from the grounds of an army base. Aware of that event, Ríos Montt nonetheless showed up to attend an FRG rally. Outraged that the general in charge of the army when their loved ones were abducted and murdered would choose the day of their funeral to visit town and make a campaign speech, the procession filed toward Ríos Montt to confront him with the most damning evidence of all: the coffins of the dead. Violent altercations ensued before FRG handlers removed Ríos Montt from the scene.

For the mourners who joined the demonstration, insult was added to injury when, in subsequent TV interviews, FRG officials claimed that the coffins contained not human remains but rocks, metal objects, wooden batons, and other makeshift weaponry, which they claimed had been concealed in the coffins in preparation for an attack. The FRG also alleged that Barillas, who was covering developments "live on air" for *La Voz de la Parroquia* (The Parish Voice), was present not to report but to foment anger and incite unrest. Renewed threats soon came his way in the form of letters and telephone calls, culminating on July 4, when his house was bombed. Two days later, his sister received word that her children would be killed if her brother did not shut up. Barillas left Rabinal and hid out in the houses of friends and colleagues in Guatemala City until he obtained a visitor's permit and was able to travel to Toronto.

The courage shown by Barillas in confronting Ríos Montt and the FRG was not matched by the Guatemalan judiciary. Ríos Montt's defeat in the

2003 elections resulted in him losing immunity from prosecution. Though he was placed under house arrest in March 2004, no legal action was advanced within the country. On July 7, 2006, however, Spanish judge Santiago Pedraz issued an international arrest warrant, calling for the extradition of Ríos Montt to stand trial in Madrid, along with seven other culprits, on charges of "genocide, torture, terror, and illegal detention." A year and a half of equivocation ended on December 17, 2007, when the Guatemalan Constitutional Court ruled that Spain did not have legal jurisdiction in the cases submitted. As he had done repeatedly, Ríos Montt denied any knowledge of massacres committed under his rule, insisting that when he assumed power "communism had won and Guatemala was lost," and firm in his belief that "the army was defending the interests of our country." Legal proceedings constituted not just character assassination, his supporters maintained, but "political defamation." Where is the evidence? his lawyers asked. Where is the burden of proof in the case against him?

If testimony gathered by REMHI and the truth commission was not enough, the revelations of the death-squad dossier hinted at the likelihood that, buried somewhere in state security files, are institutional records not only of government tolerance of repression but also of its planned, systematic execution. The existence of such an archive had long been denied. A cabinet of horrors of the army's own concoction has yet to be found, and admitted to, but we now have a vast trail of paper that directly implicates the National Police as the accomplices, indeed, the architects, of state terror.

The discovery was inadvertent, the result of Guatemala's human rights prosecutor, Sergio Morales, sending his staff to confirm the removal of explosives from a police storage facility located in a residential neighborhood of Guatemala City. On further investigation of the site, Morales's inspectors found that five buildings housed an estimated seventy-five million documents: National Police records of its own activities and doings. "We opened up one of the file cabinets in the first room we entered," recalls Carla Villagrán, "and there were dozens of folders marked with the names of some of the most famous cases of political assassination in Guatemala." Villagrán and her associates found case folders filled with the opposite of what one might expect: instead of keeping track of how inquiries into crimes were progressing, the reports indicated their actual plotting and perpetration.

After a nearby building was set on fire, Morales moved decisively to gain legal access to the files and to safeguard them against sabotage. "The files contain a wealth of information [that] will help us understand how repression worked and where the orders came from," observes Claudia Samayoa of Guatemala's National Human Rights Movement. "It is becoming clear that the police force was a repressive arm of the military." Within three years of its odious contents coming to light, the atrocity archive had a director, Gustavo Meoño, and a staff of two hundred trained personnel committed to the preservation of documented acts of terror, the tracks of which may allow thousands of Guatemalans one day to know the fate of disappeared relatives and next of kin. "We've made a complete inventory of everything we have now, and we update it every day," Meoño told Kate Doyle of the National Security Archive. "I want an archive that is ordered, organized, and accessible. I want the research to continue indefinitely, so nothing can destroy it or interrupt the work." Doyle points out that Guatemala's National Police received professional training from the United States for almost twenty years after the overthrow of Jacobo Arbenz. U.S. complicity is palpable, she argues, more than just a logistical prop. "I record, therefore I am," Doyle notes of the bureaucracy of terror, whose officers, "consumed by the hunt for subversives," were deployed not to maintain social order but to violate it.

Though Frank La Rue, presidential commissioner for human rights, told Reuters correspondent Eduardo García that "the State's obligation is now to protect these documents, so that we can start working on them," Berger's priorities lay elsewhere. Human rights activists found themselves under renewed attack and intimidation, their requests for protection to the Ministry of the Interior slighted and ignored. The military budget increased during Berger's first year in office, even though army ranks had in theory been reduced by half, to fifteen thousand personnel; the entrepreneurial interests of the armed forces, therefore, grew and diversified. Former soldiers, without any rehabilitation, became police officers. In terms of economic policy, Berger pursued an agenda that favored not the needy but big business, awarding two controversial concessions to Canadian mining companies in Sipacapa and El Estor, thereby violating Convention 169 of the International Labor Organization, which establishes the right of indigenous peoples to be consulted when their lands and resources are the target of development. Despite the publication, in July 2006, of a glossy brochure proclaiming "30 months of achievements and still going strong," the latest UN human development index placed Guatemala last in all Latin America. Not even the recruitment of Rigoberta Menchú as a goodwill ambassador could counter negative statistics and opinions as the tenth anniversary of the peace accord approached. When it arrived, the UNRG, the insurgent collective that, along with government and military officials, had signed a halt to hostilities, refused to take part in any ceremony or commemoration. All-important "structural changes," URNG declared, "have not happened. The evils that created the armed conflict remain present." No one summed up the situation more pertinently than anthropologist Linda

Green. In effect, peace is impossible because of (1) the impunity enjoyed by "those responsible for the orchestration of a brutal counterinsurgency war, which facilitates an ongoing militarized state structure, albeit in civilian disguise; and (2) a neo-liberal economic model that creates conditions most favorable for transnational elites" while impoverishing the poor even more. A decade of peace gave no cause for celebration.

COLOM (2008–2012) AND THE FAILURE OF STATE

In 2002, Amnesty International described the Guatemala over which Alfonso Portillo presided as a "corporate mafia state." The human rights agency saw little improvement as the presidential elections of 2007 drew near. "Clandestine groups openly flout the rule of law and have a knock-on effect on the administration of justice," it lamented, concluding that "the freedom [of these groups] to act with impunity [goes] unchallenged." The outgoing vice president, Eduardo Stein, was equally sober in his assessment. Guatemala, he told the BBC, is in danger of becoming a "narco-state." Is not the country, asked *El País* on January 21, 2008, already a "failed state"? A week after Álvaro Colom assumed the presidency, columnist M. A. Bastenier wondered if the failure of state had made Guatemala the Somalia of Latin America.

Colom, defeated in two previous election bids, won at his third attempt as leader of the National Unity of Hope (UNE). In a second-round victory on November 4, Colom secured 53 percent of the vote, compared to the 47 percent garnered by Otto Pérez Molina of the Patriot Party (PP). Campaigning with slogans like "Your hope is my commitment" and "Life, development, and peace," Colom takes pride in his affiliation with Maya culture, claiming to be inspired by its spiritual tendencies. A textile magnate, his social-democrat credentials may be traced back to his uncle, Manuel Colom Argueta, a former mayor of Guatemala City whose presidential aspirations and pledges of political reform ended with his assassination in 1979; a file with Colom's uncle's name on it is among the most incriminating of those found in the National Police Archive. Colom acknowledges that organized crime has attempted to penetrate UNE ranks, but cites the case of Manuel de Jesús Castillo Medrano as evidence of corruption being held at bay: Castillo Medrano was expelled from the party following media exposure that connected him to drug trafficking and the orchestration of car thefts. Allegations of shady dealings, however, continue to be leveled at UNE and its membership.

Colom is a soft-spoken, articulate man whom I met and conversed with at a political forum in Ottawa in 1995, when he headed FONAPAZ, a national development agency charged with improving living conditions in rural areas. He struck me then as earnest and well-intentioned, certainly a more progressive choice for president than Pérez Molina, a retired general and self-declared hard-liner who, in his campaign speeches, advocated that the solution to lawlessness was to deploy army patrols on the streets, double the size of the police force, and reimpose the death penalty. Pérez Molina's military background includes a spell at the U.S. School of the Americas, an institution from which he and many fellow graduates returned to Guatemala better versed in the theory of anticommunism, which they subsequently put into practice. Pérez Molina applied his U.S. training to counterinsurgency operations in Ixil country, and served as chief of army intelligence and the presidential guard. His résumé also includes acting as the military's representative in the negotiations leading up to the signing of the peace accord. The waging of war, however, not the pursuit of peace, is what Pérez Molina knows best. Francisco Goldman goes so far as to implicate him in the plot that took the life of Bishop Gerardi. Pérez Molina is sixty, and his presidential ambitions run high.

Political crisis, including demands for his resignation, beset Colom after a well-known and respected lawyer, Rodrigo Rosenberg Marzano, was assassinated on May 10, 2009. Fearing for his life, and believing that two of his clients, businessman Khalil Musa and his daughter Marjorie Musa, had lost theirs because of what they had confided in him, Rosenberg only days before he was murdered made a video in which he bared his soul. The video, he instructed the colleague who helped him make it, should be released in the event of his demise.

"Sadly," Rosenberg begins, "if you are watching this video and listening to me, it is because I am dead." He asserts that his death "has a first name and a second," Álvaro Colom, whom he labels "a thief, a murderer, and a coward." Rosenberg informs us that Colom approached Khalil Musa with a view to having him serve on the board of directors of Banrural, the state-owned bank for rural development. After agreeing to do so, Musa was distressed to find out that Banrural was enmeshed in all sorts of illegal transactions, among them "laundering money, pilfering public funds, and running fictitious programs headed by the president's wife, Sandra de Colom." Rosenberg describes Banrural as "a front for narcotics trafficking," and calls it "a den of robbers, drug peddlers, and assassins." Musa's knowledge of this, which he shared with his daughter and was about to make public, is the reason they were killed. Rosenberg states clearly that he realizes he may well be next: "Am I going to be yet another statistic because of what I have documented proof of?" Foreseeing the worst, he expresses the hope that his death will mark "the beginning of a new way forward for Guatemala."

National salvation under Colom, who denies all involvement in Rosenberg's assassination and who dismisses the late lawyer's allegations as "completely false," is difficult to imagine. The president lurches from one expediency to the next, criticized (among others) by Carmen Aida of the Myrna Mack Foundation, who is of the opinion that "he has improvised everything, forming a government in which only one woman and one indigenous Maya have been given appointments." Aida believes that the Colom administration "has social-democrat airs, but no authentic competence." Accused of poor judgment and unreflective behavior, he provoked jibes and consternation from the outset: during his inaugural discourse, he spoke passionately about "the privilege of the poor" while wearing a $30,000 gold watch.

Reporting to congress on his first year in office, Colom disclosed that, in 2008, homicides exceeded six thousand, one in three killings related to the drug trade, and three times more firearms now circulate in Guatemala than at the height of the armed conflict. "I well understand the reluctance of judges to sign arrest warrants for drug traffickers," news coverage in *Prensa Libre* records Colom conceding. "They know that if they do so, almost certainly they will be assassinated the next day." In an earlier report in the newspaper, he admitted that drug lords were buying legitimate businesses and taking over commercial operations, and that not all Guatemalan territory was under government control.

The one positive sign is the realization that impunity has to be dealt with if state authority is to survive. A significant retreat from the abyss is the establishment of the International Commission against Impunity in Guatemala (CICIG), a UN initiative that received congressional sanction in August 2007. Headed by the distinguished Spanish jurist Carlos Castresana, CICIG can count on the legal expertise of 150 special appointees, whose Herculean task is to foster in Guatemala respect for the rule of law. Castresana's optimism is measured. "The elite realize that if they do not lend us their support in remaking Guatemala, including helping out financially, then they will lose everything." A sea change is taking place, Castresana believes, in the mindset of the elite, and in that of state officials too. Hitherto, they considered allowing CICIG to enter and operate in Guatemala "a loss of sovereignty." Castresana puts it emphatically the other way around. "What CICIG is all about," he stresses, "is giving back to the country the sovereignty it has lost."

As Guatemala teeters, it remains difficult not to look back and lament, yet again, the overthrow of Jacobo Arbenz Guzmán. In October 1995, more than four decades after his removal from the presidency by a CIA-backed coup, Arbenz's remains were returned to the country that he tried to modernize and change, but for which the United States had set an alternate, Cold War agenda—one that in many quarters has yet to thaw. The idea of meaningful reform, however, was not repatriated with him. What was repatriated, fourteen years after his remains, were the ashes of his wife, María Vilanova. Perhaps her posthumous return to Guatemala will one day be more than symbolic. Vilanova, who rebelled against her conservative background in El Salvador to become a critical, freethinking spirit, is said to have held political views that influenced her more moderate-minded husband. Addressing the root causes of why Guatemala is the way it is, and attempting to do something about it, as Arbenz did, is the logical place to start.

Guatemala, it does no harm to reiterate, is *not* a poor country. It is rich in resources, natural and human. Guatemala has been *made* a poor country because the allotment of its resources, especially its land resources, has been deformed by crippling geographies of inequality. Geography, as I see it, is all about resources, specifically access to (or control over) resources that pertain to land. Equitable, sustainable use of land is what makes development possible. If land is made available to those who know how to work it, for the benefit of all and not just a few, then economic development and social stability are possible. It makes short-term political sense, whatever party is in power, to engage issues relating to fair taxation and the just remuneration of agricultural labor. The fundamental issue of grossly unequal ownership of land, however, can be resolved only if it is actually addressed. If it is not, the peace that was signed into being in 1996 may prove neither as "firm" nor as "lasting" as its signatories, and the opposing constituencies they represent, had envisioned.

Genaro Castañeda, the "Q'anjob'al Canadian"
(Chapter 1 and Epilogue).

Magdalena González (Chapter 4) with her
great-granddaughter Lucía.

Rigoberta Menchú, "Nobel K'iche'" (Chapter 2 and Epilogue). Courtesy of Fototeca Guatemala, CIRMA
(Centro de Investigaciones Regionales de Mesoamérica).

Death and the Devils (Chapter 6). Photograph by Mary Ellen Davis.

Joselino González, the "Delivery Man" (Chapters 7 and 17).

General Romeo Lucas García, president of
Guatemala, 1978–1982 (Chapter 8).
Courtesy of Fototeca Guatemala, CIRMA.

General Efraín Ríos Montt, president of
Guatemala, 1982–1983 (Chapter 9), and founder
of the Guatemalan Republican Front (Epilogue).
Courtesy of Fototeca Guatemala, CIRMA.

Jorge Carpio Nicolle, who, as general director of
the newspaper El Gráfico in the early 1980s, signed
editorials denouncing the violence (Chapter 9).
He was assassinated in 1994. Courtesy of Fototeca
Guatemala, CIRMA.

General Oscar Humberto Mejía Víctores, president
of Guatemala, 1983–1986 (Chapter 10).
Courtesy of Fototeca Guatemala, CIRMA.

Entrance to the army barracks at Sacapulas. The sign on the upper right reads: "Only those who fight have the right to conquer; only those who conquer have the right to live" (Chapter 11). Photograph by Paul VanZant.

Entrance to the army barracks at Sololá (Chapter 12).

Jorge Serrano Elías, president of Guatemala, 1991– 1993 (Chapter 14). Courtesy of Fototeca Guatemala, CIRMA.

Ramiro de León Carpio, center, president of Guatemala, 1993– 1996 (Chapters 15 and 16). Courtesy of Fototeca Guatemala, CIRMA.

Jacobo Arbenz Guzmán (right), the reform-minded president of Guatemala between 1951 and 1954, in conversation with his minister of foreign affairs, Guillermo Toriello. The Arbenz government was overthrown by a CIA- *backed coup (Chapter 18). Courtesy of Fototeca Guatemala,* CIRMA.

From an educational poster put out by the UN Mission to Guatemala, in which a Spanish conquistador orders two natives to "Work faster!" The caption below reads: "When the Spaniards arrived, they defeated the Mayas and compelled them to work" (Chapter 18). Under protests from the Spanish ambassador to Guatemala, the poster was withdrawn.

From the same UN educational poster, a government official (left) informs a group of villagers: "These lands now belong to this gentleman." The new landlord (right) tells the villagers: "You will always work for me." The caption below reads: "Under the government of Justo Rufino Barrios, Indian lands were expropriated and handed over to large operators, foreigners as well as Guatemalans" (Chapter 19).

Vinicio Cerezo Arévalo, president of
Guatemala, 1986–1991 (Chapters 11, 12, and
13). Courtesy of Fototeca Guatemala, CIRMA.

Álvaro Arzú, president of Guatemala,
1996–2000 (Epilogue). Courtesy of
Fototeca Guatemala, CIRMA.

Bishop Juan Gerardi, assassinated April 26,
1998, two days after his presentation of the
Catholic Church's human rights project
Guatemala: Nunca Más. Courtesy of
the Archdiocesan Human Rights Project.

Alfonso Portillo, president of Guatemala,
2000–2004 (Epilogue). Courtesy of
Fototeca Guatemala, CIRMA.

March preceding the Mass held to honor the memory of Bishop Juan Gerardi four months after his assassination (Epilogue).

From the cover of Nunca Más, *vol. 4, an image titled "So That All Shall Know" (Epilogue). Photograph by Daniel Hernández-Salazar.*

Oscar Berger, president of Guatemala,
2004–2008 (Epilogue). Courtesy of
Fototeca Guatemala, CIRMA.

Álvaro Colom, elected president of Guatemala
in 2007 (Epilogue). Courtesy of
Fototeca Guatemala, CIRMA.

Leonardo Buch Chiroy, Maya Trekkie (Chapter 21).

At peace in the corn. The cross on the left marks the burial site of Magdalena González (Chapter 4).

SOURCES AND COMMENTARY

People began to write about Guatemala a long time ago. Our oldest records, those left by the Maya themselves, are in the form of hieroglyphic inscriptions that appear on various artifacts dating from as early as A.D. 250. Classic Maya culture, according to Gordon Brotherston (1992), expressed itself textually on the surface of alabaster, bone, jade, obsidian, onyx, paper, pottery, shell, stone, and wood. Scripts from the Classic period (A.D. 300–900) are rich and plentiful compared with the meager survivals of the Postclassic (A.D. 900–1524).

Since the foundational studies of Sylvanus G. Morley ([1915] 1975) and J. Eric S. Thompson (1950), the interpretation of Maya writing has been revolutionized by the research of Ian Graham (1975), Stephen D. Houston (1989), David H. Kelley (1976), Linda Schele and David Freidel (1990), and Linda Schele and Mary E. Miller (1986). Tatiana Proskouriakoff (1960) was the first to shift the research focus of Maya epigraphy away from issues of astronomy, religion, and the contemplation of time (see León-Portilla [1973] 1988) to the more mundane operations of war and politics, especially the rise and fall of dynastic rulers and city-states. Michael D. Coe ([1992] 1999) offers a riveting account of the deciphering of Maya script, crediting the Russian scholar Yuri V. Knorosov with the breakthrough that resolved the impasse created by the stubbornness of Thompson. The language of Maya inscription is considered by Stephen Houston, John Robertson, and David Stuart (2000) to be classic Ch'olti'an, an ancestral form of present-day Ch'orti'. Linda Schele and Peter Mathews (1998) offer a splendid synthesis of a field of studies in constant flux. While Maya elites and their ways of life command most attention, as in the volume edited by Jessica Joyce Christie (2003), the scholars brought together by Jon C. Lohse and Fred Valdez, Jr. (2004) construct a narrative from Preclassic to Postclassic times from the bottom up. The experience of being Maya in Classic times is pieced together most assiduously by Stephen Houston, David Stuart, and Karl Taube (2006).

Conquest by imperial Spain saw Maya peoples in Guatemala adapt their modes of writing to European conventions, which meant learning how to use the Latin alphabet. The practice, begun in the mid-sixteenth century, resulted in the preservation of all sorts of knowledge, enabling us to view a radically altered world through Maya eyes. Numerous texts exist, the most famous being the *Popol Vuh*, translated directly from K'iche' into English by Munro S. Edmonson (1971) and Dennis Tedlock (1985). Delia Goetz and Sylvanus G. Morley also provide access to the *Popol Vuh* in English, via the Spanish translation of Adrián Recinos (1950). Victor Montejo (1999a) tells the creation story for a younger audience, ably assisted by the marvelous illustrations of Luis Garay. Inspired work by Karen Bassie-Sweet (2008) links the sacred geography of the *Popol Vuh* with specific places, locales, and topographical features. Another key text is the *Annals of the Cakchiquels,* which Daniel G. Brinton (1885) and Adrián Recinos and Delia Goetz (1953) translated directly from Kaqchikel into English. In the preparation of their "definitive edition," Judith M. Maxwell and Robert M. Hill II (2006) collaborated with native speakers of the language. Robert M. Carmack (1973) provides the best available guide to these and other indigenous documents, which the three volumes edited by David Carrasco (2001) help contextualize in the Mesoamerican world at large.

In English-language historiography, we first read of Mayas and Spaniards courtesy of Thomas Gage, whose experiences in Guatemala in the seventeenth century make fascinating reading. Gage's portrayal of the Maya lot, like the cleric himself, is not without its blemishes and idiosyncrasies, but his trenchant observations of conquest in action are striking, if not entirely trustworthy. A. P. Newton (1928) tampers with Gage's righteous, self-serving text far less than does J. Eric S. Thompson (1958). Two centuries passed before another Englishman, Henry Dunn, published an account of his stay in Guatemala. Dunn ([1829] 1981) has worthwhile insights, but it was the American traveller John Lloyd Stephens ([1841] 1969) who opened up the Maya world as never before. Stephens, whose insights are enhanced by the superb illustrations of his artist companion, Frederick Catherwood, forged a travel-writing genre that influenced the likes of Caroline Salvin ([1873–1874] 2000), Anne and Alfred Maudslay ([1899] 1979), Thomas Gann (1926), and Aldous Huxley (1934). The genre is exemplified in our day by Ronald Wright (1989), Anthony Daniels (1990), Peter Canby (1992), and Stephen Connely Benz (1996), among others less engaging. Alfred Maudslay, who first ventured to Guatemala in 1872, pioneered the scientific study of the Maya from a Western academic perspective, which is wonderfully evoked in Ian Graham's biography of him. Graham (2002) shares with his readers an infectious admiration not only for Maudslay the archaeologist but also for Maudslay the artist and photographer. The Maya present as well as the Maya past is showcased in the tribute organized by John M. Weeks (2001) for Robert M. Carmack, a distinguished researcher in our day.

Scholarly studies that situate Guatemala in the Spanish scheme of empire tend to be overshadowed by the literature available on Mexico; the lands and peoples conquered by Hernán Cortés, it seems, were destined to attract greater attention than those conquered by Pedro de Alvarado (Mackie [1924] 1978). The standard set decades ago by Murdo J. MacLeod is an enduring benchmark; MacLeod ([1973] 2008) assesses recent contributions in a new edition of his classic work. William L. Sherman (1979) fills a large gap in our awareness of how Spaniards controlled and exploited the indigenous population. Miles L. Wortman (1982) emphasizes economic and social matters, while Adriaan C. van Oss (1986, 2003) concentrates on the role of the Catholic Church. Christopher H. Lutz (1994) furnishes us with a vivid urban history of Santiago de Guatemala; the art and architecture of the colonial capital receive detailed treatment at the hands of Sidney D. Markman (1966) and Verle L. Annis (1968). Ralph H. Vigil (1987) charts the life and times of Alonso de Zorita, a Crown official who toiled to impose government authority in the mid-sixteenth century by enforcing laws aimed at improving native welfare. In his ambitious social history, Robinson A. Herrera (2003) includes the experiences of blacks and mixed bloods, and Martha Few (2002) examines those of women, a persecuted lot. Wendy Kramer (1994) sheds light on the turbulent first years of conquest; the event or process itself is reinterpreted and envisioned quite distinctly by Florine G. L. Asselbergs (2004), who has also teamed up with Matthew Restall (2007) and contributed to the volume edited by Laura Matthew and Michel R. Oudijk (2007) to promote greater awareness of indigenous roles. Native presence is emphasized as paradigms shift and a new conquest history is written (Universidad Francisco Marroquín 2007).

Robert M. Carmack (1981), Nancy M. Farriss (1984), Robert M. Hill II (1991), Grant D. Jones (1989, 1998), and Sandra L. Orellana (1984) examine in depth the fate of Maya peoples under Spanish rule. My own research endeavors, alone or in collaboration with others (Lovell [1985] 2005, 2000; Cook and Lovell [1992] 2001; Lovell and Lutz 1995, 1996; Lovell and Swezey 1990), to assess the cultural and demographic repercussions of conquest. Readers who wish to track down the provenance of sources quoted in Chapters 1 and 18 are referred to these works for archival or bibliographic particulars. Michael Taussig (1984, 1987) addresses the fears and the terror tactics that charge all colonial encounters, as do Inga Clendinnen (1987), Paul Sullivan (1989), and

Dennis Tedlock (1993). There is no more visceral indictment of Spanish rule in Guatemala than Severo Martínez Peláez's *La Patria del Criollo,* now available in an English-language edition. For Martínez Peláez ([1970] 2009), "the colonial regime was a regime of terror," responsible for making "Indians" in the first place and exploiting them relentlessly thereafter.

For the nineteenth and early twentieth centuries, E. Bradford Burns (1980, 1986), Paul J. Dosal (1995), Virginia Garrard-Burnett (2000), David McCreery (1990, 1994), and Ralph Lee Woodward, Jr. (1990, 1993) elaborate empirically the more conceptual schema of Oliver La Farge (1940), Robert A. Naylor (1967), and Carol A. Smith (1984). Robert G. Williams (1994) sets the emergence of Guatemala as a "coffee republic" in a comparative Central American context, as do Lowell Gudmundson and Héctor Lindo-Fuentes (1995). The case studies presented in Chapter 19 are derived from the work of several scholars: Charles Wagley (1941, 1949) and John M. Watanabe (1990, 1992) on Santiago Chimaltenango; Robert Burkitt (1930), Jackson S. Lincoln (1945), Benjamin Colby and Pierre van den Berghe (1969), and David Stoll (1993) on Nebaj; Oliver La Farge (1947) and Shelton H. Davis (1970) on Santa Eulalia; and David McCreery (1988) on San Juan Ixcoy. Our understanding of the transformations that occurred in Guatemala in the century after independence has been advanced considerably by René Reeves (2006).

The ill-fated Guatemalan Revolution of 1944–1954—and especially what a decade of rural conflict and agrarian reform represented for Maya communities—is open to at least two interpretations. In terms of popular gains, Robert Wasserstrom (1975) believes it amounted to very little; Jim Handy (1994) champions the opposite view, drawing on considerably more archival documentation than Wasserstrom. Handy, whom I consider by far the more convincing of the two, emphasizes an array of internal factors more than the part played by external agents. Interference in Guatemalan affairs by the U.S. government and corporate interests is well documented by Richard Immerman (1982), Piero Gleijeses (1991), and Nick Cullather ([1999] 2006). The words of Ambassador John Peurifoy's wife and of President Arbenz, quoted in Chapter 20, can be found in the damning exposé of Stephen Schlesinger and Stephen Kinzer ([1982] 2005). In the late 1940s, Gore Vidal ([1995] 1996) lived in Guatemala, where he befriended fellow writer and president of congress Mario Monteforte Toledo, from whom he learned about local customs and corruption. Irascible to some, temperamental to all, Vidal has some pointed but pertinent remarks to make about U.S. hegemony and political intrigue, in effect anticipating the overthrow of Arbenz by some four years in his novel *Dark Green, Bright Red* ([1950] 2005). Effecting "regime change" elsewhere in the world is now acknowledged by many Americans, including government officials in Washington, as something that does not always serve the long-term interests of the United States. Such an epiphany, alas, does not apply to Guatemala, whose people continue to suffer, more than half a century later, from an act of infamy that President Clinton saw fit to acknowledge when he visited the country in 1999.

Coming to grips with the political turmoil that has wracked Guatemala since the overthrow of Arbenz is no easy task. Richard N. Adams (1970) is a useful point of departure, and contains insightful remarks about power structures and the modern military establishment, the latter analyzed at length by Jennifer Schirmer (1998). Stephen M. Streeter (2000) offers a thorough dissection of the immediate post-Arbenz years; Eduardo Galeano (1969) remains indispensable for examining key events of the 1960s. Thereafter, Patrick Ball, Paul Kobrak, and Herbert F. Spirer (1998), Karen Brandow and Thomas F. Reed (1996), George Black (1984), Robert S. Carlsen (1997), Angela Delli Sante (1996), Ruth Gidley, Cynthia Kee, and Reggie Norton (1999), Greg Grandin (2004), Duncan Green (1992), Jim Handy (1984), Catherine Nolin Hanlon and Finola Shankar (2000), Jennifer K. Harbury (1997), Susanne Jonas (1991), Paul Kobrak (1999), Deborah Levenson-Estrada (1994), Beatriz Manz (2004), James Painter (1987), Victor Perera (1993), Victoria Sanford (2004), Robert H. Trudeau (1993), and Daniel Wilkinson (2002) steer the reader through more recent upheavals. The despicable orchestration behind acts of "disappearance," which in Guatemala usually means abduction, torture, and death, is unveiled by the tenacious Kate Doyle (1999, 2007). Frank M. Afflitto and Paul Jessilow (2007) choose to examine the impact of state terror not on those eliminated by it but on relatives and next of kin left alive to deal with it as quotidian hell. Linda Green (2006–2007), David Holiday (2000), Susanne Jonas (2000), Liisa North and Alan Simmons (1999), William Robinson (1998), Rachel Sieder et al. (2002), Jack Spence et al. (1998), William Stanley and David Holiday (2002), and Ruth Taylor (2000) scrutinize the transition from war to peace. The troubled passage is grappled with most innovatively by Diane M. Nelson (2009). Ongoing violence in the form of mob lynchings and the high incidence of female homicides are analyzed, respectively, by Angelina Snodgrass Godoy (2000) and Victoria Sanford (2007, 2008).

Robert M. Carmack (1988) pays special attention to the impact of violence on Maya peoples, while James Dunkerley (1988, 1994) fits contemporary Guatemalan politics into a larger isthmian scenario. Mario Payeras (1983) articulates the goals of the guerrilla insurgency; the Guatemalan Church in Exile (1989) makes public those of the Guatemalan military, spelled out in Chapter 12. From a report published by Cultural Survival and the Anthropology Resource Center (1983) I lift the gruesome testimony of the massacre that took place at Finca San Francisco, one of a litany of atrocities chronicled by the pertinacious Ricardo Falla (1983, 1984, 1994). Falla's account (*Quiché Rebelde*) of how serving as a priest in San Antonio Ilotenango in the late 1960s changed him as much as his parishioners is available in English translation (2001). With the publication of the Catholic Church's *Guatemala: Nunca Más,* for which the Human Rights Office of the Archdiocese of Guatemala (1999) secured a concise English-language edition, and the UN Commission for Historical Clarification's *Guatemala: Memory of Silence* (1999), we now have detailed transcripts of what is still one of the twentieth century's least-known and most chilling acts of war. Online versions of the former may be accessed in English at http://shr.aaas.org/guatemala/ceh/report/english/toc .html.

I have attempted to indicate, chapter by chapter, the newspaper sources that inform much of Part Two. On the second floor of the National Library in Guatemala City, the Hemeroteca Nacional strives to maintain its impressive collection of newspapers and periodicals, dating back to the nineteenth century. Two of the newspapers I draw on, *El Gráfico* and *El Imparcial,* are no longer in circulation. Online searches via the Internet are possible, but deny one tactile pleasure and *in situ* sensation. Anyone who seeks out these sources needs to be wary and alert. Newspapers in Guatemala, observes a character in Francisco Goldman's novel *The Long Night of White Chickens* (1992), "have to be read to be believed." There are times I would prefer *not* to believe what I read in the Guatemalan press, but that would constitute an act of denial. Guatemalan newspapers furnish Goldman (1999, 2002, 2007) with abundant material concerning the murder of Bishop Gerardi, but his novelist's eye for human foibles is what lends his accounts of the crime macabre theatricality and genuine pathos.

For many years the Network in Solidarity with the People of Guatemala (NISGUA) published its quarterly *Report on Guatemala* with an activist U.S. readership predominantly in mind. The *Report* complemented information obtained from its own sources in Guatemala with liberal use of material presented by local news outlets: print media for the most part but with a sprinkling of radio and television coverage too. In my Epilogue, I have drawn extensively on what the *Report*'s correspondents have to say, especially concerning the presidency of Oscar Berger and, after him, the election of Álvaro Colom. NISGUA's decision, in 2007, to cease printing a quarterly update deprives its faithful following of hard-copy bulletins, but logging on to the website www.nisgua.org allows access to news and analysis as well as activist networking. The same strategy applies to Rights Action (www.rights

action.org), for which the tireless Grahame Russell gives his all, ensuring that Canadian business and commercial ties are monitored and commented on in addition to U.S. connections. Canada's solidarity links to Guatemala are examined by Kathryn Anderson (2003). Another indispensable source is the Guatemala Scholars Network (www.vanderbilt.edu/gsn), whose periodic newsletters keep researchers informed, connected, and motivated.

Seeing, the saying assures us, is believing. Images in our digital age, however, perhaps even more than words, are manipulated and tampered with as never before. Our trust in delivery, therefore, needs to be fine-tuned. Photography in Guatemala, which dates back to the medium's earliest applications, has had many notable practitioners, their work nowhere more resourcefully guarded for posterity than in the Fototeca archive of the Centro de Investigaciones Regionales de Mesoamérica (CIRMA). No visit should be made to Antigua without stopping by to admire the setting, and marvel at the holdings, of this remarkable institution, a visit that (with any luck) will coincide with an exhibit of photographs drawn from CIRMA's unrivalled collection. Two catalogs (CIRMA 1998, 2005) are available, with an ample selection of images of life in Guatemala from 1870 on, and informative explanatory texts. Also helpful for purposes of orientation is the essay by Enrique del Cid (1994) that appeared in newspaper form in *El Imparcial* in 1962. Guatemala is fortunate to have figured in the travel itinerary of Eadweard Muybridge (Burns 1986; Solnit 2003) when coffee production was gearing up, a feature he captured in all its diverse complexity. The incomparable photographs of Muybridge, who spent six months in Guatemala in 1875, adorn several books dealing with coffee and development in Guatemala, including those of Regina Wagner (2001) and Robert G. Williams (1994). Accomplished photographers from all over (Parker 1982; Namuth 1985) have recorded Guatemala's demons (Simon 1987) as well as its delights (Becom 1997; Vecchiato 1989). In terms of documenting the trajectory from war to peace, Jonathan Moller (2004) has created an extraordinary body of work, as has James Rodríguez (MiMundo.org). Two Guatemalans whose photography encapsulates their country's pain, yet transcends it, are Luis González Palma (1999) and Daniel Hernández-Salazar (Maldonado 2007), both of whom enjoy deserved international acclaim.

Anthropological research on Guatemala has produced many distinguished contributions, often set in the context of one specific Maya community. The best community studies, among them a model of the genre carried out by Robert M. Carmack (1995), show an awareness of the importance of history, even if many float ungrounded in a timeless ethnographic present. Four collections of essays—those edited by Clarence L. Hay et al. (1940), Sol Tax (1950), Carl Kendall, John Hawkins, and Laurel Bossen (1983), and Victoria R. Bricker and Gary H. Gossen (1989)—allow an appraisal to be made of how the field has evolved. The talented Maud Oakes (1951a, 1951b) crafted not one but two classic accounts. Oliver La Farge can be credited with three: one as sole author (1947), one with Frans Blom (1926–1927), and another with Douglas Byers (1931). There are occasions, or so it seems to me, when the postmodern soul-searching of anthropologists (see Watanabe 1995) could profit from a sanguine reading of neglected or forgotten predecessors.

Several investigations, however, including those by Edward F. Fischer (2002), Edward F. Fischer and Carol E. Hendrickson (2002), Brent E. Metz (2006), and Diane M. Nelson (1999) indicate that methodological as well as textual innovation (see Zimmerman 1995) is alive and well. This is especially so regarding strategic ways, the reservations of David Stoll (1999) notwithstanding, in which Mayas may be engaged in the telling of their stories, indeed encouraged to take charge of narration themselves. Working closely with Andrés Xiloj, for example, enabled Dennis Tedlock ([1982] 1985) to imbue his translation of the *Popol Vuh* with living K'iche' authority. A similar disposition on the part of Barbara Tedlock ([1982] 1992) permeates her portrayal of how ancient concepts of time and space are kept alive in the daily routines of the present. James D. Sexton (1981, 1985, 1992) accommodates the narration of life histories adroitly, as do David Carey, Jr. (2001) and Hilary E. Kahn (2006). Having myself witnessed, in this giddying era of globalization, the performances of Mayas in the marketplace (see Chapter 21), I am particularly struck by the tactical fieldwork and incisive narratives of Walter E. Little (2004), Edward F. Fischer and Peter Benson (2006), and Liliana R. Goldín (2008).

Pedro Gaspar González (1995, 1998), Rigoberta Menchú (1984, 1998), and Victor Montejo ([1982] 1984, 1987, 1991, 1995, 1999a, 1999b) speak to us more directly, three Maya voices now heard among a growing concert of others, women notably among them (Anderson and Garlock 1988; Berger 2006; Hooks 1993; Smith-Ayala 1991). Linda Green (1999) weaves the painful experiences of Maya women into an illuminating discussion of fear as a way of life. Green's disclosures are echoed in the work of Judith Zur (1998) and Jennifer Reade and Catherine Nolin (2008). Richard Wilson (1991, 1993, 1995) does the same for the Q'eqchi' subjects of his fieldwork, whom he sees turning political repression into cultural resurgence. In a dazzling piece of scholarship, Greg Grandin (2000) demonstrates that, in the late eighteenth and nineteenth centuries, the K'iche' of Quetzaltenango not only shaped their own destiny but also influenced the ways in which the Guatemalan state implanted itself around them. Language and dress (England 1995; Deuss [1981] 1990; Hendrickson 1995; Mayers 1966; Schevill 1993, 1997; Warren

1994) are rich repositories of culture and identity; age-old traditions endure (Cook 2000; Stanzione 2003; Molesky-Poz 2006) even as they mutate and change (Deuss 2007).

If rebirth and renewal signal a new Maya order (Fischer and Brown 1996; Gálvez Borrell and Esquit Choy 1997; Montejo 2005; Smith 1991; Warren 1992, 1998; Wright 1992), the gains have not been achieved without tremendous costs (Smith 1990). As Mayas regroup and rebuild, they do so remembering not only the dead and the disappeared but also the exiled and the displaced (Burns 1993; Fink 2003; Foxen 2008; Hagan 1995; Loucky and Moors 2000; Manz 1988; Nolin 2006; Taylor 1998; Vlach 1992). Perhaps the writers of the *Popol Vuh* had some form of solace in mind when they recorded: "Whatever might be is simply not there: only murmurs, ripples, in the dark, in the night."

Adams, Richard N. 1970. *Crucifixion by Power: Essays on Guatemalan National Social Structure, 1944–1966.* Austin: Univ. of Texas Press.

Afflitto, Frank M., and Paul Jesilow. 2007. *The Quiet Revolutionaries: Seeking Justice in Guatemala.* Austin: Univ. of Texas Press.

Anderson, Kathryn. 2003. *Weaving Relationships: Canada-Guatemala Solidarity.* Waterloo, ON: Wilfred Laurier Univ. Press.

Anderson, Marilyn, and Jonathan Garlock, eds. 1988. *Granddaughters of Corn: Portraits of Guatemalan Women.* Willimantic, CT: Curbstone Press.

Annis, Verle L. 1968. *The Architecture of Antigua Guatemala.* Guatemala: Universidad de San Carlos.

Asselbergs, Florine G. L. 2004. *Conquered Conquistadors: The Lienzo de Quauhquechollan/ A Nahua Vision of the Conquest of Guatemala.* Leiden: CNWS Publications.

Asturias, Miguel Angel. [1950] 1968. *Strong Wind.* Trans. Gregory Rabassa. New York: Delacorte.

———. [1954] 1971. *The Green Pope.* Trans. Gregory Rabassa. New York: Delacorte.

———. [1960] 1973. *The Eyes of the Interred.* Trans. Gregory Rabassa. New York: Delacorte.

Ball, Patrick, Paul Kobrak, and Herbert F. Spirer. 1998. *State Violence in Guatemala, 1960–1996: A Quantitative Reflection.* Washington: American Association for the Advancement of Science.

Bassie-Sweet, Karen. 2008. *Maya Scared Geography and the Creator Deities.* Norman: Univ. of Oklahoma Press.

Becom, Jeffrey. 1997. *Maya Color: The Painted Villages of Mesoamerica.* Photographs by Jeffrey Becom. Text by Jeffrey Becom and Sally Jean Aberg. New York: Abbeville Press.

Benz, Stephen Connely. 1996. *Guatemalan Journey.* Austin: Univ. of Texas Press.

Berger, Susan. 2006. *Guatemaltecas: The Women's Movement, 1986–2003.* Austin: Univ. of Texas Press.

Black, George. 1984. *Garrison Guatemala*. With Milton Jamail and Norma Stoltz Chinchilla. New York: Monthly Review Press.

Blom, Frans, and Oliver La Farge. 1926–1927. *Tribes and Temples*. 2 vols. New Orleans: Tulane Univ. Press.

Brandow, Karen, and Thomas F. Reed. 1996. *The Sky Never Changes: Testimonies from the Guatemalan Labor Movement*. Ithaca: Cornell Univ. Press.

Bricker, Victoria R., and Gary H. Gossen, eds. 1989. *Ethnographic Encounters in Southern Mesoamerica: Essays in Honor of Evon Zartman Vogt, Jr.* Albany, NY: Institute of Mesoamerican Studies.

Brinton, Daniel G. 1885. *The Annals of the Cakchiquels*. Philadelphia: Library of Aboriginal American Literature.

Brotherston, Gordon. 1992. *Book of the Fourth World: Reading the Native Americas through Their Literature*. Cambridge: Cambridge Univ. Press.

Burkitt, Robert. 1930. "Explorations in the Highlands of Western Guatemala." *The Museum Journal* 21(1): 41–72.

Burns, Allan F. 1993. *Maya in Exile: Guatemalans in Florida*. Philadelphia: Temple Univ. Press.

Burns, E. Bradford. 1980. *The Poverty of Progress: Latin America in the Nineteenth Century*. Berkeley: Univ. of California Press.

———. 1986. *Eadweard Muybridge in Guatemala, 1875: The Photographer as Social Recorder*. Berkeley: Univ. of California Press.

Canby, Peter. 1992. *The Heart of the Sky: Travels among the Maya*. New York: HarperCollins.

Carey, David, Jr. 2001. *Our Elders Teach Us: Maya-Kaqchikel Historical Perspectives*. Tuscaloosa: Univ. of Alabama Press.

Carlsen, Robert S. 1997. *The War for the Heart and Soul of a Highland Maya Town*. Austin: Univ. of Texas Press.

Carmack, Robert M. 1973. *Quichean Civilization: The Ethnohistoric, Ethnographic, and Archaeological Sources*. Berkeley: Univ. of California Press.

———. 1981. *The Quiché Mayas of Utatlán: The Evolution of a Highland Guatemalan Kingdom*. Norman: Univ. of Oklahoma Press.

———. 1995. *Rebels of Highland Guatemala: The Quiché-Mayas of Momostenango*. Norman: Univ. of Oklahoma Press.

———, ed. 1988. *Harvest of Violence: The Maya Indians and the Guatemalan Crisis*. Norman: Univ. of Oklahoma Press.

Carrasco, David, editor-in-chief. 2001. *The Oxford Encyclopedia of Mesoamerican Cultures: The Civilizations of Mexico and Central America*. 3 vols. New York: Oxford Univ. Press.

Centro de Investigaciones Regionales de Mesoamérica. 1998. *Picturing Guatemala: Images from the CIRMA Photography Archive*. Guatemala: CIRMA.

———. 2005. *Images of Guatemala: 57 Photographers from the CIRMA Photography Archive and the Guatemalan Photographic Community*. Guatemala: CIRMA.

Christie, Jessica Joyce, ed. 2003. *Maya Palaces and Elite Residences: An Interdisciplinary Approach.* Austin: Univ. of Texas Press.

Cid, Enrique del. 1994. "First Photographers Who Worked in Guatemala." Trans. David Haynes and Birgitta B. Riera. In *The Daguerreian Annual: Official Yearbook of the Daguerreian Society,* 35–45. Eureka, CA: The Daguerreian Society.

Clendinnen, Inga. 1987. *Ambivalent Conquests: Maya and Spaniard in Yucatan, 1517–1570.* Cambridge: Cambridge Univ. Press.

Coe, Michael D. [1992] 1999. *Breaking the Maya Code.* Rev. ed. New York: Thames and Hudson.

Colby, Benjamin, and Pierre van den Berghe. 1969. *Ixil Country: A Plural Society in Highland Guatemala.* Berkeley: Univ. of California Press.

Commission for Historical Clarification. 1999. *Guatemala: Memory of Silence.* Guatemala: Litoprint.

Cook, Garrett W. 2000. *Renewing the Maya World: Expressive Culture in a Highland Town.* Austin: Univ. of Texas Press.

Cook, Noble David, and W. George Lovell, eds. [1992] 2001. *"Secret Judgments of God": Old World Disease in Colonial Spanish America.* Rev. ed. Norman: Univ. of Oklahoma Press.

Cullather, Nick. [1999] 2006. *Secret History: The CIA's Classified Account of Its Operations in Guatemala, 1952–1954.* 2nd ed. Stanford: Stanford Univ. Press.

Cultural Survival and the Anthropology Resource Center. 1983. *Voices of the Survivors: The Massacre at Finca San Francisco, Guatemala.* Peterborough, NH: Transcript Printing.

Daniels, Anthony. 1990. *Sweet Waist of America: Journeys around Guatemala.* London: Hutchinson Books.

Davis, Shelton H. 1970. "Land of Our Ancestors: A Study of Land Tenure and Inheritance in the Highlands of Guatemala." PhD diss., Harvard University.

Delli Sante, Angela. 1996. *Nightmare or Reality?: Guatemala in the 1980s.* Amsterdam: Thela Publishers.

Deuss, Krystyna. [1981] 1990. *Indian Costumes from Guatemala.* Nottingham, UK: Charles Goater and Son.

———. 2007. *Shamans, Witches, and Maya Priests: Native Religion and Ritual in Highland Guatemala.* London: The Guatemalan Maya Centre.

Dosal, Paul J. 1995. *Power in Transition: The Rise of Guatemala's Industrial Oligarchy, 1871–1994.* Westport, CT: Praeger.

Doyle, Kate. 1999. "Death Squad Diary: Looking into the Secret Archives of Guatemala's Bureaucracy of Murder." *Harper's,* June.

———. 2007. "The Atrocity Files: Deciphering the Archives of Guatemala's Dirty War." *Harper's,* December.

Dunkerley, James. 1988. *Power in the Isthmus: A Political History of Modern Central America.* London: Verso.

———. 1994. *The Pacification of Central America.* London: Verso.

Dunn, Henry. [1829] 1981. *Guatemala, or The Republic of Central America in 1827–8.* Detroit: Blaine Ethridge.

Edmonson, Munro S., trans. 1971. *The Book of Counsel: The Popol Vuh of the Quiché Maya of Guatemala*. New Orleans: Tulane Univ. Press.

England, Nora. 1995. "Linguistics and Indigenous American Languages: Mayan Examples." *Journal of Latin American Anthropology* 1(1): 122–149.

Falla, Ricardo. 1983. "The Massacre at the Rural Estate of San Francisco, July 1982." *Cultural Survival Quarterly* 7(1): 43–44.

———. 1984. "We Charge Genocide." In *Guatemala: Tyranny on Trial*, 112–119. Ed. Susanne Jonas, E. McCaughan, and E. Sutherland Martínez. San Francisco: Synthesis.

———. 1994. *Massacres in the Jungle: Ixcán, Guatemala, 1975–1982*. Trans. Julia Howland. Boulder: Westview Press.

———. 2001. *Quiché Rebelde: Religious Conversion, Politics, and Ethnic Identity in Guatemala*. Trans. Phillip Berryman. Austin: Univ. of Texas Press.

Farriss, Nancy M. 1984. *Maya Society under Spanish Rule: The Collective Enterprise of Survival*. Princeton: Princeton Univ. Press.

Few, Martha. 2002. *Women Who Live Evil Lives: Gender, Religion, and the Politics of Power in Colonial Guatemala, 1650–1750*. Austin: Univ. of Texas Press.

Fink, Leon. 2003. *The Maya of Morganton: Work and Community in the Nuevo New South*. Chapel Hill: Univ. of North Carolina Press.

Fischer, Edward F. 2002. *Cultural Logics and Global Economies: Maya Identity in Thought and Practice*. Austin: Univ. of Texas Press.

Fischer, Edward F., and Peter Benson. 2006. *Broccoli and Desire: Global Connections and Maya Struggles in Postwar Guatemala*. Stanford: Stanford Univ. Press.

Fischer, Edward F., and R. McKenna Brown, eds. 1996. *Maya Cultural Activism in Guatemala*. Austin: Univ. of Texas Press.

Fischer, Edward F., and Carol E. Hendrickson. 2002. *Tecpán Guatemala: A Modern Maya Town in Global and Local Context*. Boulder: Westview Press.

Foxen, Patricia. 2008. *In Search of Providence: Transnational Mayan Identities*. Nashville: Vanderbilt Univ. Press.

Fuentes, Carlos. 1985. *Latin America: At War with the Past*. Toronto: CBC Enterprises.

Galeano, Eduardo. 1969. *Guatemala: Occupied Country*. Trans. Cedric Belfrage. New York: Monthly Review Press.

———. 1991. *The Book of Embraces*. Trans. Cedric Belfrage, with Mark Schafer. New York: W. W. Norton.

Gálvez Borrell, Víctor, and Alberto Esquit Choy. 1997. *The Mayan Movement Today: Issues of Indigenous Culture and Development in Guatemala*. Guatemala: Facultad Latinoamericana de Ciencias Sociales.

Gann, Thomas. 1926. *Ancient Cities and Modern Tribes: Exploration and Adventure in Maya Lands*. London: Duckworth.

García, Eduardo. 2005. "Rescued Police Files Hold Guatemala's Dark Secrets." *Guatemala Scholars Network News,* October 2005.

Garrard-Burnett, Virginia. 2000. "Indians are Drunks and Drunks are Indians: Alcohol and Indigenísmo in Guatemala, 1890–1940." *Bulletin of Latin American Research* 19(3): 341–356.

Gidley, Ruth, Cynthia Kee, and Reggie Norton, eds. 1999. *Guatemala: Thinking About the Unthinkable.* London: Association of Artists for Guatemala.

Glassman, Paul. 1988. *Guatemala Guide.* Champlain, NY: Passport Press.

Gleijeses, Piero. 1991. *Shattered Hope: The Guatemalan Revolution and the United States, 1944–54.* Princeton: Princeton Univ. Press.

Godoy, Angelina Snodgrass. 2000. "Lynchings and the Privitization of Justice in Post-War Guatemala." *Report on Guatemala* 21(2): 8–11, 13.

Goldín, Liliana R. 2008. *Global Maya: Work and Ideology in Rural Guatemala.* Albuquerque: Univ. of New Mexico Press.

Goldman, Francisco. 1992. *The Long Night of White Chickens.* New York: Atlantic Monthly Press.

———. 1999. "Murder Comes for the Bishop." *The New Yorker,* March 15.

———. 2002. "Victory in Guatemala." *The New York Review of Books,* May 23.

———. 2007. *The Art of Political Murder: Who Killed the Bishop?* New York: Grove Press.

González, Pedro Gaspar. 1995. *A Mayan Life.* Trans. Elaine Elliot. Rancho Palo Verdes, CA: Yax Te' Press.

———. 1998. *Return of the Maya.* Trans. Susan G. Rascón, with Fernando Peñalosa and Janet Sawyer. Rancho Palo Verdes, CA: Yax Te' Press.

González Palma, Luis. 1999. *Poems of Sorrow.* Santa Fe, NM: Arena Editions.

Graham, Ian, ed. 1975. *Corpus of Maya Hieroglyphic Inscriptions.* Vol. 1. Cambridge, MA: Peabody Museum of Archaeology and Ethnology, Harvard University.

———. 2002. *Alfred Maudslay and the Maya: A Biography.* Norman: Univ. of Oklahoma Press.

Grandin, Greg. 2000. *The Blood of Guatemala: A History of Race and Nation.* Durham: Duke Univ. Press.

———. 2004. *The Last Colonial Massacre: Latin America in the Cold War.* Chicago: Univ. of Chicago Press.

Green, Duncan. 1992. *Guatemala: Burden of Paradise.* London: Latin America Bureau.

Green, Linda. 1999. *Fear as a Way of Life: Mayan Widows in Rural Guatemala.* New York: Columbia Univ. Press.

———. 2006–2007. "The Peace Accords a Decade Later." *Report on Guatemala* 27(4): 4–8.

Guatemalan Church in Exile. 1989. *Guatemala: Security, Development, and Democracy.* Mexico City: Guatemalan Church in Exile.

Gudmundson, Lowell, and Héctor Lindo-Fuentes. 1995. *Central America, 1821–1871: Liberalism before Liberal Reform.* Tuscaloosa: Univ. of Alabama Press.

Hagan, Jacqueline M. 1995. *Deciding to be Legal: A Maya Community in Houston.* Philadelphia: Temple Univ. Press.

Handy, Jim. 1984. *Gift of the Devil: A History of Guatemala.* Toronto: Between the Lines.

———. 1994. *Revolution in the Countryside: Rural Conflict and Agrarian Reform in Guatemala, 1944–1954.* Chapel Hill: Univ. of North Carolina Press.

Harbury, Jennifer K. 1997. *Searching for Everardo: A Story of Love, War, and the CIA in Guatemala*. New York: Warner Books.

Hay, Clarence L., Ralph L. Linton, Samuel K. Lothrop, Harry L. Shapiro, and George C. Vaillant, eds. 1940. *The Maya and Their Neighbors*. New York: D. Appleton Century.

Hendrickson, Carol. 1995. *Weaving Identities: Construction of Dress and Self in a Highland Guatemala Town*. Austin: Univ. of Texas Press.

Herrera, Robinson A. 2003. *Natives, Europeans, and Africans in Sixteenth-Century Santiago de Guatemala*. Austin: Univ. of Texas Press.

Hill, Robert M., II. 1991. *Colonial Cakchiquels: Highland Maya Adaptations to Spanish Rule, 1600–1700*. Fort Worth: Harcourt, Brace, Jovanovich.

Holiday, David. 2000. "Guatemala's Precarious Peace." *Current History* 99(634): 78–84.

Hooks, Margaret, ed. 1993. *Guatemalan Women Speak*. Washington, DC: Ecumenical Program on Central America and the Caribbean.

Houston, Stephen D. 1989. *Maya Glyphs*. London: British Museum.

Houston, Stephen, John Robertson, and David Stuart. 2000. "The Language of Classic Maya Inscriptions." *Current Anthropology* 41(3): 321–338.

Houston, Stephen, David Stuart, and Karl Taube. 2006. *The Memory of Bones: Body, Being, and Experience among the Classic Maya*. Austin: Univ. of Texas Press.

Human Rights Office of the Archdiocese of Guatemala. 1999. *Guatemala: Never Again!* Maryknoll, NY: Orbis Books.

Huxley, Aldous. 1934. *Beyond the Mexique Bay*. London: Chatto and Windus.

Immerman, Richard. 1982. *The CIA in Guatemala: The Foreign Policy of Intervention*. Austin: Univ. of Texas Press.

Jonas, Susanne. 1991. *The Battle for Guatemala: Rebels, Death Squads, and U.S. Power*. Boulder: Westview Press.

———. 2000. *Of Centaurs and Doves: Guatemala's Peace Process*. Boulder: Westview Press.

Jones, Grant D. 1989. *Maya Resistance to Spanish Rule: Time and History on a Colonial Frontier*. Albuquerque: Univ. of New Mexico Press.

———. 1998. *The Conquest of the Last Maya Kingdom*. Stanford: Stanford Univ. Press.

Kahn, Hilary E. 2006. *Seeing and Being Seen: The Q'eqchi' Maya of Livingston, Guatemala, and Beyond*. Austin: Univ. of Texas Press.

Kelley, David H. 1976. *Deciphering the Maya Script*. Austin: Univ. of Texas Press.

Kendall, Carl, John Hawkins, and Laurel Bossen, eds. 1983. *Heritage of Conquest: Thirty Years Later*. Albuquerque: Univ. of New Mexico Press.

Kobrak, Paul. 1999. *Organizing and Repression in the University of San Carlos, Guatemala, 1944 to 1966*. Washington, DC: American Association for the Advancement of Science.

Kramer, Wendy. 1994. *Encomienda Politics in Early Colonial Guatemala, 1524–1544: Dividing the Spoils*. Boulder: Westview Press.

La Farge, Oliver. 1940. "Maya Ethnology: The Sequence of Cultures." In *The Maya and Their Neighbours*, 282–291. Ed. C. L. Hay et al. New York: D. Appleton Century.

————. 1947. *Santa Eulalia: The Religion of a Cuchumatán Indian Town.* Chicago: Univ. of Chicago Press.

La Farge, Oliver, and Douglas Byers. 1931. *The Year Bearer's People.* New Orleans: Tulane Univ. Press.

León-Portilla, Miguel. [1973] 1988. *Time and Reality in the Thought of the Maya.* Trans. Charles L. Boiles, Fernando Horcasitas, and the Author. Norman: Univ. of Oklahoma Press.

Levenson-Estrada, Deborah. 1994. *Trade Unionists against Terror: Guatemala City, 1954–1985.* Chapel Hill: Univ. of North Carolina Press.

Lincoln, Jackson S. 1945. *An Ethnographic Study of the Ixil Indians of the Guatemalan Highlands.* Chicago: Microfilm Collection of Manuscripts on Middle American Cultural Anthropology, University of Chicago.

Lión, Luis de. [1985] 2003. *El tiempo principia en Xibalbá.* Guatemala: Magna Terra.

Little, Walter E. 2004. *Mayas in the Marketplace: Tourism, Globalization, and Cultural Identity.* Austin: Univ. of Texas Press.

Lohse, Jon C., and Fred Valdez, Jr. 2004. *Ancient Maya Commoners.* Austin: Univ. of Texas Press.

López, Fernando, and Christina Albo. 2000. "Guatemala's Prison System on the Verge of Collapse." *Report on Guatemala* 21(3): 8–11.

Loucky, James, and Marilyn M. Moors, eds. 2000. *The Maya Diaspora.* Philadelphia: Temple Univ. Press.

Lovell, W. George. [1985] 2005. *Conquest and Survival in Colonial Guatemala: A Historical Geography of the Cuchumatán Highlands, 1500–1821.* 3rd ed. Montreal: McGill-Queen's Univ. Press.

————. 2000. "The Highland Maya." In *Mesoamérica,* 392–444. Ed. Richard E. W. Adams and Murdo J. MacLeod. Vol. 2, pt. 2, of *The Cambridge History of the Native Peoples of the Americas.* Cambridge: Cambridge Univ. Press.

Lovell, W. George, and Christopher H. Lutz. 1995. *Demography and Empire: A Guide to the Population History of Spanish Central America, 1500–1821.* Boulder: Westview Press.

————. 1996. "'A Dark Obverse': Maya Survival in Guatemala, 1520–1994." *The Geographical Review* 83(3): 398–407.

Lovell, W. George, and William R. Swezey. 1990. "Indian Migration and Community Formation: An Analysis of *Congregación* in Colonial Guatemala." In *Migration in Colonial Spanish America,* 18–40. Ed. David J. Robinson. Cambridge: Cambridge Univ. Press.

Lutz, Christopher H. 1994. *Santiago de Guatemala, 1541–1773: City, Caste, and the Colonial Experience.* Norman: Univ. of Oklahoma Press.

Mackie, Sedley J., ed. and trans. [1924] 1978. *An Account of the Conquest of Guatemala in 1524 by Pedro de Alvarado.* Boston: Longwood Press.

MacLeod, Murdo J. [1973] 2008. *Spanish Central America: A Socioeconomic History, 1520–1720.* Austin: Univ. of Texas Press.

Maldonado, Oscar Iván, ed. 2007. *So That All Shall Know: Photographs by Daniel Hernández-Salazar.* Austin: Univ. of Texas Press.

Manz, Beatriz. 1988. *Refugees of a Hidden War: The Aftermath of Counterinsurgency in Guatemala.* Albany: State Univ. of New York Press.

———. 2004. *Paradise in Ashes: A Guatemalan Journey of Courage, Terror, and Hope.* Berkeley: Univ. of California Press.

Markman, Sidney D. 1966. *Colonial Architecture of Antigua Guatemala.* Philadelphia: American Philosophical Society.

Martínez Peláez, Severo. [1970] 2009. *La Patria del Criollo: An Interpretation of Colonial Guatemala.* Trans. Susan M. Neve and W. George Lovell. Durham: Duke Univ. Press.

Matthew, Laura, and Michel R. Oudijk, eds. 2007. *Indian Conquistadors: Indigenous Allies in the Conquest of Mesoamerica.* Norman: Univ. of Oklahoma Press.

Maudslay, Anne C., and Alfred P. Maudslay. [1899] 1979. *A Glimpse at Guatemala and Some Notes on the Ancient Monuments of Central America.* New York: Blaine Ethridge.

Maxwell, Judith M., and Robert M. Hill, II. 2006. *Kaqchikel Chronicles: The Definitive Edition.* Austin: Univ. of Texas Press.

Mayers, Marvin K., ed. 1966. *Languages of Guatemala.* The Hague: Mouton.

McCreery, David. 1988. "Land, Labor, and Violence in Highland Guatemala: San Juan Ixcoy (Huehuetenango), 1890–1940." *The Americas* 45(2): 237–249.

———. 1990. "State Power, Indigenous Communities, and Land in Nineteenth-Century Guatemala, 1820–1920." In *Guatemalan Indians and the State: 1540 to 1988,* 96–115. Ed. Carol A. Smith. Austin: Univ. of Texas Press.

———. 1994. *Rural Guatemala, 1760–1940.* Stanford: Stanford Univ. Press.

Menchú, Rigoberta. 1984. *I, Rigoberta Menchú: An Indian Woman in Guatemala.* Ed. Elisabeth Burgos-Debray. Trans. Ann Wright. London: Verso.

———. 1998. *Crossing Borders.* Trans. and ed. Ann Wright. New York: Verso.

Metz, Brent E. 2006. *Ch'orti'-Maya Survival in Eastern Guatemala: Indigeneity in Transition.* Albuquerque: Univ. of New Mexico Press.

Molesky-Poz, Jean. 2006. *Contemporary Maya Spirituality: The Ancient Ways Are Not Lost.* Austin: Univ. of Texas Press.

Moller, Jonathan. 2004. *Our Culture is Our Resistance: Repression, Refuge, and Healing in Guatemala.* New York: PowerHouse Books.

Montejo, Victor. [1982] 1984. *El Kanil: Man of Lightning.* Trans. Wallace Kaufman. Carrboro, NC: Signal Books.

———. 1987. *Testimony: Death of a Guatemalan Village.* Trans. Victor Perera. Willimantic, CT: Curbstone Press.

———. 1991. *The Bird Who Cleans the World and Other Mayan Fables.* Trans. Wallace Kaufman. Willimantic, CT: Curbstone Press.

———. 1995. *Sculpted Stones.* Trans. Victor Perera. Willimantic, CT: Curbstone Press.

———. 1999a. *Popol Vuh: A Sacred Book of the Maya.* Trans. David Unger. Illustrated by Luis Garay. Toronto: Groundwood Books.

———. 1999b. *Voices from Exile: Violence and Survival in Modern Maya History.* Norman: Univ. of Oklahoma Press.

————. 2005. *Maya Intellectual Renaissance: Identity, Representation, and Leadership.* Austin: Univ. of Texas Press.

Morley, Sylvanus G. [1915] 1975. *An Introduction to the Study of the Maya Hieroglyphs.* New York: Dover Publications.

Namuth, Hans. 1985. *Los Todos Santeros: A Family Album of Mam Indians in the Village of Todos Santos Cuchumatán, Guatemala, 1947–1987.* London: Dirk Nishen.

Naylor, Robert A. 1967. "Guatemala: Indian Attitudes toward Land Tenure." *Journal of Inter-American Studies* 9(4): 619–639.

Nelson, Diane M. 1999. *A Finger in the Wound: Ethnicity, Nation, and Gender in the Body Politic of Quincentennial Guatemala.* Berkeley: Univ. of California Press.

————. 2009. *Reckoning: The Ends of War in Guatemala.* Durham: Duke Univ. Press.

Newton, A. P., ed. 1928. *The English-American: A New Survey of the West Indies.* London: George Routledge and Sons.

Nolin, Catherine. 2006. *Transnational Ruptures: Gender and Forced Migration.* Burlington, VT: Ashgate Publishing.

Nolin Hanlon, Catherine, and Finola Shankar. 2000. "Gendered Spaces of Terror and Assault: The *Testimonio* of REMHI and the Commission for Historical Clarification in Guatemala." *Gender, Place, and Culture* 7(3): 267–288.

North, Liisa L., and Alan B. Simmons, eds. 1999. *Journeys of Fear: Refugee Return and National Transformation in Guatemala.* Montreal: McGill-Queen's Univ. Press.

Oakes, Maud. 1951a. *Beyond the Windy Place: Life in the Guatemalan Highlands.* New York: Farrar, Straus, and Young.

————. 1951b. *The Two Crosses of Todos Santos: Survivals of Mayan Religious Ritual.* Princeton: Princeton Univ. Press.

Orellana, Sandra L. 1984. *The Tzutujil Mayas: Continuity and Change, 1250–1630.* Norman: Univ. of Oklahoma Press.

Oss, Adriaan C. van. 1986. *Catholic Colonialism: A Parish History of Guatemala.* Cambridge: Cambridge Univ. Press.

————. 2003. *Church and Society in Spanish America.* Amsterdam: Askant.

Painter, James. 1987. *Guatemala: False Hope, False Freedom.* London: Catholic Institute for International Relations and Latin America Bureau.

Parker, Ann, and Avon Neal. 1982. *Los Ambulantes: The Itinerant Photographers of Guatemala.* Photographs by Ann Parker. Text by Avon Neal. Cambridge, MA: MIT Press.

Payeras, Mario. 1983. *Days of the Jungle: The Testimony of a Guatemalan Guerrillero, 1972–1976.* Trans. George Black. New York: Monthly Review Press.

Perera, Victor. 1993. *Unfinished Conquest: The Guatemalan Tragedy.* Berkeley: Univ. of California Press.

Proskouriakoff, Tatiana. 1960. "Historical Implications of a Pattern of Dates at Piedras Negra." *American Antiquity* 25: 454–475.

Reade, Jennifer, and Catherine Nolin. 2008. *Empowering Women: Community Development in Rural Guatemala.* Saarbrücken: VDM Verlag.

Recinos, Adrián, and Delia Goetz, trans. 1953. *The Annals of the Cakchiquels.* Norman: Univ. of Oklahoma Press.

Recinos, Adrián, Delia Goetz, and Sylvanus G. Morley, trans. 1950. *Popol Vuh: The Sacred Book of the Ancient Quiché Maya.* Norman: Univ. of Oklahoma Press.

Reeves, René. 2006. *Ladinos with Ladinos, Indians with Indians: Land, Labor, and Regional Ethnic Conflict in the Making of Guatemala.* Stanford: Stanford Univ. Press.

Restall, Matthew, and Florine G. L. Asselbergs. 2007. *Invading Guatemala: Spanish, Maya, and Nahua Accounts of the Conquest Wars.* University Park, PA.: Penn State Press.

Robinson, William. 1998. "Neo-Liberalism, the Global Elite, and the Guatemalan Transition." *Report on Guatemala* 19(4): 6–13.

Salvin, Caroline. [1873–1874] 2000. *A Pocket Eden: Guatemalan Journals, 1873–1874.* South Woodstock, VT: Plumsock Mesoamerican Studies.

Sanford, Victoria. 2004. *Buried Secrets: Truth and Human Rights in Guatemala.* New York: Palgrave MacMillan.

———. 2007. "Women in Danger: Feminicide and Impunity." *Report on Guatemala* 28(2): 8–10.

———. 2008. "From Genocide to Feminicide: Impunity and Human Rights in Twenty-First Century Guatemala." *Journal of Human Rights* 7: 104–122.

Schele, Linda, and David Freidel. 1990. *A Forest of Kings: The Untold Story of the Ancient Maya.* New York: William Morrow.

Schele, Linda, and Peter Mathews. 1998. *The Code of Kings: The Language of Seven Sacred Maya Temples and Tombs.* New York: Scribner.

Schele, Linda, and Mary E. Miller. 1986. *The Blood of Kings.* New York: George Braziller.

Schevill, Margot Blum. 1993. *Maya Textiles of Guatemala.* With a historical essay by Christopher H. Lutz. Austin: Univ. of Texas Press.

———, ed. 1997. *The Maya Textile Tradition.* With photographs by Jeffrey Jay Foxx. New York: Harry Abrams.

Schirmer, Jennifer. 1998. *The Guatemalan Military Project: A Violence Called Democracy.* Philadelphia: Univ. of Pennsylvania Press.

Schlesinger, Stephen, and Stephen Kinzer. [1982] 2005. *Bitter Fruit: The Story of the American Coup in Guatemala.* Rev. and expanded ed. Cambridge, MA: Harvard Univ. Press.

Sexton, James D., ed. and trans. 1981. *Son of Tecún Umán: A Maya Indian Tells His Life Story.* Tucson: Univ. of Arizona Press.

———, ed. and trans. 1985. *Campesino: The Diary of a Guatemalan Indian.* Tucson: Univ. of Arizona Press.

———, ed. and trans. 1992. *Ignacio: The Diary of a Maya Indian of Guatemala.* Philadelphia: Univ. of Pennsylvania Press.

Sherman, William L. 1979. *Forced Native Labor in Sixteenth-Century Central America.* Lincoln: Univ. of Nebraska Press.

Sieder, Rachel, Megan Thomas, George Vickers, and Jack Spence. 2002. *Who Governs?: Guatemala Five Years After the Peace Accords.* Cambridge, MA: Hemispheric Initiatives.

Simon, Jean-Marie. 1987. *Guatemala: Eternal Spring, Eternal Tyranny.* New York: W. W. Norton.

Simonds, Merilyn. 1999. *The Lion in the Room Next Door*. Toronto: McClelland and Stewart.

Skvorecky, Josef. 1984. *The Engineer of Human Souls*. Toronto: Lester and Orpen Dennys.

Smith, Carol A. 1984. "Local History in Global Context: Social and Economic Transitions in Western Guatemala." *Comparative Studies in Society and History* 26(2): 193–228.

———, ed. 1990. *Guatemalan Indians and the State: 1540 to 1988*. Austin: Univ. of Texas Press.

———. 1991. "Maya Nationalism." *NACLA Report on the Americas* 25(3): 28–33.

Smith-Ayala, Emilie. 1991. *The Grandaughters of Ixmucané: Guatemalan Women Speak*. Toronto: The Women's Press.

Solnit, Rebecca. 2003. *River of Shadows: Eadweard Muybridge and the Technological Wild West*. New York: Viking.

Spence, Jack, David R. Dye, Paula Worby, Carmen Rosa de León-Escribano, George Vickers, and Mike Lanchin. 1998. *Promise and Reality: Implementation of the Guatemalan Peace Accords*. Cambridge, MA: Hemispheric Initiatives.

Stanley, William, and David Holiday. 2002. "Broad Participation, Diffuse Responsibility." In *Ending Civil Wars: The Implementation of Peace Agreements*, 461–462. Ed. Stephen John Stedman, Donald S. Rothchild, and Elizabeth M. Cousens. Boulder: Lynne Rienner Publishers.

Stanzione, Vincent. 2003. *Rituals of Sacrifice: Walking the Face of the Earth on the Sacred Path of the Sun*. Albuquerque: Univ. of New Mexico Press.

Stephens, John L. [1841] 1969. *Incidents of Travel in Central America, Chiapas, and Yucatan*. 2 vols. New York: Dover Publications.

Stoll, David. 1993. *Between Two Armies in the Ixil Towns of Guatemala*. New York: Columbia Univ. Press.

———. 1999. *Rigoberta Menchú and the Story of All Poor Guatemalans*. Boulder: Westview Press.

Streeter, Stephen M. 2000. *Managing the Counterrevolution: The United States and Guatemala, 1954–1961*. Athens: Ohio University Center for International Studies.

Sullivan, Paul. 1989. *Unfinished Conversations: Mayas and Foreigners between Two Wars*. New York: Alfred A. Knopf.

Taussig, Michael. 1984. "Culture of Terror, Space of Death: Roger Casement's Putomayo Report and the Explanation of Torture." *Comparative Studies in Society and History* 26(3): 467–497.

———. 1987. *Shamanism, Colonialism, and the Wild Man: A Study in Terror and Healing*. Chicago: Univ. of Chicago Press.

Tax, Sol, ed. 1950. *Heritage of Conquest: The Ethnology of Middle America*. New York: Macmillan.

Taylor, Clark. 1998. *Reweaving the Torn: Return of Guatemala's Refugees*. Philadelphia: Temple Univ. Press.

Taylor, Ruth. 2000. "Puppet, Champion, or Chameleon? Portillo Takes Over the Presidency." *Report on Guatemala* 21(1): 2–5, 13.

————. 2002. "Coffee and Land: Can Crisis Lead to Positive Change?" *Report on Guatemala* 23(2): 7–11.

Tedlock, Barbara. [1982] 1992. *Time and the Highland Maya*. Rev. ed. Albuquerque: Univ. of New Mexico Press.

Tedlock, Dennis, trans. 1985. *Popol Vuh: The Mayan Book of the Dawn of Life*. New York: Simon and Schuster.

————. 1993. "Torture in the Archives: Mayans Meet Europeans." *American Anthropologist* 95(1): 139–152.

Thompson, J. Eric S. 1950. *Maya Hieroglyphic Writing: An Introduction*. Washington, DC: Carnegie Institution of Washington.

————, ed. 1958. *Thomas Gage's Travels in the New World*. Norman: Univ. of Oklahoma Press.

Trudeau, Robert H. 1993. *Guatemalan Politics: The Popular Struggle for Democracy*. Boulder: Lynne Rienner Publishers.

Universidad Francisco Marroquín. 2007. *Quauhquechollan: A Chronicle of Conquest*. Guatemala: Mayaprin, S.A.

Vecchiato, Gianni. 1989. *Guatemala Rainbow*. San Francisco: Pomegranate Artbooks.

Vidal, Gore. [1950] 2005. *Dark Green, Bright Red*. London: Abacus.

————. [1995] 1996. *Palimpsest: A Memoir*. New York: Penguin.

Vigil, Ralph H. 1987. *Alonso de Zorita: Royal Judge and Christian Humanist, 1512–1585*. Norman: Univ. of Oklahoma Press.

Vilanova de Arbenz, María. [2000] 2003. *Mi esposo, el presidente Arbenz*. Guatemala: Editorial Universitaria de la Universidad San Carlos de Guatemala.

Vlach, Norita. 1992. *The Quetzal in Flight: Guatemalan Refugee Families in the United States*. Westport, CT: Praeger.

Wagley, Charles. 1941. *Economics of a Guatemalan Village*. Menasha, WI: American Anthropological Association.

————. 1949. *The Social and Religious Life of a Guatemalan Village*. Menasha, WI: American Anthropological Association.

Wagner, Regina. 2001. *The History of Coffee in Guatemala*. Trans. Eric Stull. Guatemala: Villegas Editores.

Warren, Kay B. 1992. "Transforming Memories and Histories: The Meaning of Ethnic Resurgence for Mayan Indians." In *Americas: New Interpretive Essays*, 189–219. Ed. Alfred Stepan. New York: Oxford Univ. Press.

————. 1994. "Language and the Politics of Self-Expression: Mayan Revitalization in Guatemala." *Cultural Survival Quarterly* 18(2&3): 81–86.

————. 1998. *Indigenous Movements and Their Critics: Pan-Maya Activism in Guatemala*. Princeton: Princeton Univ. Press.

Wasserstrom, Robert. 1975. "Revolution in Guatemala: Peasants and Politics under the Arbenz Government." *Comparative Studies in Society and History* 17(4): 443–478.

Watanabe, John M. 1990. "Enduring Yet Ineffable Community in the Western Periphery of Guatemala." In *Guatemalan Indians and the State: 1540 to 1988*, 183–204. Ed. Carol A. Smith. Austin: Univ. of Texas Press.

————. 1992. *Maya Saints and Souls in a Changing World.* Austin: Univ. of Texas Press.

————. 1995. "Unimagining the Maya: Anthropologists, Others, and the Inescapable Hubris of Authorship." *Bulletin of Latin American Research* 14(1): 25–45.

Weeks, John M., ed. 2001. *The Past and Present Maya: Essays in Honor of Robert M. Carmack.* Lancaster, CA: Labyrinthos.

Wilkinson, Daniel. 2002. *Silence on the Mountain: Stories of Terror, Betrayal, and Forgetting in Guatemala.* Boston: Houghton Mifflin.

Williams, Robert G. 1994. *States and Social Evolution: Coffee and the Rise of National Governments in Central America.* Chapel Hill: Univ. of North Carolina Press.

Wilson, Richard. 1991. "Machine Guns and Mountain Spirits: The Cultural Effects of State Repression among the Q'eqchi' of Guatemala." *Critique of Anthropology* 11(1): 33–61.

————. 1993. "Anchored Communities: Identity and History of the Maya-Q'eqchi'." *Man* 28(1): 121–138.

————. 1995. *Maya Resurgence in Guatemala: Q'eqchi' Experiences.* Norman: Univ. of Oklahoma Press.

Woodward, Ralph Lee, Jr. 1990. "Changes in the Nineteenth-Century Guatemalan State and Its Indian Policies." In *Guatemalan Indians and the State: 1540 to 1988,* 52–71. Ed. Carol A. Smith. Austin: Univ. of Texas Press.

————. 1993. *Rafael Carrera and the Emergence of the Republic of Guatemala, 1821–1871.* Athens: Univ. of Georgia Press.

Wortman, Miles L. 1982. *Government and Society in Central America, 1680–1840.* New York: Columbia Univ. Press.

Wright, Ronald. 1989. *Time among the Maya: Travels in Belize, Guatemala, and Mexico.* Markham, ON: Penguin.

————. 1992. *Stolen Continents: The Americas through Indian Eyes Since 1492.* Boston: Houghton Mifflin.

Zimmerman, Marc. 1995. *Litterature and Resistance in Guatemala: Textual Modes from 'El Señor Presidente' to Rigoberta Menchú.* 2 vols. Athens, OH: Ohio Univ. Press.

Zur, Judith N. 1998. *Violent Memories: Mayan War Widows in Guatemala.* Boulder: Westview Press.

INDEX

CPSIA information can be obtained at www.ICGtesting.com
Printed in the USA
LVOW11s1159221215

467427LV00003B/8/P